STEALING MANHATTAN

The Untold Story of America's Billion Dollar Gem Heist Masterminds

NEW YORK TIMES BESTSELLING AUTHOR

BURL BARER

WITH PUNCH STANIMIROVIC

WILDBLUE
P R E S S

WildBluePress.com

STEALING MANHATTAN published by:
WILDBLUE PRESS
P.O. Box 102440
Denver, Colorado 80250

Publisher Disclaimer: Any opinions, statements of fact or fiction, descriptions, dialogue, and citations found in this book were provided by the author and are solely those of the author. The publisher makes no claim as to their veracity or accuracy and assumes no liability for the content.

WILDBLUE PRESS is registered at the U.S. Patent and Trademark Offices.

ISBN 978-1-960332-01-1 Hardcover
ISBN 978-1-952225-44-4 Trade Paperback
ISBN 978-1-952225-43-7 eBook

Cover design © 2023 WildBlue Press. All rights reserved.

Cover Design by Tatiana Vila, www.viladesign.net

Interior Formatting by Elijah Toten, www.totencreative.com

STEALING MANHATTAN

For Howard Lapides

Foreword by Burl Barer

This book is a true crime author's dream—an exclusive on the greatest untold American crime story of the 20th century, including the most astonishing mega-heist ever conceived: over one billion dollars in diamonds, gold, precious gems, and negotiable currency stolen from New York's diamond district under the cover of darkness by sophisticated safe crackers, alarm specialists, and security experts. No weapons, no violence. As everything stolen was fully insured, those who accomplished this theft saw it as a victimless crime. Yes, they got away with it.

This is one version of a one hundred percent true story recalled from memory and supported by extensive research and interviews with primary participants. Any errors of fact are unintentional, and all conversations quoted are adapted and reconstructed from individual recollections and are presumed accurate in essential content.

I was granted unprecedented access to the world's greatest gem heist masterminds including the personal memoirs of the remarkable genius, "Mr. Stan," the ultimate gentleman thief.

Mr. Stan was a respected member of New York high society, a trusted and admired example of charm, grace, courtesy, and integrity in all aspects of his life and career. He was well known as a historic artifact collector, real estate investor, champion of the underdog, gracious entertainer, and President of *Gemstones Trading International* with five offices in New York's diamond district.

His lovely younger wife, Branka, was a brilliant artist and friend of Phillip Pearlstein, Walter Chrysler, and Joan Crawford. Together, Stan and she were a power couple beloved and admired for their sophistication, generosity, honesty, and ethics.

What Mr. Stan's friends and associates didn't know was that Stan and Branka oversaw six or more teams of highly trained and disciplined specialists who, in the midnight hour, looted the vaults of the jewelry manufacturing firms insured for one hundred million or more.

Their only son, "Punch," was sent at age ten to the world's most expensive and elite boarding school in Switzerland. He returned educated, erudite, multi-lingual, and a world-class athlete who pulled his first multi-million-dollar heist at age fifteen.

Punch then recruited the security firms to work with him instead of against him. With teams of acrobats, strongmen, safe crackers, locksmiths, and alarm experts, the final added co-conspirator was the addition of the Lacka safe manufacturing company. They trained Punch in how to open all their top-of-the-line safes.

Here then is the first volume in the Stealing Manhattan trilogy: the one hundred percent true story of America's first family of altruistic outlaws whose creative antics in the redistribution of wealth spanned two generations and three decades of outrageous adventures both here and abroad, and whose talent and techniques form the foundation of every cinema-style heist by the notorious international gem thieves known as the Pink Panthers.

Foreword by Branka DiGangi

My son dreamed of being the world's greatest gem heist mastermind. He could never achieve that goal because his father already held that title. Not only did he mastermind the most astonishing series of diamond heists in history, but he was never caught, never prosecuted, never spent a day in prison, never hurt anyone in the process, and only robbed firms that were fully insured or over-insured.

Our son followed his father's path. He created new techniques and methods later used worldwide by the notorious Pink Panthers who, despite reports to the contrary, originated not in Serbia, but in New York's diamond district when my former husband, Mr. Stan, and our only son, Paul, were stealing Manhattan.

Introduction by Paul "Punch" Stanimirovic

I became a diamond thief to make my father proud of me. For a glorious period in the 1990s, I was King of the New York streets until SWAT teams, helicopters, hundreds of police officers, and one smart dog, captured me. They couldn't keep me, and they couldn't stop me.

I walked out of jail and hid in plain sight for four years using dozens of names and identities, hosting lavish events, and hanging out with superstars. If I were to name-drop every show-business celebrity who visited my home, partied in my nightclub, or went skiing with me in the Swiss Alps, the combined weight would tear through this page, or knock the screen off your Kindle, Nook, or Kobo.

There are days when I only remember the thrill of the heist, the pulse-pounding excitement of slithering down the back of 47th Street in Manhattan as a black-attired heist-ninja backed up by my hand-picked crew of professionals dedicated to my father's precision planning.

I'm sure you're curious about my dad, the man I regard as a true genius. Had he been caught doing a heist, he would already be famous. Now, he will be. Who else pulled off mega-heists totaling over one billion dollars and got away with it? Nobody.

My mother? Oh, she is beautiful and fabulous. I want you to really get to know my parents, charming and sophisticated outlaws, who honestly got away with everything. This is their story, and mine, as told by our friend and confidant, Burl Barer.

Chapter One
Mr. Stan

The only reason the world's greatest gentleman thief survived childhood is that he wasn't Jewish.

Vojislav Stanimirovic—call him Stan—was born March 19, 1937, in Novi Sad, Serbia, the Kingdom of Yugoslavia, two years before the Nazis invaded Poland.

It was in Novi Sad that more than 1,400 Jews were lined up in four rows on the frozen Danube River—men women and children—and shot in the back. The ice cracked, and their dead bodies were carried down to Belgrade and beyond for weeks.

"I was only five when the Nazis came," Stan recalled in his memoirs. "They grabbed me for playing outside after sunset. The Jewish Synagogue was directly behind our residence, so when the Nazis saw me at play, they assumed I was Jewish. When they understood who I was, that I wasn't Jewish, and my family's high social position, they didn't kill me; instead, they did other things."

When the Nazis were done with him, he was never again a joyful child of exuberant self-expression. He became taciturn, withdrawn, pensive, and silent except for sudden outbursts of excess anger and unchanneled rage.

His most immediate response to his own personal Nazi invasion was to join the Junior Partisan Rebels, and he wasn't the only child fighting the Nazis.

"My brother and my cousin were also in the resistance at an early age. We dropped homemade explosives down on the German tanks from the second floor of buildings as the tanks went down the street."

In March 1944 when he was only seven, the Germans sought out all remaining Jews and transported about 1,600 to Auschwitz. One month later, Jewish property was plundered completely.

"I saw things no child should see. Bodies of the dead hanging from trees, headless corpses by the side of the road. I had to step around the rotting shells of former friends. This left lasting impressions on me."

His life and family spared the Holocaust, Stan was blessed with an enviable upbringing with all the benefits of an advanced education and interaction with society's elite.

"My father, Nick, was a man of wealth and success prior to the Communist take-over in Yugoslavia after World War II. His best friend, super-spy, Dusko Popov, was Ian Fleming's inspiration for James Bond. They raised their pinkies in the air when drinking tea," recalled Stan, "They were like brothers, and had great fun together. Both men were distinguished in service to their country. My father became greatly respected as a Colonel in the Military Police."

Stan's mother, Jeleca, educated in Vienna's finest schools, wrote the Encyclopedia for Yugoslavia. She passed her writing talents on to her son.

"I majored in journalism at Belgrade College and pursued my athletic interests with dedicated Olympian aspirations," Stan said proudly. I excelled at what I loved: boxing, wrestling, and gymnastics."

Stan was also trained in both classical ballet and contemporary ballroom dancing, "I found ballet too effeminate in form and presentation for a manly man such as I," remarked Stan in half-jest. "I did, however, realize the beauty and grace inherent in the art form, and the combination of sensitive precision and effortless artistry triggered an exceptionally open and welcoming response from beautiful women."

Physically fit and mentally sharp, Stan didn't dance around difficult contemporary issues. He consistently championed social justice and earned the reputation as a troublemaker who penned excellent and often controversial contributions to *Political Magazine.*

Using the term, "controversial," may be underselling their primary characteristics. Stan's in-depth exposé of the tragic post-war conditions of the country's war orphans, predominantly Jewish, fermented violent outrage against its well-meaning author.

"I never thought this would happen," confessed Stan. "I was raised in a military family, and when I finished my mandatory service, I stayed on in the Reserve as a journalist and correspondent reporting to Belgrade. This was a perfect arrangement—I made a decent living doing what I loved doing. I was a true journalist, not part of a propaganda machine. My article in the Spring edition of *Politika* Magazine disgraced my parents and determined my destiny. Why? Ask anyone who read it."

The problem was that so many people did read it, and what they read was a blatant condemnation of the government for ignoring the plight of orphaned children from World War II. These children, suffering in squalor, needed more than decent conditions. They cried out for love, guidance, a big brother, and a mentor. To these children, Stan was their champion, their protector.

Stan was pressured to just shut up. He was repeatedly advised that no one cared about war orphans. So many of them were Jews. The publisher demoted Stan to working on

Western comic strips, a calculated reduction in Stan's direct impact on reader opinions and values.

Angry readers believed that Stan should have simply parroted the party line. In truth, the stories were about the journalist's own disillusionment with the insincere claims of Communism.

"I saw how class distinction and prejudice caused corrosive disunity and separation in our country," said Stan. "Especially with thousands of little Jewish orphans. They had no parents, and they had no rights. It was a shock, a sin, and a scandal."

"I saw them abused, neglected, and estranged from society. This was not any form of Communism; this was clearly cruelty. As a journalist, I had a responsibility to PURSUE AND PRESENT the best available version of the truth. I authored articles for publication, but most of them never made it to press after the first one."

Unaware that Stan's father was the highest-ranking Colonel in the nation's Military Police, local hard-core Communists decided to personally punish the author. They forced Stan from his home to torture him in a local barn.

"They hung me upside down while they poked blades of broken scissors into smoldering coals, then used those blades to slice dangerously close to my testicles and my rectum. Thank God my father found out, and before those thugs could do anything more, the Military Police burst in, took control, and cut me down."

"My father rescued me from extreme punishment for the crime of humanitarian compassion but reactivated my military service and not in a way my journalism talents would be used. Reassigning me in the military was seen as some sort of patriotic punishment."

The young Stanimirovic viewed his proactive writings on behalf of mistreated children as the very essence of patriotism—no patriot wants his beloved homeland shamefaced before all humanity for cruelty to innocents.

Words are endowed with great power, and Stan chose his words carefully both in public and in print, communicating heartfelt compassion for the oppressed and righteous indignation at the oppressors.

His first published revelation of the government's endemic antisemitism and sanctioned child abuse garnered attention in the USA via translation into English.

Stan decided to abandon Yugoslavia and make a run for the border. Stan deserted the army and made his way out of the country. In the process, he encountered an incredibly sexy Romani woman whose wiles he found irresistible.

"It was dangerous traveling alone, so we pretended we were husband and wife. That sort of ruse has obvious advantages."

It took much bravery and significant effort to traverse the rocky terrain that led him to a safe border crossing. When he first made it into Italy, he thought he was still in Yugoslavia,

"That's because I saw a giant red star—the sign of Communist Yugoslavia. It was a Texaco sign."

Stan jumped the fence to Italy with a woman who was, in Stan's words, "pure fire. We made love in the train car. Oh, she was a Romani indeed. She read my palm and said my future was glorious. Of course, I had preplanned my glorious future before meeting her."

Prior to his escape, he'd contacted the Hebrew Immigrant Assistance Society (HIAS), apprising them of his controversial features in the magazine, his defense of Jewish orphans, and his own impressive credentials including his refinement at the finest schools in Vienna.

It was in one of the few remaining post-war refugee camps in Italy that Stan sat down with pencil and paper and computed the amount that HIAS was promising him, plus what his talents and abilities would bring him in additional revenue. By his own estimation, he would be a self-made millionaire within twenty-four months.

Politics was a highly emotional issue among many refugees from Yugoslavia ever since it became ruled by the Communist regime of Marshal Tito following World War II. Stan was not into partisan politics but was into compassionate capitalism. The more money he had, the more he could share, the more he could help those of lesser wealth.

Stan traveled to New York from Italy in 1957 wearing a well-tailored suit and carrying a Serb Croat/English Dictionary his mother gave him and a hard-earned international reputation as a champion of oppressed children. He also possessed a man's ultimate asset: charm, which is the ability to get the answer "yes" without ever asking the question.

It was because of his honestly earned reputation for integrity that upon arrival in the USA that he was referred for employment by HIAS. His willingness to take on any paying work with an attitude of consummate professionalism was more than impressive. He worked in a staple factory and at the airport cleaning restrooms.

Fellow Serbians alerted to Stan's arrival in the United States were eager to guide him, support him, exploit him, or corrupt him.

"Oh, they were waiting for me, all right," confirmed Stan in personal correspondence. "I met Nikola Kavaja, notorious for his attempts to assassinate Marshall Tito, the President of Communist Yugoslavia, and Alex "Texas" Karalanovic who shared Nikola's disdain for Tito. I wasn't interested in their politics, but they did capture my interest in other matters. We all had what is called today a side-hustle—a way of making extra money, off the books, to augment our monthly salaries."

Stan's side hustle presaged "White Men Can't Jump" by decades, and the hustle was a winner. Stan would take bets on his ability to jump over a 1957 Corvette in a single leap. For the average untrained American, such a feat seems impossible, but Stan was a well-trained Serbian athlete.

Hired to clean bathrooms at the airport, Stan arrived for work so impeccably dressed that the other workers assumed he was an airline executive or Captain of a flight crew until he put on his work coveralls. His cleaning was so exemplary, he was soon offered higher and higher positions.

A man of astonishing insight, Stan was an adaptive learner and an amazing strategist with a true gift for relating to people in all social classes. He acquired an array of skills and business connections prior to, and during his first marriage to the beautiful and astonishingly wealthy Amy Schreiber, daughter of Abe Schreiber, who among many other things, owned Schreiberville, one of those bungalow rental vacation spots in the Catskills' Swan Lake area.

More rustic and less formal, the bungalows competed with other bungalow colonies rather than vacation spots such as the luxurious Swan Lake Hotel.

The bungalow colony had different neighborhoods from poor to rich. At night, Jackie Mason, Nipsy Russell or some other Borscht belt comedian performed. There was often a live band, and sometimes a movie. It was at Schreiberville that Stan met Amy. He was there giving dance lessons; a suave Eastern European Patrick Swayze living out his own *Dirty Dancing* scenario.

When fall came, Stan secured a position at the Adams School teaching art as therapy for disturbed children. Amy was earning $800 a week as a speech therapist. As a friendly co-worker, Amy brought him cake and coffee every day.

That was the extent of their relationship until Amy came to Stan's apartment one morning to borrow a book. Sensing there was an undercurrent of non-platonic intent, Stan took a well calculated risk.

"She was midsentence in some superficial small talk when I set down my coffee, walked over, and intended to sweep her off her feet with an unexpected kiss of passion.

She saw me coming and met me more than halfway in intention and even more in passion. I don't know who was more surprised, or if neither of us was surprised at all. Well, that one kiss preceded several more. Suffice it to say, she forgot to borrow the book. Instead, she asked me if I would marry her."

"Yes," replied Stan.

Amy took him home to meet her parents. They were immediately captivated by his charm, grace, and engaging personality. The wedding was a lavish affair displaying the talents of three Rabbis, special guest stars, and a menu featuring a plethora of kosher delicacies.

Because of his fame defending Jewish orphans, and his complete familiarity with all things Judaica, there was no need for him to convert to Judaism; he was presumed Jewish, and he didn't bother to correct anyone. He chose to be considered among the Chosen People. His actual upbringing in the Christian Orthodox Church was kept secret.

Everyone has secrets. Amy's secret was her active bisexuality.

"I returned home one afternoon earlier than she anticipated. My wife and her friend, or lover…I know this is all sounds so cliché," said Stan. "Trust me. Living an emasculating cliché is much worse than it sounds."

Stan stopped cold, stunned, and mortified by the sight of his wife's little feet kicking in orgasmic delight. To a traditional man such as him, seeing his beautiful wife being sexually pleased by another woman was devastating and emasculating.

Outraged, he turned on his heels, went into the kitchen and grabbed the biggest and sharpest knife he could find.

With all the focus and deadly determination at his comm and, he ran back into the bedroom like Norman Bates in *Psycho,* knife raised with killer intent. He swung that blade down as hard as he could right between the two women and into the thick cushiony mattress, gutting it right down the middle as if it were a large fish.

"I looked right into Amy's eyes as I did it," he explained to the authors, "and the look on her face was sheer terror. I'm sure she thought she and the other woman would suffer the same fate as the mattress."

With no further comment nor threat of personal violence, he simply walked out of the house and had the marriage annulled. He did not reveal to anyone the reason for the annulment and spoke not an unkind word about his first spouse. What he did retain were all the incredible upper-crust New York contacts, and bestowals from Amy's father for not revealing the reason for the annulment, including a Deli in Manhattan and another in Upstate New York, and a wedding gift of an Alpha Romeo Spider.

"This is where I learned the construction trade," said Stan," and the reason that I was the best sandwich maker was because I had my own deli after I married Amy."

If Amy's sexual infidelity scarred him emotionally, he kept those scars as concealed as those of the flesh hiding behind the stylish clothing of his personality in multi-layers of charm.

It was again his intellect, wit, wisdom, and financial generosity that drew the attention of another beautiful woman of New York old money, Leslie Olmsted, allegedly the great granddaughter of Frederick Law Olmsted, the architect of New York's Central Park.

Despite the Sara Lawrence College records' firm assertion that Leslie was not a direct descendent of the famed architect, Leslie was, for whatever reason, poised on the brink of undeniable wealth that was not available to her in her high school and college years.

"Leslie graduated fifth in her high school graduating class, and came to New York to attend Sarah Lawrence in September 1957," said Stan. "I didn't meet her at that time, but later after my divorce from Amy. Leslie had a quick, short-lived marriage to a Mr. Beauchamp that lasted less time, I believe, than it takes to watch *Gone with the Wind*. She immediately took back her family name and was Olmsted when I met her and Olmsted again after she left me."

When they met, Stan didn't know about her trust fund. She was several years away from tapping that, and she was financially struggling.

"Leslie had lost her apartment," recalls Stan. "I think her LSD experiments had her sidetracked."

Aside from admiring her paisley wallpaper and writing her name in the air with the bright red tip of a cigarette, young Leslie was not as enamored with Timothy Leary and Ram Dass as she was with Peter Max. As an artist she delighted in the visuals of psychedelia more than any quest for oneness with the universe.

Before her marriage to Stan, she wrote these lines: "After college I shall be married, honeymooned and ensconced in a New York apartment. Then the future becomes unclear, although my hope is to do work in graphic design—this desire having grown out of studies in stage designing and painting here at Sarah Lawrence."

Leslie's career took off and soon, as Editor in Chief for Carnegie Hall Magazine, Leslie appreciated Stan lending his journalistic skills. They collaborated on writing and editing numerous feature articles for the magazine.

Traveling to California in the early days of their marriage, the couple invested in what seemed an excellent opportunity—land in Southern California's Antelope Valley.

There is no valley, and there haven't been any indigenous antelope in the region for numerous decades. What Antelope Valley did have was the city of Palmdale, "The Glittering Jewel of the High Desert," a city whose future rested upon the projected and controversial construction of the Palmdale International Airport and expanded participation of the aerospace industry in the Palmdale economy.

The airport never got off the ground, and Palmdale became the bipolar real estate market poster child by its rapid cycle of high expectations and economic depressions that tarnished its brassy reputation.

When Stan discovered that the property in Antelope Valley was worth less at the end of his marriage to Leslie than it was on their honeymoon, he wrote her a check for half the community property's value: zero dollars and zero cents.

The couple did create one lasting and valuable contribution to society—a baby boy named Sasha Alexander Frederick Stanimirovic.

His name was edited and rewritten as Alex F. Olmsted when Leslie could no longer deal with what no one outside their home ever witnessed: Stan's unexpected anger outbursts that terrified Leslie.

"I was like a volcano inside but calm on the outside. I only erupted when I believed it was safe, that I was with people who, unlike the Nazis, loved me and wished me no harm. You take the heat of that anger, or perhaps outrage and indignation are better words, fuel it with alcohol, and…," The dramatic pause in Stan's narrative wasn't for effect, it was from emotion,

Stan promised to change, stop drinking, and go into therapy for his anger issues. "I did consult a therapist who confirmed that I suffered from what they now call PTSD, and what they used to call being shell shocked if you were a soldier in the war. Stop drinking? No. Change?" Stan shrugs, smiles, and asks, "How many Serbian men does it take to change a lightbulb? Only one, but the lightbulb itself must want to change."

If Leslie anticipated a quick resolution to Stan's issues, disappointment arrived faster and more efficiently. An escalating argument triggered Leslie going into labor for the birth of their only child.

"She didn't want me with her for the birth," recalled Stan. "She didn't want to see me at all. In fact, she even wrote on our apartment wall, in a moment of anger, 'Stan will never change'."

The day Leslie left him was the last time Stan saw his son, Alex.

Stan saw his own father again in 1962 when Stan went to Paris, France, to finalize a lucrative business arrangement with two young Serbians with significant New York connections: Bruno Sulak and his best pal, Biki.

"Biki's brother owned a Manhattan furniture store, and a Polish cousin, The Professor, taught French at a New York college," Stan explained. "Bruno and Biki would acquire silver and other valuable artifacts in Europe which I would purchase for resale in New York. By the very nature of the plan, everyone made money. Of course, Bruno became the most famous gentleman thief in the history of France. I bought many wonderful items from him over the years, but I was never given the backstory of conditions under which he may have acquired some of those items. Why would he confess crimes to me when we have a lucrative and legal business relationship? No, Bruno would not be so foolish as to interrupt our pleasant stream of natural cash flow."

While making money was second nature to Stan, his first nature was romancing women. The most signific heart he captured was that of a teenage Jewish girl from former Yugoslavia blessed with a fashion model's figure and fresh-faced beauty.

Unlike Stan, Amy, or Leslie, she didn't come from money, nor did she have the advantages of being high society in either the USA or Yugoslavia. That would all change with astonishing rapidity, making her the mink adorned better half of New York City's ultimate power couple.

Chapter Two
Branka

"1968,' said actor/producer Tom Hanks, "was the year that changed America." It was also the year that America forever changed the life of 18-year-old Branka Teofilovich, a gifted artist attending the University of Beograd.

"I received an art scholarship to New York's Parson's Academy. To me, New York City was a near-mythical city far away and far beyond someone such as I."

The prestigious yet partial scholarship was achieved by the advocacy of American Ambassador, Henry J. Taylor, and Branka's Aunt, Radmilla Marianovic, who worked for the Yugoslavian Embassy during the reign of Marshal Tito when that famed dictator came to America in 1962 for a historic meeting with United States President John F. Kennedy.

Tito returned to Yugoslavia, but Aunt Rada stayed in the USA where she became beloved, famed, and acclaimed for her remarkable party planning abilities and her undeniable talent in the kitchen. Ambassadors and Presidents hired her to cater their lavish events, and Rada lived in a twenty-room apartment made for the Saudi Royal Family, and then utilized by Sudanese Ambassadors. It was through Rada, employed by diverse Ambassadors, including Ambassador Taylor, that the lovely Branka took her first airplane ride.

"Good evening, ladies and gentlemen, this is your Captain speaking. if you look to your right, you will notice the New York skyline…"

Branka, mesmerized by the city coming out of the mist, felt a tear begin to roll down her cheek. She caught that single tear on the tip of her finger and used it to trace the New York skyline on the airplane's windowpane.

"I believed that in America, all my dreams of art and freedom, love and fulfillment, would come true," recalls Branka. "I was more excited than apprehensive. I entered the United States the same night that Richard Nixon was elected President. We both thought, no doubt, that our future was unspeakably glorious. From the moment I arrived in New York, my life was transformed. Suddenly I was among the elite of New York society."

Awaiting her upon arrival was a young Puerto Rican fellow, her driver, holding a sign with her name misspelled: Ms. Bianca Teofilovich. In her white miniskirt sprinkled with yellow daisies offsetting her long tan legs and the long hair cascading down to her perfectly formed posterior,

The young driver tried to impress her with his professionalism but fumbled both her single suitcase and his best pickup lines when he remembered that she didn't speak English.

With Branka in the passenger seat and the young driver behind the wheel, our artistic immigrant was whisked away to uptown Manhattan where she would live in that twenty-room mansion on Park Avenue.

Welcome to America.

Aunt Rada knew only the best people, the well to do who did very well and for whom extravagance in the service of hospitality was no vice. Rada wanted her niece to meet the up and coming within the ranks of the already established. Hence, Aunt Rada invited Branka to a high-class party on 5th Avenue and 50th Street in New York City.

The party was extravagant, celebrities and antiques were wall to wall, and those walls were adorned with rare paintings and valuable items crafted from pure silver. Parked downstairs was the owner's Alpha Romero; Parked upstairs like a benevolent monarch was the party's host, an alpha Romeo—the wealthy and influential entrepreneur known simply as Mr. Stan.

"Who owns this place?" asked Branka. "It looks like a museum. Who could afford this artwork, this exceptional wealth? Whoever it is, they either bought it or stole it, or perhaps both."

"As soon as I saw our suave Serbian host," recalls Branka, "I was attracted to him. He was exceptionally charming, and a graceful ballroom dancer as well."

"He pursued me aggressively that night," says Branka. "He didn't know I was ... what's the expression? Barely legal. I was smitten, I admit. When we found out that were from the same Communist country, that really lit the fuse on romantic fireworks. This older handsome man was really something. I couldn't get him off my mind. The party was long over, but I was not over him at all."

Mr. Stan was a man who moved fast. He immediately asked her to return, but not simply for a visit or a romantic tryst.

"You should move in with me," said Stan, half in jest. Branka heard no jest whatsoever. At first, she was slightly taken aback, but she didn't find the offer offensive or embarrassing. At that same opulent party, she met Stan's best friend, The Professor, an erudite Polish fellow who told Branka that he taught French at New York University.

"He was always dressed beautifully," recalls Branka, "complete with scarf and a cashmere long coat, sleek black gloves and the type of hat that gave him the air of a 1940s movie star. His cars were always Jaguars or Lincoln Town Cars. He had a most fascinating career and a multi-hued past. He was the only member of his family who survived the Nazi death camps. He was in the French Foreign Legion, an accomplished paratrooper, spoke numerous languages, a former Olympian, and the fastest man in Poland when it came to the 100m race."

Young Branka knew nothing of him beyond his demeanor and those above-mentioned highlights. The same could be said regarding her knowledge of the charming Mr. Stan.

"I asked Aunt Rada and her employer, Mr. Taylor, about Mr. Stan. I was told that Stan was a much-admired businessperson who ran a few of the most exceptional buildings in Manhattan, was very rich, and he comes from one of the most prestigious families in Novi Sad, Serbia. I admit I was young, easily influenced, and headstrong. After all, I said to Rada, Stan is respected and rich, and his best friend is a French Professor. They are professionals. How bad can it be?"

She had no idea.

The Professor's real name was Andre Montrose, although when he immigrated to America his name was Andrzej Zalenski. That name change was legal. His subsequent use of the names Alec Belmont, Marc Conti and Carl Martin for criminal purposes were not.

The Professor was regarded by the NYPD's Major Case Squad as an international man of mystery suspected of being either a mastermind of crime in disguise, or an educated, eccentric intellectual who perhaps justified forays into the outer fringes of criminality as sociological experiments or the flexing of unused mental muscles.

In the pop culture parlance of 1968, The Professor and Mr. Stan were the Frankie Lee and Judas Priest of New York high society.

"They were the best of friends," confirms Branka with a smile. "I must credit or perhaps blame the Professor for assuring that Stan and I became a couple. I decided to take Stan up on his offer, but tears were shed from day one."

Branka made her decision and rode to Stan's apartment in the limo used by the Sudanese Ambassadors courtesy of Aunt Rada. When she arrived at Stan's door, suitcase in hand, she discovered she wasn't the only female in residence.

"The other woman was his live-in flight attendant who made sure he kept his tray table in an upright position. One look at her, and all hell broke loose. I let him have it, but good," she remembers. "I told him that he was no good, and I started sobbing as only a heartbroken and distraught teenager can sob."

Branka laid down an ultimatum: "Either she goes, or I go." Any indecision on Stan's part evaporated in the heat of reason supplied by his best friend, The Professor. "Keep Branka," said the Professor. "She is a diamond."

The only interaction between Branka and either of Stan's previous wives was when Leslie Olmstead came to the apartment to retrieve various personal items that originally belonged to her mother.

"She didn't want to see Stan. Their divorce was not yet final, but was in process," recalls Branka, "so she came when he was in Europe on business, and I was there to help her get those things she wanted. There was a painting, however, that she left behind because it was too large to fit in her trunk."

Leslie paused and looked Branka over from top to bottom, offered a knowing, compassionate smile, and shared from the heart.

"Stan is really wonderful," said Leslie. "He is a true loyal friend, an entertaining conversationalist, talented, brilliant. He knows how to do almost anything and do it well except two things: He is not a good husband and he's not a good father. Otherwise, he's wonderful."

Branka was unaware of Stan's anger issues, and even if she were informed, she was so in love that she would ignore them anyway.

Branka was soon Stan's lawfully wedded wife and an integral aspect of his remarkable lifestyle. As with all whirlwind romances, the participants seldom see each other's flaws or deep personal scars.

"Once we were married," says Branka, "I was aware that my husband's body, amazingly perfect in every way, was marked by well-concealed and seldom revealed scars in what I will call personal areas. The older ones were from the night of the Nazis, and others were from his escape from Communist Yugoslavia."

"My husband was a man of discipline," Branka recalls, "not only his own discipline, but he would inflict discipline upon me in unexpected ways at unexpected times. But I was young, madly in love with this charismatic man of exquisite taste who shared my national origin and my love of all forms of art."

Soon she would also be forever wed to a new art form: The art of the heist.

"What did I know of sophisticated criminals? Nothing at all. The concept never crossed my mind. I was a naïve young girl from Serbia. All I knew of America, and American culture, I learned amid luxury in his Manhattan apartment."

When did Stan become a gentleman thief? He was already doing heists when Branka married him.

Stan was encouraged by his new pals from the old country to experience the adrenaline augmented comradery of what Stan later termed "planning and executing altruistic non-violent exercises in the redistribution of wealth."

"Victimless crimes. He was forever hooked," says Branka. "For him, it was his greatest pleasure, his beloved indulgence."

Others say that Stan's criminal trajectory went from risky hobby to full time obsession when he used his new skills as retaliation for a wrong done him by a client for whom he was doing construction work.

"That is a classic story," says Branka, "and I have heard it told many times, but never exactly the same."

The skeleton of the story goes something like this:

Stan was doing work for a local construction firm when he purchased a brand-new Pontiac GTO. Putting the car through its paces on the streets of New York, Stan lost control of the muscle car and crashed directly into an NYPD precinct headquarters.

Aside from the affrontery of full-frontal damage, the cops found the accident absurdly amusing. Stan, sensing their suspicion of his decidedly foreign accent, suggested they call the construction company for assurance that he was an upstanding, responsible individual.

The construction company did exactly the opposite. and went so far as to term Stan a criminal.

Stan was incredulous. According to legend, he decided to make them correct at their own financial peril. Stan enlisted the aid of his pal Biki who was in New York to visit his brother who owned a furniture business in Manhattan, and his Polish cousin, alias the Professor. A few payoffs later, Stan and his pal Biki from France stood triumphantly in front of a formidable vault containing a great deal of money, the bulk of it belonging to the offending construction firm.

"It was supposed to be easy," recounts Stan in one version of events. "We were given the combination to the vault in advance from our inside connection. But no matter how many times we tried it, it didn't work. I was so angry and frustrated that I grabbed a hammer and threw it at the side of the vault. The hammer tore through the vault as if it were made of paper Mache! There was nothing secure about that vault at all. It was all impressive from the front, but it was as easy to tear open as a bag of potato chips. That was, as far as anyone knows, the first vault ripped open from the side for a successful heist."

After that, they hit every soft vault in the Diamond District.

"One of the techniques I pioneered," admits Stan casually, "was to penetrate the vault from underneath the floor because it was just a normal floor that could be cut through easily. We used hydraulics and we even had a full time Croatian hydraulics expert in my crew by the name of Nikola."

"When I married Stan," states Branka, "he was managing his legitimate business concerns, but also doing highly sophisticated heists, almost baffling in their brilliance, which were almost all inside jobs committed for a very altruistic reason. I would have to say that he was always a gentleman, and he saw himself somewhat like Robin Hood."

Stan, the epitome of generosity, did favors for people that he liked—never for money, and he was paid back with trust by the Mellon family, the DuPonts, Vanderbilts, Olmsted, Rockefeller, and Chrysler. They owned buildings that needed attention and security, and they paid Stan to oversee these properties and manage them. His "Stan's Construction" was for the elite of New York who wanted custom quality projects. Among those who formed a strong relationship with Mr. Stan were Andy Warhol, Pierre Balmain, and Phillip Pearlstein.

He also invested in restaurants and built his own Anita's Chile, Dubrovnik, and did the construction for Tavern on the Green. He remodeled New York's museums and made a fortune from all the old storage units that had prewar skeleton key locks. These units had remained untouched and unpaid for decades, and the building owners wanted them cleaned out. Stan was told that he could keep or sell anything of value.

"My husband found wealth like you will never believe," recounts Branka, "old books that cost, today, $1.5 million— paintings and antique furniture —and this was like a gift from heaven. We opened Gallery Antiques and I partnered with the Manhattan Antique Flea markets. Walter Chrysler collected all manner of antiques and nostalgia, paying top dollar and loving the rarities we offered."

As for the heist aspect, planning those was part of his daily routine. Up at 5:05 a.m., Stan did a few hundred pushups, then went for his morning walk in Central Park, and then would convene with his best friend, the Professor, to plan detailed heists over demitasse cups of strong coffee. Then he would begin addressing his myriad business interests.

"My first heists weren't diamonds and precious gems," admits Stan, "they were antiques of astonishing value—rugs, paintings, and incredible handcrafted silver artifacts at a time when high-end antique dealers were experiencing an economic downturn and they needed an immediate influx of cash. As with the later diamond heists, the sudden theft of their priceless inventory meant a windfall of operating capital." Stan's sterling reputation earned him the nickname, *Stan Silver.*

His later heists were primarily executed in New York's Diamond District. Notorious for its long standing and almost impenetrable criminality, any novice diamond buyer or diamond seller would be taken advantage of to the greatest degree possible.

"The district," commented former NYPD Detective Bo Dedle, "is crawling with liars and thieves who rob the customers and rob each other."

The diamond dealers and manufacturing firms were not the biggest crooks in the district. That title belongs to the insurance and security companies.

Chapter Three
The Protection Scam

"It was a protection racket, plain and simple," recalls jeweler Benny Shmeckle* "except it was legal. These insurance companies were saying we had to pay two thousand dollars a week for insurance, and we would say that we didn't need it. No one was robbing us, why do we need insurance? Well, the next thing you know, we would be robbed. No coincidence. 'Buy our insurance, buy our security or else.' Well, it was a racket. And then a miracle—along came Mr. Stan with a most brilliant idea…"

The true twist in the tale is that the robberies done on behalf of the insurance companies to force payment and compliance were arranged by the Mafia. Yes, there has always been a close linkage between insurance and crime. After all, who knows the protection racket better than the Mob?

The insurance company would request the Mob to rob a certain jeweler, and the Mob would make sure the job got done right by farming it out to reliable professionals who had no idea who was really hiring them, or why. The Mob's contact was Alex "Texas" Karalanovic, a successful immigrant with a dubious past linked to old-world criminality and intense political activism that boiled over into occasional overt terrorism.

As a hot-headed teenager, Alex attempted assault on Yugoslavian dictator Marshall Tito at the Waldorf Astoria when Tito visited New York.

If Alex would have had a gun instead of a knife, Tito would be dead.

"Alex's mother was married to an American in Iowa," Branka recalls. "He couldn't be deported. He got in a lot of trouble when he was younger back in the old country—he stole a car that had important papers in it belonging to the American Ambassador. His joy ride earned him four years in prison."

It was behind bars that teenage Alex met a charming, educated and, refined light-fingered fellow known as Biki. Together they escaped prison and made it first from Yugoslavia to Paris. Biki, of course, introduced Alex to his best friend, Bruno Sulac and all of them became close friends and associates of Mr. Stan.

"Alex had a cab company and he drove a blue van," says Branka. "I remember he always had a yarmulke in his glove compartment for when he sold diamonds on 47th Street so people would think he was Jewish. In truth, he was a criminal from Italy with the School of Turin."

"Everything is tied in and connected," comments Paul. "My father, Alex and the Professor all connected in New York. Stan went to Paris to meet Biki in 1962 and they became fast friends. It is now far too late for the Feds to put together the pieces and build a case that has been cold for over twenty years."

Yes, it was Stan and the Professor who did the work for hire, unaware of who hired them.

When Stan heard the Jewish merchants bemoaning this protection racket, he had an epiphany of brilliant, diamond-like clarity. He would right this wrong by turning the game on its head.

Stan consulted with the put-upon Jewish merchants being extorted, and advised them to buy even more insurance, and load up their safes with each other's merchandise to increase their insured inventory.

"The brilliant thieves would acquire office space under the vaults or rent property next door or even next door to next door—drill through the walls of two businesses to get to our safes," a willing victim confirmed. "We would come to work in the morning, and everything would be gone—everything! Well, we were highly insured for more than we ever actually had on hand. The insurance company paid us the full value in two weeks. We all made a fantastic profit."

The diamond district is a hotbed of clever, yet common criminals, but Mr. Stan was not a common criminal. He was distinguished by his honesty, his ethics, and most of all by the fact that you could trust him one hundred percent. The police never arrested Stan for what he did in the diamond district because they never caught him, nor could they directly link him to any specific heist.

Detective Thomas Connolly had been investigating a series of diamond district heists for several months, but these athletic acrobatic criminals were beyond anything the NYPD had ever encountered and were responsible for over forty spectacular heists in the diamond district.

"They were fantastic," said Connolly, "like something out of a movie. They swung on ropes from building to building."

Obviously, this wasn't the work of pasta-stuffed overweight Mafia thugs. No, these were incredibly athletic individuals of great skill with precision planning.

After many frustrating months, Connolly finally watched this crew in the act on August 12, 1970, by using military night vision goggles developed for use during the Vietnam War.

"Yes, it is one hundred percent true what the investigators said about Stan's crew," says Branka. "They repelled off buildings like acrobats. This system of escape was designed by Stan as he was very smart in figuring out ways to escape.

What he really wanted was the James Bond Jet Pack so after a heist the crew could just fly away."

"They only caught one fellow," Branka remembers, "who gave his name as Raymond Smith. That wasn't his real name, and when he was released on his personal recognizance, they never saw him again."

No one ever used their real name if arrested. Their fake name was fully validated with an address and the name of someone who would vouch for them, so they could make bail or be released on their own recognizance.

"We always had people on the outside ready and waiting to validate the name, address and reputation of the individual arrested," confirmed Branka. "They would say, 'of course we know Mr. Smith, he's been at this address for twenty years and he works at such and such.' and they would sound concerned about Mr. Smith making it to work today. Everything looked and sounded official to make sure we got them out of jail."

Raymond Smith, prior to release, allegedly ratted out Mr. Stan as the man behind the brilliant and daring heists. Connolly waited and watched, keeping an eye on the dapper Mr. Stan.

"[Stan and his wife, Branka] had been under surveillance for four months for mega jewel burglaries that they had carried out in the Manhattan Diamond District." Detective Tom Connolly later confirmed.

The police officers didn't go to Stan's apartment to arrest him for heists, or even question him regarding any potential involvement. They went to his apartment to shake him down for a payoff.

Of all the days to pull their shakedown, the NYPD had to pick one immediately following the world-famous Vizcaya Museum Heist. To this day, Branka shudders at the mention of that horrific home invasion coupled with outright extortion by corrupt cops who humiliated her, terrorized her, and dragged her off to jail.

"That nightmare altered my life and the life of my husband completely," she laments. "Stan and I are forever linked to the infamous and highly publicized Vizcaya Museum Heist."

Chapter Four
Vizcaya

In truth, there never was a Vizcaya Museum Heist. In fact, there was never even a robbery or burglary. There is more than one version of that story, and the truth has never before been revealed. The Miami Herald told it this way:

Three robbers lured an elderly guard at the Vizcaya Museum from his office, overpowered him and stole a valuable antique silver collection.

That was the guard's well-rehearsed story, and he livened it up with colorful details on how these dangerous men tricked him, jumped him, tied him up, and then stole the museum's collection of priceless silver. Newspapers ran diagrams of the Museum with notes showing the progress of the midnight hour criminals who trussed up our elderly guard and made off with the boodle.

It was a complete lie.

There were no robbers, no one tied him up, and there never was a daring heist. It was all a scam by the long-time guard who had a longtime gambling problem that put him at the mercy of a local bookie with ties to one of the most feared enforcers for the Chicago outfit, Harry "The Hook" Aleman.

The guard had been pilfering minor treasures from the museum for quite a while. Now, he needed to pay his gambling debts.

He quietly let it be known that he had items for sale of significant value. The guard had previously sold singular items to Alex "Texas" Karalanovic, owner of a New York taxicab company as well as business investments in Texas. He, in turn, sold silver pieces to Mr. Stan, a known buyer and collector of fine art, antiques, and silver.

When you compare that original Miami Herald story with what the Vizcaya Museum says today, you can easily discern that there is no similarity between the two narratives.

Here is what the Vizcaya Museum says about that event:

On March 22, 1971, three individuals from New York City raided the Vizcaya and stole approximately $1,500,000 in artwork and silver items, some of which were of historical value. This trio of reputed jewel thieves was arrested on March 25, 1971. Sergeant Tom Connolly from the New York Police Department raided the luxurious Manhattan apartment of Vojislav Stanimirovic and his wife Branka and arrested them. The couple's accomplice, Alexander Karalanovic, was also arrested, and all three were charged with suspicion of possession of stolen property... From the Stanimirovics' apartment, approximately $250,000 of the stolen goods was recovered. Sergeant Connolly stated that included in the theft was a silver bowl that once belonged to Napoleon Bonaparte and was virtually priceless. According to Sergeant Connolly, the three perpetrators had been under surveillance for four months for unrelated mega jewel burglaries that they had carried out in the Manhattan Diamond District. NYPD Captain Thomas Kissane said that the vast majority of the precious items stolen from the Vizcaya were not ever recovered.

Depending upon who's telling the story, it is either a clever combination of creative criminality, nail-biting crowd-pleasing bravado, or an over-the-top comedy best portrayed by the cast of "My Cousin Vinny."

In Branka's version, the famous museum heist begins with nothing more than a delightful opportunity for a romantic sun-drenched celebration of her husband's birthday.

"Ambassador John H. Taylor, employer of Aunt Rada, asked my husband to do him a favor: pick up Taylor's new Rolls Royce in Florida and bring it up to Manhattan. Where in Florida? The Vizcaya Museum and Gardens. When? The weekend of my husband's birthday, March 19, 1971."

The Vizcaya, a famed National Historic Site, was once the winter residence of industrialist James Deering and was designed as a palatial Italian Villa on tropical Biscayne Bay. He filled it with European art, state of the art technology and surrounded it with beautiful gardens.

Branka was excited to go away with Stan for his birthday. Just the two of them alone together in lovely Florida at the glorious, enchanting Vizcaya, followed by a pleasant drive up the coast in Mr. Taylor's Rolls Royce. Visions of rekindled romance put a sparkle in her eyes and a fresh spring in her step.

Ambassador Taylor purchased two first-class tickets to Ft. Lauderdale, and Branka was one happy passenger until they landed and were about to retrieve their luggage.

Pulling up to the terminal was an unexpected and unwelcome sight: Stan's friend of questionable legality and cocaine proclivities, Alex "Texas" Karalanovic in a white Cadillac convertible loaded with Stan's fishing poles sticking up from the back seat, and a Cuban cigar clamped between his teeth.

"Hey, Stan," he called out, "I rented this until you get the Rolls!"

Branka knew immediately that this wasn't going to be a birthday weekend of candlelight, roses, and fine wine, and Stan sure as hell didn't bring her to Florida to sit on her hands while he went sport fishing.

Something was up, and she was visibly upset. Stan tried to calm her down but telling women to calm down is like telling cats to do synchronized swimming.

She became as animated as a Warner Bros. cartoon, and one can easily picture the steam rising as her temperature increased. Stan was scary when angry, but even he knew better than to mess with his beautiful young wife in public.

Alex knew both well enough to have serious concerns about the impact of Branka's suspicion about the upcoming sideline assignment—pick up some merchandise being sold by the overnight guard. He had a significant fortune in suitcases secured in a conveniently located closet on the Estate. The key to that closet was provided by the guard.

"It is very simple," said Alex. "There are seven suitcases full of stuff from a guard who works nights at the museum. I've bought from him before. If you're going to be at the Vizcaya, you can bring a couple of the suitcases back to New York for me, and I'll bring the rest."

All Stan and Branka had to do was roll the suitcases out of the closet and into a van that was already parked nearby on the estate, as was Taylor's Rolls-Royce.

Now, here is an astonishing never-before-revealed twist to the tale. You can scour the internet and the crime books of the world and never find this story because it has never been revealed until now:

There was a daring double-cross, a second treasure, and a late-night fake robbery at the Museum long after Stan and Branka drove off to New York in Taylor's Rolls Royce with two of the eight Louie Viton suitcases. Alex summoned some backup, including Stan's boyish tousle-haired protégé, Billy the Kid because there was the Cadillac, the guard's van and Alex's blue van as well.

Stan, driving the Cadillac rental, arrives at the Vizcaya at ten in the morning where he sees Alex's blue van and Taylor's white Rolls Royce parked in the restricted parking area. Alex and the guard have gone off somewhere for a meeting and will return when the guard's shift begins at 4 pm.

Having arrived at the Estate, Stan and Branka became enchanted with the beautiful expanse of glorious gardens, and Branka's dream of a romantic getaway became a reality.

"Vizcaya is very romantic, indeed," says Branka, a blush on her cheeks, "and Stan was very virile; I was a younger woman. We had a most exciting time exploring everything a couple in love could do on the beautiful grounds of the Vizcaya Estate."

Do the math: One handsome husband, one beautiful, younger wife, and twenty-three acres of exquisite gardens. "We explored the Estate in the most romantic manner possible, the details best left to your imagination."

Climaxing their adventure at the Vizcaya, the couple realized that the closet containing the suitcases was right in front of them, and the Rolls Royce was easily accessible They simply unlocked the closet, removed the eight suitcases, loaded five of them into Alex's van, and the final two into the trunk of the Rolls-Royce.

When Alex and the guard returned at 4 p.m., Stan and Branka said their goodbyes, but the guard became angry.

"Put everything back in the closet! "

"No," said Stan, "we're not putting anything back. We did exactly what you wanted, and we're leaving."

The reason the guard was angry is that he had planned to double-cross everyone by having the heist be a robbery taking place on his shift, with him being tied up while the robbers load up the van with treasure. He would then identify the van and get everyone caught and arrested.

He would have the money to pay off his bookie, plus he would be a hero for getting the swag back. That's the way he planned it, and he was determined to stick to that plan no matter what.

Alex didn't know about the double cross, but he was informed that there was more treasure to be had if he and a few other guys could load up the van with more merchandise. The guard had his fake robbery all arranged for later that night.

Alex was no slouch when it came to last minute necessities—he was on the phone in a heartbeat, summoning a few trusted associates vacationing in Orlando, and securing the required cash for the transaction.

Alex and his crew came during the guard's shift; they loaded up the other items in Alex's blue van and waved goodbye to the cooperating guard who promptly told numerous lies to the police and gave an accurate description of a van that was later found abandoned on the New Jersey Turnpike. That van wasn't Alex's, it was the guard's own van.

Who drove it away, what was in it, and what was happening?

Two teenagers drove the guard's van away filled with rarities from the museum's current display and dutifully left in on the turnpike so everything could be recovered. Their reward for being fall guys in an aspect of the plan never shared with Alex or Stan was a quick conviction and prison time.

What about the contents of the suitcases and other boodle loaded in Alex's blue van? All the suitcases wound up at Stan and Branka's apartment, Alex delivered them along with what other non-display items the guard had selected for his own private sale.

A Florida newspaper story confirms that, "the stolen silver was recovered from the van and was identified by the owners who allowed it displayed at the museum." The recovered silver was indeed displayed at the museum; the items in the suitcase were also from Vizcaya, but not from the displayed collection.

The Vizcaya guard never mentioned Stan and Branka, the suitcases or the Rolls Royce. He had one story and he stuck to it—late night robbers who tied him up.

The NYPD cops who arrested Stan, Branka, and Alex had no knowledge of the Vizcaya Museum Heist. These cops were allegedly in the pocket of one of New York's five Mafia families. That is an important detail, a detail of such magnitude that its significance eluded their son, Paul, for many decades.

"This all happened before I was born," says Paul, "but I heard the story all my life, and I used to tell the story as if it were about a bunch of crooked cops robbing my folks. It's not. This is the story of how some over-eager, allegedly corrupt, mobbed-up cops handed my father the keys to the master lock, threw wide the gates of financial opportunity, and forever sealed Mr. Stan's fortune and his soon-to-be son's future."

When these cops saw all the incredible silver, art, antiques, and precious gems, they assumed it must all be stolen. No, it wasn't all stolen. Most of the items taken from the apartment had no connection to the Vizcaya, and were, Branka insists, acquired legally.

"The cops decided to extort money from us," recalls Branka. "They wanted a six thousand dollar cash payoff. Thankfully, Stan didn't have six thousand in cash on him. At least that's what he told the cops. They pressured him, but he insisted that he simply didn't have the cash."

Of course not.

If he gave these guys cash, it would be divided up, stuffed in their pockets, and end of story. The Mafia family for whom the cops worked would never hear about the six thousand cash, let alone where it came from. Plus, there would be nothing to keep these jerks from coming back again for more cash.

"Gentleman," said Stan in words such as these, "follow me and I will show you something astonishing. I assure you that when you leave tonight, both our futures will be assured and trouble-free."

Intrigued, these crooked cops dutifully followed him to what can only be described as "The Treasure Room." It might have taken car jacks to lift their jaws off the floor when they beheld what Mr. Stan so readily revealed. When negotiations were over, the cops called for backup. They needed two vans and more men to load up all the valuables. And then they loaded Stan and Branka and heaped humiliation on young Branka who was tossed in the local slammer and treated like crap. She was terrified, alone, and scared.

Stan, dapper as ever, entered the men's unit as if a conquering hero. Everyone admired Mr. Stan except the asshole cops who robbed him. The inmates were impressed because he was being held on one hundred thousand dollars bail, an amount usually reserved for someone charged with first degree murder.

No problem.

The Professor, Andre Montrose, showed up with cash in hand to pay the bail, but the authorities still held Stan and Banka a while longer to make sure the money was neither counterfeit nor stolen.

"Almost everything those cops stole from us," insists Branka, "was purchased or acquired legally. They took rare books, Tiffany lamps, and antique silver items my husband collected and paid for. The cops took merchandise estimated at a value of over one million dollars."

One million buys a lot more than six thousand, especially when men of a certain standing and reputation in the community must make sincere amends for the regrettable actions of underlings.

Do I need to draw you a picture?

Had the cops sought permission from a Mafia family to rob Mr. Stan, the permission would never be granted. Mr. Stan is not the man you rob; he is the man you admire and respect. He is a man of his word, and a man you can trust.

All five New York Mafia families knew his standing among the famed financiers and developers whose roots were deeper in the city's corrupt soil than any of them. The heads of the five families comprehended the situation perfectly, and you should grasp that in the world of criminals there are thugs and punks and semi-illiterate opportunists devoid of any moral compass. and then you have the elite of the elite—the top floor, the penthouse atop the pinnacle of crime's hierarchy is the one who can do that which is the greatest and most prestigious act of all—a diamond heist where no one is hurt, and even the victims are, in the final analysis, perfectly happy. That, of course, was Mr. Stan, a man of means but by no means a punk thug armed robber or "I hope nobody is home" burglar.

They owed Mr. Stan more than heartfelt condolences for the affront to his privacy, safety, and dignity. Gentlemen do not treat other gentlemen with such crude thuggery, and there would be sincere assurances that such a tragic error was never sanctioned by them, that no such event would ever happen again, and while Mr. Stan, his lovely wife, and his friend Alex were arrested, the charges were "on suspicion of possessing stolen property" and that's as far as it went. As far as Branka was concerned, it went far too far.

"It was a horrible and demeaning experience. We had just returned from a lovely trip to Florida for Stan's birthday, visited the Vizcaya Gardens, picked up some suitcases that we were asked to pick up, and brought Ambassador Taylor's Rolls Royce back to New York. And suddenly I'm being treated as some sort of criminal."

Arrested on Friday and released on Monday while Stan was still in jail, Branka returned home to find ….

"Nothing! I found nothing at all! The entire apartment had been completely cleaned out—looted one hundred percent. I didn't even have underwear or a change of clothes," recalls Branka, "Where did it go? It went to the home of the Virdens, a family of Croatians from Serbia. I go there, and I see this woman wearing my dress! All our possessions are now in this other family's home. All the cash I had in my bedroom is now in Mr. Virdan's pocket. If I wanted what was in his pockets, I had to take what was in his pants. He wanted sex with me first before he would return anything."

The thief suggested that he and Branka run off together to California, a trip financed by the money he stole from her apartment.

"Are you crazy? What are you thinking? You steal everything I have, and then expect me to have sex with you and run off with you? It was horrible," says Branka, "we had everything taken from us except our prestige, my looks, and Stan's charm."

It wouldn't be long before they were back in the highlife again but in the meantime, it was Aunt Rada to the rescue. She was living in the twenty-room luxury apartment utilized on and off by the Sudanese Ambassadors. In an apartment that size, whose residents were seldom in residence, it was easy to move Stan and Branka in without anyone ever noticing. There was plenty of food and delightful accommodations; it served as an excellent launching pad for the next stage of Stan and Branka's career in the realm of high society reputations and higher yield heists.

The lovely Branka is as famed for her minimizing as she is for her ability to select the most lucrative and easily accomplished heists. Hence, one must magnify Stan's and her complicity in any criminal endeavor in which Branka may portray her husband and herself as almost innocent bystanders.

Regardless of appropriate credit or ignoble complicity, the question New York's five Mafia families had to ask themselves was, "How do you make amends to a man whom you so admire?"

Every crime boss knows that having a judge in your pocket is nothing compared to having a US Ambassador up your sleeve, plus open checkbooks from the wealthiest families in New York. The heads of the five families would give dearly to be as connected and respected as Mr. Stan.

How is it that the charming rogue millionaire heist master never was arrested, detained, questioned, or mistreated again by the boys in blue or the anti-crime leaders? Simple. He had established his ascendency over them most graciously.

He didn't seek revenge for the robbery because the robbery was his revenge for the attempted shakedown, and its outcome a demonstration of true power born of insight, wit, wisdom and a mind that saw in full color 70mm what others only saw in 16mm black and white.

Despite being "linked" to the Vizcaya Heist in the museum's history brochure, they were never prosecuted for anything related to the heist itself, and their prestige in New York's high society did not drop by even a percentage point. Mr. Stan continued to manage the most prestigious buildings in New York City and was the go-to man for any repairs, construction or painting on the city's famed museums and galleries.

You can imagine their old-money clients explaining the Vizcaya incident away with the honest explanation that Mr. Stan was always buying antiques, silver, art and artifacts, so it is certainly possible to innocently purchase stolen merchandise.

"It was probably some absurd misunderstanding," one darling dowager with a large hat and larger purse would say to Branka. Ever so gracious, Branka would never say, "Actually, my husband and I made off with 1.5 million dollars in rarities and brought them to Manhattan in the trunk of a new Rolls Royce belonging to the former United States Ambassador to Switzerland!"

The intense press coverage—over one hundred newspaper stories in the USA alone—made Mr. Stan even more famous in Serbia than he already had become because of his business success.

3 Seized With $250,000 In Allegedly Stolen Items

SPECIAL TO THE NEW YORK
TIMES MARCH 25, 1971

The police seized more than $250,000 in allegedly stolen antique silver, Jewelry, paintings, and other items last night at a cooperative apartment house at 27 West 55th Street.

An art importer, his wife and a taxi driver were arrested and charged with possession of stolen property and illegal possession of a deadly weapon—an automatic pistol.

The authorities in Florida were notified in connection with the more than $500,000 in antique silver, stolen from the Vizcaya Museum in Miami Monday.

Those arrested were identified as Vojistan Stanimirovic, 34 years old and his wife, Branka, 22, of the 55th Street address, and Alexander Karilanovic, 31, of 110 East 36th Street.

Alexander "Texas" Karilanovic and Mr. Stan had a falling out sometime later when Alex helped himself to one of Mr. Stan's heists.

That ended their professional relationship, and Alex retired to Florida.

Soon, when the Serbian Diaspora of the 1980s and 1990s was fully underway, people came to America with the singular goal of meeting Mr. Stan in hopes of finding employment. They were, of course, one hundred percent rewarded and assimilated.

No one man did more to employ and integrate newly arrived refugees into mainstream middle-class America than Mr. Stan. From doormen at the exclusive residence hotels to Security Guards for Holmes and Wells Fargo, Mr. Stan was the man who could assure your future by his extensive social contacts and his own personal generosity.

Of all the surprise repercussions of the Vizcaya incident, one incident was entirely conceivable: a baby. Yes, the adrenalin rush of that whole fracas not only stimulated Mr. Stan's criminal evolution, but also planted a seed that in the fullness of gestation became little Paul Stanimirovic. Branka, once an innocent eighteen-year-old art student who came to America less than three years before, was married, pregnant and, forever associated with a world-famous heist that never happened.

Chapter Five
Birth of a Bandit

Little Paul (Pavle) was born May 10th, 1972, in Roosevelt Hospital, Midtown, New York City. His mother took him strolling in a bassinet alongside Mia Farrow's sister with whom she was close.

Within the year, the child made his first visit to Yugoslavia, and upon return to New York, his father started Stanley Construction and Stan's Paint Company.

Stan's Paint was both a legitimate paint company employing an army of honest immigrants from Eastern Europe and the front for a small precision heist team of trained professionals.

Here is a most basic chronology of a Stan's Paint Quickie:

A white van pulls up to The Gallery on Madison Avenue, and five painters carry in the drop cloths, paint cans, brushes and appropriate signage. A quick coat of paint soon glistens on the gallery benches, and "Wet Paint" signs and drop cloths route patrons away from the painters' work.

Next on their "to-do" list are two priority items: the wall safe and the display cases. In the one-minute maximum that it takes one painter to crack and loot the safe, the other painters smash and grab multi-millions in diamonds, dumping the rocks into three-fourths filled cans of paint.

Within one minute, the safe's contents, the diamonds and the five painters are gone. The white van casually flows to the sea of similar vans on the streets of New York. No witness can identify the white clad, white masked painters in the nondescript white van. Even if the van were stopped for being suspiciously white, a search would find no precious gems—only painters from a most reputable painting company delivering paint, brushes and drop cloths.

For Stan's Paint Company, this was business as usual. It was all about speed, all about precision, all about doing everything as if it were a choreographed performance: How long does it take to open a door? How long for a response team to follow through? Every question was answered in stop-watched minutes, seconds, and seconds' fragments.

Precision timing, precision practice, precision performance.

No matter how expansive Stan's business interests, there was always time for travel and family outings. In 1974, the family visited California, Florida, and Yugoslavia.

"I have only olfactory memories of the first two visits," says Paul, "but I recall perfectly the different scents and aromas. We visited my mother's hometown of Vircin. I loved it. When my mother left there, she ran away from heaven."

Branka has two equally gorgeous sisters who delighted in their sibling's successful marriage to such a wealthy Serbian-American. "And they also," says Paul, "enjoyed playing with me and spoiling me. My mother and her sisters were like the Gabor sisters or the Kardashians, except better looking of course."

Aunt Rada's only son, Uncle Paul, came to America in late 1975 determined to become one hundred percent American.

"Rada is my mother by birth," says Uncle Paul. "My sister and I were raised by my grandmother who survived the Nazis because her non-Jewish friends hid her and kept her from being smoke and ashes. My sister and I regard Branka as if she were our sister rather than a cousin. We were all raised together. Every year they would visit us in Yugoslavia, and I dreamed of going to America and making something of myself—the opportunities in what was then Communist Yugoslavia were limited, severely limited. Once in America, I had no interest in going back to Yugoslavia and I know for a fact that while Yugoslavia can be beautiful, there is something wonderful about America to me. I'm very proud to be an American citizen. In 1976, my mother, Stan, Branka and I purchased a new house in Fort Lee, New Jersey."

It was in that house, in 1977, that Branka experienced the unforgettable sight of her baby boy, not yet five years old, held with a gun to his head. Little Paul felt the cold steel against his temple and saw the haunting images of his parents humiliated, tied up and robbed. This was Little Paul's first taste of the betrayal and duplicity that his family would deal with all their lives.

Chapter Six
The Home Invasion

10:15 p.m.

The doorbell of the family residence rang at exactly 10:15 p.m., shortly after Uncle Paul left to go on a date to Studio 54.

Uncle Paul had lots of dates with beautiful women because he was, by his own admission, remarkably good-looking. If being good-looking were a fault, you can't blame the man—it was simply a fact of life.

Branka opened the door and welcomed Mr. Kardash and Mr. Kikila, two men from whom Stan and she purchased artwork and antiques.

"I didn't like those two men," says Uncle Paul. "They were not good to have in your home. It wasn't any of my business, but if it were my business, I wouldn't do business with them."

Kardash and Kikila had recently enlisted Stan's expertise on a multi-million-dollar jewelry heist in Paterson, New Jersey. They knew the location and how to get in, but when it came to safes, the combination of Kardash and Kikila couldn't open a K-Mart lockbox.

These two were not in Stan's league. They were lower-level Damon Runyon characters with more bravado than brains. Branka let them in and went to put on a fresh pot of coffee. Mr. Kardash politely excused himself to use the bathroom.

"There wasn't a bathroom on the main floor," Branka said. "He went up the stairs and I didn't think anything of it."

Kardash went directly to Little Paul's bedroom, grabbed the child from his bed, put a gun to the little boy's head and carried him downstairs.

The evening's social atmosphere screeched to a halt when Stan and Branka saw a .357 to their child's temple. Kardash cocked the gun and ordered the shocked parents to get on the floor where they were tied up with lengths of rope Kikila had concealed under his jacket.

The two men then looted the home of at least one million dollars in diamond jewelry recently brought home from a safety deposit box.

"One man carried me," recalls Little Paul, "gun to head, directing the other what to grab and load into a pillowcase. My father, by miracle or ingenuity, broke free from his bonds just like an action hero—fast, strong athletic and dangerous. He quickly freed my mother and confronted the two thieves as if he were bulletproof. Why they didn't shoot, I don't know, but I remember being tossed to the floor, hearing the crashing of glass, my mother crying and calling my name."

The two men smashed through a large window to the outside and ran like hell with Stan in hot pursuit. Meanwhile, the diamond jewelry was falling out of the pillowcase, leaving a dazzling multi-faceted trail on the grass all the way to Fort Lee Park. The two thieves kept running, and Stan kept chasing them. Branka called the police. Little Paul hid under Uncle Paul's bed.

"That's where I was at 4:00 in the morning when Uncle Paul came home to me under his bed, sobbing and terrified."

"When the police arrived," recounts Branka, "they asked me who the jewelry belonged to, and I told them it belonged to my husband and me, and I told them who robbed us," says Branka. "The police listened, consulted among themselves, and … you won't believe this—they arrested me. I was still on probation from that Vizcaya nonsense, so they took me into custody again on suspicion of possessing stolen merchandise. They wanted to charge my husband also, but he quickly figured out what was the most likely scenario when the police arrived, and he didn't come home, which didn't surprise me. He had an excellent attorney, David Lenefsky, who made sure that Stan wasn't charged with anything serious, and simply advised to exercise due diligence when purchasing valuable merchandise just in case it was of dubious origin. He did have to report to a probation officer every so often. He would bring that person lovely gifts, and they would cover for him. Yes, Stan learned that in America everything, and almost everyone, has a price."

Recalling this most stressful night of danger and despair, Branka gives a slow sigh before she puts the inevitable twist in the tale:

"All the jewels Kardash and Kikila stuffed into that pillowcase were ones I had recently brought home from a safe deposit box. I did that because an associate of those two crooks told Stan and me that there was a buyer in town seeking to purchase high end merchandise. It was a setup to get us to bring that jewelry to the house, so we could be robbed. None of it was from the Patterson, New Jersey heist that Stan did for them. That heist, as with all of them, was an inside job done for the insurance money, and those items were sold off long before this home invasion. Kardash and Kikila were never arrested, never prosecuted. Do you think I ever got all that jewelry back from the police? Ha! Of course not."

Branka was arrested once again on suspicion of possession of stolen merchandise. She made bail and hired Les Bierman a local lawyer who looked like Harrison Ford to represent her.

A careful examination of the jewelry in her possession revealed that it was all one hundred percent legitimate with only two items suspected of being stolen before being lawfully acquired.

"My parents were set up by people they employed," explains Paul. "Buca and his wife, Milica, pretended to be friends with my mother, and my parents helped them tremendously. It was they who sent in Kardash and Kikila to rob my folks. My uncle wanted to go after them in Paterson New Jersey where they were hiding. but my father decided not to pursue and to wait and let it marinate. And that's exactly how it played out.

"Finally, one Christmas not that long ago, Buca himself, drunk and sobbing comes begging forgiveness. He said that if my father would not forgive him, he would kill himself. I had never seen a grown man crying, and he looked like Brutus or Bluto from the Popeye cartoons. In fact, that's who I thought he was back when I was little. My father told the crying man that he was forgiven, and then turned his back and walked away."

Stan, Branka and Little Paul left Fort Lee behind and relocated their residence temporarily to the home of a known political extremist in Astoria. This peculiar living arrangement was simply a way station, a needed pit stop before getting back on the road to prominence. Mr. Stan was not wanted by the N.J. police for any criminal charges, but they did want to "talk to him" about the home invasion robbery.

Branka knew that her little boy had nightmares from the home invasion, and she was concerned for both his mental and physical wellbeing. If something such as that happened again, she didn't want him to have another gun to his head.

To assure his personal safety, he was sent off to live where there would be no guns, no beatings.

"I spent the next three years, on and off, in the enormous apartment of a peculiar, mostly sad older lady for whom

Aunt Rada cooked and cared. The lady was crazy about me. She would dress me up in itchy wool sailor suits and then take pictures of me. I never saw the pictures because she never remembered to put film in the camera."

Her name was Joan Crawford. She used to be an actress.

Chapter Seven
Joan Crawford

Crawford was a true long-time friend of Stan and Branka because Mr. Stan managed her prestigious Manhattan apartment building residence. He had control of all the remodeling and painting of New York's most desirable addresses. Crawford was especially fond of Aunt Rada and her amazing baking skills, most notable being Rada's lemon cake with powdered sugar.

"I always loved Rada," says Paul. "She never yelled or got angry at me. Aunt Rada was my weekly savior because I knew I was safe and would not get beaten or punished. She and I would watch TV together, and on Sunday I would watch Abbott and Costello, Bugs Bunny and Kung Fu movies. Aunt Rada wasn't exactly a housekeeper. She oversaw management of Ambassador Taylor's household and lived in a 20-room apartment made originally for the Saudis, and then the Sudanese Ambassadors. Joan Crawford lived across the hall, and Rada spent a great deal of time with Joan as well."

In September 1973, Crawford moved from apartment 22-G to a smaller apartment next door (22-H) at the Imperial House, 150 East 69th Street. Living on the same floor was former Ambassador Taylor—yes, he of the Vizcaya Rolls-Royce—and his artist wife.

"I was as familiar with them as I was with Joan Crawford," said Paul. "Mr. Taylor gave me rides in his fancy car, and he always took me to the Barnum and Bailey Circus."

Rada was employed by the Taylors until Mr. Taylor had a stroke. He passed away February 24, 1984. Until then, Paul was the official Taylor/Crawford delivery boy.

"They sent me back and forth with notes on three-by-five cards. Looking back, it was all insider trading regarding Pepsi-Cola—Joan tipping off the Taylors. You should have seen me in a little sailor suit driving my toy cars on the parquet floors."

If you had been there in Joan Crawford's apartment in the year of her death, you would have thought that she never smiled, was never happy, and had a mean streak. You would mostly be right, except when it came to Rada and Little Paul.

"She was never mean to me, and while she looked strict and cold, she could be warm as one of Rada's cakes, right out of the oven. Rada was her friend, and I was there to be with Rada, not Joan, but it became a habit that I spent all my time with Joan and her doggie, Princess."

Little Paul was Joan Crawford's last true love, and they spent innumerable hours together.

"She taught me card games, told me stories about people from the old days that meant nothing to me, about how she loved her brother and took care of him, and she would tell me that she worked hard, very hard to get what she wanted in life."

Little Paul enjoyed amusing her because he was a natural-born performer. She called him her little Fred Astaire.

"I didn't know what it meant but said it so lovingly that I assumed it was a compliment."

In the years he lived there, Joan Crawford became less social and sociable. She hardly ever left her bed except to play with him.

"She thought it was great fun chasing me around the apartment while I giggled, and the dogs barked," says Paul. "That game stopped when Crawford hurt herself by crashing into some furniture. After that, she and I mostly shared time in her room where she sat propped up on her bed like royalty. The bed was covered in papers which I did my best to not disturb."

She showed him photographs of her glory days, and his childish questions such as "How did you get old?" and "Why don't you look like that now?" only seemed to amuse her.

"How old do I look," she would ask as if it were a comedy routine.

"At least one hundred years old."

"And Betty?"

"Who's Betty?"

"Exactly!"

She never failed to find that exchange entertaining in its predictability and the honesty of Little Paul's ignorance about Betty Davis.

"Perhaps it was my innocence that gave her the freedom to tell me things that she wouldn't tell another adult. Two days before my birthday, which was two days before she died, she had me get up on the bed, so she could hold me close, and tearfully asked me if I would do something for her—if I would make her a promise—a promise on Mother's Day, especially for her."

"She was holding me, softly crying as she spoke, and told me that on my birthday she was leaving me her dog, Princess, the dog whom I loved and played with all the time. I didn't comprehend leaving me meaning other than giving me. "

Princess, a black and white Shih Tzu, was her favorite. She had other dogs, older poodles, but Princess was beautiful, and she had her own doggie bed, and cute doggie furniture, and even her own room.

"I was thrilled that she was going to make Princess my dog. I couldn't imagine a more wonderful birthday gift. I can still hear her voice asking me to promise to always love and take care of Princess."

"Do you promise? Do you really promise?"

"I promised that I would, and she cried some more, and thanked me. She was softly sobbing, holding me, squeezing me. She had become sadder and needier in the past few weeks, not as pleasant as before. She was always much more pleasant to me and Rada than she was to anyone else but that Mother's Day she was not the woman she was before, but I was a child, and I was thinking only of me, and how much I wanted that dog."

"It's Mother's Day," I reminded her, as there were none of her children or grandchildren there. "I'm going with my mommy, but I will be back on my birthday. Aunt Rada is making a seven-layer cake!"

When he returned on May 10th, he eagerly looked for Princess, but she wasn't there.

"Where's Princess?"

"She was given away," said Aunt Rada.

"I went ice-cold inside," remembers Paul. "In my entire life, to this very day, I have never experienced such a depth of disappointment, such a feeling of cruel deception. I believed that Joan Crawford's tearful request that I love and care for Princess, and that she was giving me Princess, was an intentional lie to a small child."

On that day, little Paul Stanimirovic despised Joan Crawford.

"This was the worst day of my life. Worse than having a gun to my head when those men robbed my parents. They lit the candles on my cake, Joan gave me a birthday card and told me to make a wish. I blew out the candles and I wished she would die."

He didn't know that his mother told Rada to give the dog to someone else because Branka feared that the dog would be one more trigger for, or recipient of, Mr. Stan's temper.

"After I blew out the candles," Paul recalls, "Joan gave me one hundred shares of stock in Pepsi-Cola. I just wanted out of there. I still had a mouth full of cake when I was almost pushed out of the apartment, and swiftly taken to the Taylors apartment across the hall. They weren't home, and I watched a great deal of commotion at Joan's apartment."

Something was wrong, terribly wrong. Rada was crying and people who worked in the building were showing up in tears. Paul watched as Joan was taken out on a stretcher. Joan Crawford was dead.

"Had I known then what I know now," says Paul, "I would not have held such resentment towards her, but I was a little boy who was having a dreadful and disappointing birthday. There was no way for me to see things other than how I saw them. Today I can take some solace in the fact that I was Joan Crawford's last true love, and the last person she spooned in her bed, the last person she held tight and confided that which, at the time I didn't comprehend."

Crawford didn't die of a heart attack as her obituary said. No, she was in increasing pain from the cancer inside her. She wasn't going to treat the cancer because she was a Christian Scientist. Instead, she was going to outsmart it. She had Little Paul give her more pills, many more pills.

Little Paul continued staying with Rada after Joan's death, spending time with the Taylors.

After Mr. Taylor's death, Rada packed up her things and told Mrs. Marian Taylor that she was going back to Yugoslavia. That was when Barton G. the soon-to-be famous restauranteur and entrepreneur, recruited Rada to work for him. Rada stayed with Barton until she retired at age eighty-nine in 2017.

"Rada's son, Uncle Paul, was never involved with my father in illegal activities. He was a handsome lady's man and a very formidable fighter. His niece is married to actor Christian Bale," remarks Paul. "At least someone in the family made it into showbiz. Lord knows my father had the opportunity."

True. Famed casting director Marion Dougherty began her career in a New York restored brownstone managed and maintained by Mr. Stan. It was there that Stan met Woody Allen, Mia Farrow and other residents and frequent visitors.

"She thought Stan could be a movie star," confirms Branka. "Or a successful character actor. He was also encouraged by his friend Charles Bronson, an actor who often stayed at our home when he was out from California."

Stan had the looks, the charm, and a unique accent. Marion Dougherty saw him as like Charles Boyer or other exotic accented romantic lead. As Stan could do anything, he probably could have done it.

"This is one reason we went to California when Marion went out to Los Angeles to be head of casting for Paramount," says Branka. "Stan wanted to see what Hollywood and Hollywood's players were like, to be blunt, he found it too gay, and I don't mean too jovial."

Branka believed the family member destined for a career in showbiz was Little Paul, a natural-born entertainer and mimic.

"I always believed my son's future would be as an actor or entertainer. I seriously wanted to send him to acting school at an early age, but Stan wouldn't hear of it. Despite all his friends knowing Little Paul's gifts, he convinced them to join him in mocking the idea."

"I loved entertaining people," confirms Paul, "just as I entertained Joan Crawford. The alternating comedy and drama of my childhood became a violent cartoon for the entire year after Crawford's death."

It was one injury after another for Little Paul. A hot coal became stuck to his foot for ten minutes at a family BBQ, his knee was ripped open when he fell on rebar while running, and the worst was being hit by a car driven by a drunk nurse fresh from a torrid affair with a firefighter.

"She was so busy putting on lipstick and preening in front of the rearview mirror that she didn't notice that she hit me," Paul remembers, "and I flew over the car and crashed to the ground cracking my head and breaking my hip. I spent nine months in the hospital and eleven months wearing a hip cast."

Paul's parents could have settled out of court with the woman's insurance company.

"They made us a generous offer," recalls Branka, "but Stan thought a direct confrontation lawsuit would be more rewarding. It wasn't. We lost, and the lawyer for the insurance company made constant fun of our name and being from a Communist country. He made it sound as if little Paul lied in wait for the drunk nurse, so he could leap in front of her car and almost get killed."

"When I finally got the hip cast off and the leg cast, "said Paul "I had the shock of my life when I saw my white toothpick of a leg—skin stretched over bone. I feared being crippled like that the rest of my life. Thankfully, it looked worse than it was."

Looks, while not the be-all and end-all of human worth, can be of significant value. By 1978, Stan was looking remarkably prosperous. With property holdings in Manhattan and an increasing visible presence in the life of the Diamond District, Mr. Stan was on his way to becoming the King of New York.

His reputation and public image were as flawless as the diamonds he "relocated" from the vaults of others to his own retail outlets with the excellent assistance of Aleksander "The Moth" Grbac and his childhood pal, Embrio, who joined Mr. Stan's team of gem heist professionals.

Chapter Eight
Alek "The Moth"

Alek came to New York originally to help Stan with one heist.

"His reputation proceeded him," recalls Branka. "He was already a well-established burglar in Europe and the old country. Prior to coming to work for Stan, he was partners with a three-foot-tall midget. They would put the midget in a delivery box, and have the box delivered to an establishment just before closing. Once everyone was gone, the midget got out of the box and opened the door to let in Alek. Very clever!"

Alek arrived at JFK, and everything was pre-arranged by Mr. Stan for Alek's ease and convenience, including an apartment and a safe identical to the one he was hired to open.

"Alek had never seen that kind of safe before," says Branka, "but he is a genius at figuring things out. Soon enough, he knew how to get into that safe, and that's all that mattered. If I recall properly, he did another heist before deciding to return to Europe or stay with Stan. He decided to stay."

"Alek was the first person to just come right out and tell me what my father was doing," says Paul. "Alek told me that he was a thief, my dad was too, and that they were going to teach me to be the next great thief. I said I was going to be a police officer and arrest all of them. I wanted to be included with the grownups, so being a thief was okay with me."

Alek wasn't kidding. The thievery of Mr. Stan, the Professor, Alek, and the other adventurous crew were making significant contributions to the subject matter of American cultural literacy. A perfect example is the sensational and unsolved MTA heist of 1979.

The MTA Heist

July 23, 1979, Benjamin Williams and John Kenny walked into the MTA Headquarters where both men were supervisors. It didn't take long for them to notice something was missing: six hundred thousand dollars in ten-dollar bills vanished overnight.

"This still-unsolved mystery is the biggest whodunnit in MTA history," wrote the New York Daily News thirty years later. "...the sensational and seemingly impossible theft promptly sparked a media frenzy. There was page after page of coverage, detailing the probable outline of events ad nauseam. The police were baffled, and the public began speculating what could've happened."

You can stop speculating. Someone should buy a copy of this book for the MTA. The crime is solved. We know whodunnit.

"Six hundred thousand in ten-dollar bills weighs a hell of a lot," says Branka with a coy smile. "I personally never tried carrying that amount of money, but I know people who have, or say they have. Either way, I'm sure they had their hands full."

Stan and Branka had their hands full with more and more Yugoslavian and Eastern European immigrants turning to them for financial help and employment, some of them criminals dedicated to making a big score in America.

They also had a young son who, despite his pre-teen chronological age was in the full throes of rebellion. The only thing that calmed little Paul down was active inclusion in Stan's victimless criminality.

"When the crews were getting ready for heists," says Paul, "I made sure there were fresh batteries in the flashlights, the tools were clean, and that there was plenty of fresh coffee. I was their little assistant and criminal in training."

When the crews returned with the booty, Paul would watch them divide it up and celebrate success. Those were the moments when he felt part of something, part of Mr. Stan's life, noticed and perhaps appreciated.

"Nothing could compare to the thrill of that—I didn't want to do anything other than make scores and heists. That was what the life was about, the stories, the memories. My father would light up. I wanted to light him up like that. They were all nocturnal animals, and I would sneak down the stairs and they would call me over to show me bags filled with gold and jewelry, and they would put me to work taking tags off jewelry."

It was, Paul says, like having family over for Christmas, and once they got into the stamp game, Little Paul worked even more.

"Circulated, uncirculated, all those things," Paul says "that was a whole years' worth of work. I got paid in stamps."

Stamps are an art form, and Young Paul was initially shocked to see the forms used in the art of his father's good friend and customer, Phillip Pearlstein.

"I was a kid, and Mr. Pearlstein had nude female models. I was a bit surprised to see them at first," he recalls, "but I soon became comfortable with that. My parents took me everywhere, and when we went to see Mr. Pearlstein, he would give me a paintbrush, paint and a canvas to keep me entertained in general and enthralled with art in specific.

Both my parents were artists, and I recall my mother and Mr. Pearlstein having great conversations on the topic. He admired my mother's art and was always so positive and supportive. I knew him then as a nice man who was a friend of my parents. His college pal and former roommate, Andy Warhol, was also one of my father's friends and a client as well. Today, of course, I know Pearlstein's fame for Modernist Realism nudes. and why he is so admired and respected. His immediate gifting me a paintbrush and canvas means even more today, as an adult and an artist, than it did back when I was a mere child. I also think seeing my parents, especially my mother, so enthralled and joyful in his presence had a very positive impression on me. My mother to me was always beautiful, but when discussing art, she became as dazzling as a diamond."

By the 1980s, Branka wore exquisite diamonds with casual grace and a complete lack of pretension. Her physical beauty matched by a most pleasant endearing and captivating personality allowed her to command attention without appearing to seek it. Her innate grace and intrinsic allure allowed her enviable access to the gem-packed vaults of New York's prestigious jewelry manufacturing firms.

It was Branka, bedecked in fabulous furs and exquisite jewelry, who "cased the joints," bringing back detailed information about the vaults, the goods, the access and alarms.

"There was one time when neither my persona nor Stan's charm could get us the information we needed," recalls Branka. "It was a gold jewelry manufacturing company with heavy security and surrounded by barbed wire. We rented an empty warehouse across the street and made our plans from there. First Stan went to visit to either buy or sell jewelry, but he wasn't able to see where the vault was located. Next, I went, and I even had a hidden video camera, but that didn't work either."

It was Alek Grbac who voiced a wise idea: break into the place simply to find out the vault's location, plus it would provide information on how long it took the cops to respond to a break-in.

"We cut the barbed wire," says Alek, "and managed to approach the building. We brought our custom-built expandable ladders with us in order to reach the windows which were rather high up. We managed to open the window, and that triggered the alarm right away. I wasn't about to give up, so I jumped through the window, hit the floor, and quickly went looking for the vault."

The police sirens screaming in the distance provided impetus for him to get the hell out, but the window was too high to reach, even with a good jump.

"I didn't have expandable ladders inside the place," Alek recalls, "but there were some boxes nearby that I could stack one atop another to get close enough to leap up and grab the hand the was waving at me from the other side of the window."

Alek eagerly grabbed the hand, was pulled up and out, and made it through the hole in the barbed wire and to the rented warehouse just as the police cars came screeching up to the factory.

"He learned the vault's location," confirmed Branka, "but he also realized that there wouldn't be time to get in, get the job done and escape before the cops arrived. I remember that he and Stan were just about to forget the entire thing when Alek came up with a brilliant, if risky idea."

The idea was indeed risky, time-consuming and potentially dangerous: dig a tunnel below the foundation of the factory. That way, they wouldn't trigger any alarms and could cut in right below the vault.

It would take months of digging and would only work if the factory's foundation were the same depth as that of the warehouse.

It was.

"We removed the concrete, and sure enough," says Alek, "there was the metal bottom of the vault. We torched it, and the next thing we knew, we were standing in the middle of a vault full of gold bars."

With no alarms triggered, and no fear of the police or private security, the gold was laboriously transferred from the factory's vault to the warehouse via tunnel, the vault floor resealed and the concrete replaced. As the warehouse was no longer required, all traces of the tunnel were abandoned, and the month-to-month rental on the warehouse was abandoned as well.

Asked if she were concerned about the project's success, Branka only offers a non-committal shrug before commenting on an unrelated gold heist with which she was familiar.

"Sometimes you can take more than you can handle. Gold is heavy, very heavy. There was one where Stan and Alek and the crew ran out of bags strong enough to handle it. They tried to use trash bags," she says laughing, "and the gold tore through those bags immediately."

That was the least of their problems. There was too much gold to fit in the getaway car. The solution was to leave the tools behind and use a second car to return the crew.

Branka, Alek and Stan find these stories amusing in retrospect, although stressful when experienced in present tense.

Branka, always concerned about after-the-fact reprisals, is not eager to bring up heists and adventures not already broached by another.

Despite two newsworthy media mentions implying some sort of criminal connection to allegedly stolen silver and artifacts, Branka has never spent a day in prison unless you count the years married to Stan where she regarded his treatment of Little Paul as abusive. Stan did not agree.

What Branka viewed as abuse, Stan regarded as simply a strict, firm upbringing that accustomed the child to hardship as preparation for survival in the adult world.

"Stan accused me of spoiling my little boy by being so kind and gentle," Branka recalls. "He said he wanted the boy strong, not weak, not a sissy boy."

It only took a few days of elementary school P.E. for his teachers and the other kids to notice the welts and bruises. The school administrators took immediate action, insisting that the family see mental health and family counseling therapists.

"The counseling professionals perceived my mother and me as father's 'beloved victims.' says Paul. "That phrase was not coined of sarcasm. We were beloved. He honestly loved my mom, and more importantly, he loved me. I can hear it and I can say it, but it remains difficult to believe because I refuse to let go of my decades of desperation, I am outraged at myself for wearing my personal pain as a diadem of defiant self-pity."

All love is a quest for unity best realized within a fortress of wellbeing. A fortress is an impregnable stronghold of protection and defense. Decades before the essentially destructive concept of "tough love," Paul's father applied "torturous love."

If you can survive me, you can survive anything.

Not exactly the lyrical hook of New York, New York, but conceptually akin to *A Boy Named Sue* in which the father knew his son would have to get tough or die.

"Stan is a very complex man," Branka explains. "Leslie Olmsted was correct in her description of him. He was the best friend you could ever have, the most charming host, the most ethical businessman in all his dealings in building management, construction, and all other legitimate endeavors. But he was such a man's man that he had no interest in his own wife and child at home. In public he was exemplary. In private it was a different story."

"Perhaps an analogy will help," says Branka, "When dark clouds block the light of the sun, the light is still there, but we are deprived of it. It is the same with people. A mental problem blocks the person's reality from shining through. With Stan, the storm clouds were thick, black, dangerous, and destructive to his relationships with me and his son, Paul. All the wonderful qualities within him were never extinguished, only eclipsed."

Mr. Stan's endearing charm was authentic, and so were his sudden mood swings. It was as if a different man lived beneath Stan's charming and engaging exterior. It is now recognized that Stan suffered from extreme PTSD.

By the year that Mr. Taylor had his debilitating stroke, 1981, Paul lived full time with his parents in their new Long Island home situated on a lovely acre of wooded property paid for in cash by Stan who never set foot inside until the family moved in. He bought it because it looked good from the outside.

"From the outside, my life looked good too," recalls Paul, "or at least the same as any other kid my age who lived surrounded by vast wealth and an increasing number of Eastern European criminals."

The new home had a huge yard with a forest behind it and little streams and brooks were everywhere. Paul absolutely loved the acreage and surroundings because it was perfect for a young boy's imagination and exploration.

"I was intrigued by the silence and pure quiet nature this was my sanctuary and I climbed every tree and made clubhouses with neighbor kids—Jewish kids accepted me, and the few Black kids too."

It was naturally the best life that a child such as Paul could possibly have. —everything from baseball, football, and Theatre in the Park. Bike trails were abundant and perfect for Paul's Fuji GT BMX bicycle.

"It was a beautiful place to grow up," confirms Paul. "I loved to go to our first Antique Jewelry Store in Babylon

Village on Deer Park next to the Lo-Man Outdoor Store. My father owned the building across the street that was part apartment building and it had a bar and a few retail places. Newsday paper was there as well. Life would have been almost perfect for a child such as I were it not for my mounting resentment towards the most loveable man in the world, my father."

Paul endured two different approaches to parenting that, in moderation and with ethical regard, can blend together perfectly. A child can be maternally nurtured and paternally disciplined without either going to extremes.

"My father used to tell me that my mother doesn't love me the way he does. He used to go on how he really loves me and that is why he had to discipline me. As it turns out, had he not accustomed me to hardship, I would never have survived the events that hit me later in life. Were it not for my mother's nurturing, I would have no heart, no soul. I have become," says Paul with self-deprecating humor, "a human Tootsie-Roll Pop—hard shell on the outside, soft and chewy on the inside."

"I was growing boy having fun or having what I imagined to be fun," Paul explains. "In August of 1981, MTV came on. I was ten years old, and I was breakdancing for the girls in the summertime, had all the latest Sharper Image gadgets and gizmos in my home—I loved the modern technology. I anticipated a whole new life. The one I got wasn't the one I anticipated."

Going to a new school with new kids thrilled Paul, and he loved the décor and ambiance: sanitary hallways, tiny lockers, and mechanical water fountains. Even the scent of education intoxicated him, and he anticipated forming even more friendships. Yet, much like a Jewish kid in Yugoslavia, he was never fully accepted because of his heritage.

"I realized," says Paul, "that their prejudice was a second-generation projection from biased parents. These provincial Long Island families created imaginary versions of my parents that evaporated into mist the moment they met my mother, the blond goddess in the one hundred thousand dollar mink coat who showed up at the PTA bake sale with the best damn cookies they ever tasted."

One look at their drop-jawed husbands staring at Branka ignited flames of jealousy, envy, and genetic protectionism. A few mothers attempted to ban her from the PTA, but beauty and baked goods are not cause for expulsion.

"Having a hot mom is weird because every kid thinks his mom is beautiful, but not every kid has a mom who won the genetic lottery and could be a real cover girl or stomach-stapled centerfold."

The school principal, smitten with Branka, soon hired her as head art teacher. The Stanimirovics, immigrants from a Communist country, were feared and admired, envied, and avoided.

To fit in, Stan bought a brand-new Cadillac, the status car of preference on Long Island. Another house Mr. Stan bought was on Venetian Shores in Lindenhurst.

"It was a massive brick custom mob house that belonged to a boss of a bookie operation," explains Paul. "It had hundreds of phone lines in the basements for taking bets. We turned this into a fourplex."

As with all other purchases, Stan paid cash.

"When it comes to cash," says Paul, "my father is the most generous man on earth. He would give you as much as you needed. But if you were his son, and all you wanted was approval, you could die from approval deprivation syndrome."

This characteristic is not unusual for men of his generation and background, according to Marko Savkovich, Paul's childhood pal.

"Paul, also known as Little Paul, and I grew up together, and our fathers were the best of friends, and both were gentleman thieves, nonviolent masters of the heist, they were so much alike: athletics is very important to Serbians.

Everyone was always in incredible physical condition, and martial arts such as judo are major interests in Serbia. Mr. Stan is a real character—suave debonair charming and very clever. To me, it always looked as if he affected a perpetual scowl even when his eyes twinkled, and he was incredibly quick with Serbian humor which is a wry dark humor like the style of the famous Jewish comics from the Catskills. We had a lot of fun fishing and boating when we were kids. I'll tell you, when those criminals started arriving from Yugoslavia looking to hook up with Stan, Paul started to get rebellious, and he acted out a lot."

Little Paul did more than act out –he acted as if Rambo in First Blood (1982) the first of the Rambo movie franchise. One look at the plot and you see instant metaphors for his life.

John Rambo is pursued by a tyrannical sheriff and his deputies, forcing him to survive using his combat skills.

"My father was the tyrannical sheriff alright," confirms Paul, "and his crew were the deputies. That was my life on screen—I identified so strongly with the character of Rambo that I even had a knife exactly like his which I stole from Lo-Man's Outdoor Store."

More conventional was Paul's video game obsession. This was before Nintendo, before X Box, before PlayStation. If you wanted to play Space Invaders or Seawolf, you needed two things: a video arcade and an endless supply of quarters. Mr. Stan had rolls and rolls of real silver quarters. They weren't doing anyone any good just sitting there, bored.

Paul gave those quarters a reason to live.

"I took hundreds of rolls of quarters from my dad's collection and spent them on video games. I paid a taxi driver one hundred dollars in quarters to take two friends and me to the arcade owned by Mr. Orlando. He owned just about every arcade hall from Atlantic City to New York City, lived across the street from us and was allegedly a mob guy married to a wonderful Jewish lady. They were good friends to my family."

Orlando had a keen eye for physical detail and customer characteristics. He knew quarters, knew Mr. Stan, and was exceptionally familiar with Little Paul and his pals. Mr. Orlando did the smart thing, and the right thing: he returned all those rare quarters to Mr. Stan. Both men knew the worth of those coins was between one hundred dollars and twenty-five thousand dollars each.

Orlando later became a jeweler because he asked Stan to make him one. In return, Orlando introduced Stan to Salvatore Stagnitta of Pan American Airlines whose connections were as remarkable as Stan's daring innovations.

"Sal was very funny," remembers Branka, "and he loved us, and his family were so nice and lovable. He had two daughters and two sons. We got together to see the Godfather and we did Christmas together a few times, and Thanksgiving. Sal was so loyal to Stan, and I think that Sal was given to Stan to look after him and protect him."

"I liked Sal," says Paul, "but he was also allegedly a cleaner like the Harvey Keitel character in Pulp Fiction who would dispose of the bodies that Roy Demeo or Ice Man would kill. If that's true, neither you nor I would ever see or know that side of Sal, just as you would never know the other side of anyone. Those who knew my father as a successful jeweler would never perceive that he was the ultimate jewel thief."

Mr. Stan was the first jewel thief to boldly rent offices in the diamond district. This was ingenious as it made it possible to move around at night with impunity and the all-important keys to all the doors.

Stan's creative and elaborate heists caught the attention of Carmine Lombardozzi, Capo of the Gambino Crime family. He was also known as " The Doctor" and "King of

Wall Street" because of his brilliant mind for numbers and mathematical formulae.

He was a more old-fashioned gangster and was a serious earner of the family. Carmine Lombardozzi trusted Stan because he had watched him grow in wealth, power, and influence since 1965 while remaining almost completely under the radar.

This was appealing to the aging mobster who had dinner with Stan and family at the Mill Basin Restaurant. Also, in attendance were Carmine's six brothers.

"Lombardozzi had a yellow Rolls Royce convertible," remembers Paul, "and I heard that his driver was a former Chief of Police. This was not the traditional sight in a Brooklyn neighborhood. People talked about it then, and some talk about it to this day."

This may be a good time to get out a pencil and paper to note who connected who with whom. It was Carmine Lombardozzi and his sons Cosmo and Gus, who connected Mr. Stan to John Gotti; Salvatore Stagnitta connected the Albanian safe cracker and safe manufacturer, Lacka, with both Stan and Gotti.

Salvatore was not only a loyal Gambino soldier; he had a legitimate executive position running Pan-Am food service. He had the entire JFK Airport in his pocket, especially the Customs and Immigration Department.

"Sal and my dad became good friends," says Paul. "And there was much mutual socializing between the families. I, being a little show-off, was entertaining them all when I was a kid. I hung out with their children and celebrated Christmas and New Year and other holidays. The Fourth of July was my favorite."

"Sal was wonderful to us," agrees Branka. "He made it possible for us to fly First Class all over the world, and he kept all of us from being criminals. I recall one time we landed at JFK from Venezuela with over two million dollars in diamond jewelry packed into my suitcases. You could hardly lift them they were so heavy. Okay, I didn't fill out a customs declaration form for the suitcases full of diamonds and jewelry. Why should I? They belonged to me. Sal explained to the customs agents that I didn't declare it because it was all mine to begin with, I didn't buy it there. I took it to sell, but I didn't sell it after all. I brought it home… so?"

"My mother is amazing at minimizing," says Paul, "You think the customs agents really believed that none of the items in those suitcases originated in Venezuela? Sal bought the agents, and the agents bought the story. As for Venezuela, we went there after a successful heist. Upon our arrival, my father had me pour him some cognac. There is a picture of that, actually."

Sal was a smooth talker and quite persuasive. He was also heavily armed. Why a Pan-Am executive needed three pistols and another in an ankle holster remains a sociological conundrum, but there was no question as to Sal's high-powered influence and endearing personality. Much the same could be said about the very deadly John Gotti.

"I recall clearly the sound of John Gotti's laugh," says Paul. "It would be two in the morning, and my dad and Gotti would be laughing like crazy in the kitchen. Their relationship was interesting as my father would never have anyone murdered or any of that greed and power-hungry bullshit. Maybe for Gotti being with my father was a vacation into another world."

Other men of questionable proclivities became regular guests, much to Branka's dismay.

"It didn't feel like company," says Branka. "I felt invaded, violated as if my home were not mine."

"It didn't start out that way," remembers Paul. "At first it was just me and my mother. My father was never there because he's a workaholic. There was a fully furnished basement, and a formal dining room featuring antique furniture. It was in the dining room one day that I saw a large box that hadn't been there before. Curious, I opened the box—more like a crate actually—and inside were two machine guns. And MP5 and an Uzi. I was stunned. What were two machine guns doing in the dining room?"

Mr. Stan never allowed anyone to have a weapon on a heist, but he had his own handguns in his closet and inside his coat pockets. One was a Sig Sauer with a green wood handle, another was a 38-snub nose, and there was a .357 that Little Paul would play with when Stan wasn't at home.

Little Paul also went through his father's pockets for spare change.

"My father always had hundred dollar bills, and only hundred dollar bills. I would help myself to one or two, and he didn't seem to notice because he had so many of them. My dad may have robbed the rich, but so did I, the rich in this case being my father."

Stan honestly saw himself as a modern Robin Hood, a cross between The Saint and Raffles—the ultimate gentleman thief.

"I was like Robin Hood," insists Stan, "I stole from the predatory rich and gave to the poor, the struggling and the disadvantaged."

Although he associated with the cream of New York high society and entertained movie stars and international celebrities such as his close friends Charles Bronson and Burt Reynolds with lavish parties at his Long Island mansion, he preferred the company and cultural authenticity of the poor, the put-upon and the marginalized.

When Stan went out on the town, it was to parts of town seldom frequented by others of his social stature. "My father had an uncanny ability to find Gypsy musicians," says Paul. "He enjoyed live music and the Gypsies. He loved the Gypsies."

It was common for Stan to hand over ten thousand dollars a night for entertainment.

"He must have had Gypsy Radar. He would go out and find them playing at 3 a.m. in some place in Manhattan, or at the Grecian Cave in Astoria with Alek Grbac."

A cave was the only thing the Long Island house didn't have. What it did have was a boxer named Milan living in the garage. Milan was one of those guys that Stan brought home drunk one night. During the time that he lived at Stan and Branka's, Milan seemed to be training for the Olympics, but he was getting in shape as Mr. Stan's bodyguard.

"Whatever is needed," Milan told Little Paul, "and that means discipline."

He showed Paul what he learned in the army in Yugoslavia, skills he acquired as a pugilist, and the focus required to be a professional criminal.

"One day," recalls Paul, "he simply was gone. Poof. No explanation, at least not to me."

After Milan came John the Croatian, and then Moma, aka Bobby Fashion, the worst of the worst. Moma looked evil: stocky with a thick neck and thick hands and an acre of severe abuse scars crowded onto his flesh.

His real first name was Momćilo. He was born in Yugoslavia and came to America with his cruel and sadistic father and one unhappy sister. Moma soon ran away and joined up with Chicano gangs in East L.A. stealing, getting high and robbing people—the more honest the person the more he enjoyed robbing them—as a school student he terrorized his teachers, threatening to blow them up.

Moma then went to Chicago and did the same low level criminal behavior, then he moved to New York where he got in trouble for shooting a man in the stomach but was never arrested.

"He wanted to lead the Serbians and make trouble with the Albanians," recalls Branka. "He went in front of the United Nations building during the Serbian Protests, but it was all a show because he never really cared about politics."

"I was beaten like a dog in California," Moma told Little Paul. "That's where I grew up, but San Quentin was my first big school."

Stan allegedly saved Moma's life. Whether a metaphor or a statement as blunt as Moma's vocabulary was an honest question posed by Paul. The truth is that Moma enraged an Albanian crime crew with an impetuous act of unwarranted violence for which he was to be unceremoniously disposed.

Mr. Stan, hearing Moma's Serbian family name, intervened. As a favor, Moma's life was spared, and the regrettably psychopathic thug begged Mr. Stan to take him in, pledging his undying loyalty. Paul and Branka, among others, aren't so sure saving Moma's life was a good idea.

"My husband brought him home like a stray viper in 1982," says Branka. "He had eyes like a goat. I couldn't stand to look at him, and he was in my house. This was not a role model I wanted for my son. He was a bully and he bragged that he was friends with Chuck Norris. I wanted to call Chuck Norris and ask him what the matter with him was."

Stan, Moma, Alek, and his lifelong friend Embrio used to go out every night and carouse around enjoying such refined pastimes as playing the Ms. Pac-Man arcade video game at a Long Island Irish Pub.

On one particularly memorable evening while Branka was home in bed alone with nothing, but a million dollars' worth of jewelry scattered over her sheets to keep her warm, Embrio was hit in the head with a beer bottle by irate customers enraged by his uncanny skill on the game.

Embrio put one quarter in the slot and played Ms. Pac Man endlessly off that one coin. The all-Irish were over-served and lacking appreciative patience. In short, the beer bottle that his Embrio in the head was like the first drop of rain precipitating a torrential downpour. When the bottle smashed into his head, Embrio didn't even flinch.

"He couldn't yet speak English," Mr. Stan later commented, "He turned and asked in Serbian, 'What does he want?' We told him 'He wants to know if you are as strong as you look.'"

Embrio, built like King Kong and almost as strong as that famed creature, answered the question with an abrupt display of his fighting prowess.

"Embrio could carry a full-grown horse around as if it were a child," says Alek "So you can imagine how feeble were the men, by comparison, who would attempt to subdue him."

All hell broke loose. The altercation escalated as if real estate prices. Alek had to practically run over people to get away in his Jaguar XJ12, the same model vehicle that Ian Ogilvy drove in the classic TV series, *Return of the Saint*, while Moma was utilizing his street fighting and prison yard repertoire.

Moma, according to legend, was once stabbed with a bayonet, and it went through him completely. He took it out of himself and used it to kill the person who attacked him—at least that's the story he tells, and he has the scar to prove it.

"Moma was grabbed by two big Irish guys," Mr. Stan would say, painting a very classy mental picture somewhat at odds with the unsophisticated nature of the primary participants, "and Moma started acting. He showed the thug who was about to attack him the scar on his heart where he got stabbed. This distracted the Irish gentleman long enough for Moma to put his keys between his knuckles and then smash his fist into the Irishman's neck. Blood started gushing, and there were moments of total terror, danger, and drunken stupidity."

"This was a huge fight that everyone remembers," says Alek, who recalls those wild days with an understandable fondness. Life was good for Alek in the 1980s. He owned a huge house on the water sold to him by the exceptionally pleasant Carl Friederich who, to this day, speaks with praise when remembering Mr. Stan, his contemporary associates, and the lovely Branka.

She, however, was unamused by episodes of masculine brawling, ruefully asking the rhetorical question: "What man prefers fist fights to the intimate company of a beautiful woman?"

"Stan never slept in our bed, and he was seldom home. My bed was filled instead with gold and every stone and every piece of jewelry you can think of. It must have been at least a few million dollars' worth of gems alone. Those things don't keep you warm in bed or in your heart."

"My father," complains Paul, "had Moma and other creeps sleeping in my house and being near Moma was not good for me even though he was teaching me karate and how to make homemade weapons for prison as if they knew what would happen to me. He showed me how to fight with a blade or a knife, how to kill with your bare hands, and he showed me ways to extract information from people who think they are bad ass."

At first it was easy for Stan to overlook Moma's blatant faults and troubling personal history of crime and violence. Moma was ruthless, selfish and wouldn't know scruples if the word showed up on Scrabble. One reason Paul resents him so much is because Moma had such an influence on him.

"I am conflicted to a degree about Moma," admits Paul, "because I learned from him how to be an evil manipulator with an explosive temper, a ruthless creature devoid of humanity and that most repellent list of characteristics is what allowed me to survive when surrounded by felons without conscience in America's worst prisons."

These precognitive peeks at future events aren't spoilers, they are short term teases. If I break the fourth wall again, my editor is going to send me a repair bill.

The wall between winners and losers in the Stanimirovic saga were never solid. There were losers who became winners and assumed winners who met ignominious defeat. The best example of the former was Boško Radonjić.

Chapter Nine
Bosko

"When I first met him," recalls Branka, "he wasn't the man we think of today. He came to America three years after I did—1970—and he worked for Stan as a new immigrant, and he parked our cars. His uncle owned a parking lot and garages that Bosko took over, but he was just a mere worker like every other immigrant. There is no shame in honest work. Remember, Stan cleaned toilets at JFK Airport. After 1983, Bosko came out of prison with connections, went back to Hell's Kitchen and took over the Westies. He was really into politics and joined the Serbian Homeland Liberation Movement, a strong anti-communist organization."

Bosko's best friend was Nikola Kavalia. They were both politically obsessed while Stan was apolitical, completely neutral, and wanted everyone to get along.

Bosko and Nikola wanted to assassinate Marshal Tito, and they also wanted to hijack airplanes, and blow-up embassies. Nikola realized his long-held dream of mile high terrorism when he hijacked a jetliner flying from New York to Chicago and threatened to blow it up. He released the passengers and most of the crew in Chicago, then forced the remaining crew to fly back to New York, where he demanded another airplane fly him safely to Ireland. When he got there, he surrendered to Irish police. He served 20 years in prison and died in 2008.

"Bosko was a hardworking man of true leadership potential," recalls Branka. "It was only after being in prison, and making contacts there, that he emerged as a different man, one with strong social and political power."

Bosko and Stan remained close in friendship if not in proximity. Bosko and Stan were seldom in the same place at the same time but there was great mutual respect. Bosko always appreciated Stan giving him his start in the USA, and Stan respected Bosko's career accomplishments.

Both men were of great personal power, although manifested differently.

Mr. Stan's power was a world away from mere materialism or political concerns. Hence, Paul came to believe that there was a power greater than himself that could whip his ass at any provocation, or at none.

"Standing in sharp relief to those painful occurrences," says Paul, "were those few wonderful moments when my father was honestly proud of me."

At the Long Island Beach, Stan and Paul went to buy some hotdogs and hamburgers, and the lady remarked that Stan's son was the richest kid on Long Island, and that the kids called him Mr. Cash.

Paul's father asked what she meant by that, and she said, "I work in his school, and he is the only kid that comes in to the school cafeteria to break hundred dollar bills every day, and you should know that other kids are taking advantage of him—your son is buying lunches for the kids that don't have much."

Perhaps that story reminded him of helping the disadvantaged Jewish kids back in the old country. He smiled in a rare display of pride in his young son, a refreshing change from his primary habit of alternately beating and ignoring Paul.

From that day on, Stan's nickname for his son was Mr. Cash. It is a true compliment because it is proud acknowledgment that Paul is the secret essence of his sire—a man who spread his money around with a generosity that seemingly bordered on irrational, but in reality, was an honest manifestation of his true self.

"There was never a man more giving of his wealth," acknowledges Branka. "It wasn't that money meant nothing to him, rather he knew what money meant to those who didn't have it. For that reason, he was always giving it away to the less fortunate. Some rich people turn a blind eye to the poor, the struggling, and the disadvantaged. Stan was never that type of man. The material needs of others was one thing he couldn't ignore."

"I didn't grasp that my father had more reasons than ever to ignore me," recalls Paul. "He had become more than a legitimate self-made millionaire, admired and respected. He had acquired an addiction to creating, crafting, and executing the perfect victimless crimes—robbing millions in diamonds, gems and antiques from the often cooperative or heavily insured and the over insured. And despite what I experienced as mistreatment of me in private, he took me with him in public so I could learn by example."

Stan was training Paul to be a version of him, but that was not what Paul envisioned.

"I wanted to be an entertainer, to amuse people and make them laugh. I loved interacting with other kids my age and learning how to do things other than pick locks and steal things."

Paul, whose given name was "Pavle" preferred his school mates call him "Paul," and his family call him "Little Paul" as differentiated from "Uncle Paul," as one more way to distance himself from his origins and have him at least partially embraced by Americana, even if that embrace was only offered by kids also perceived as outsiders—Blacks and Jews, neither of whom at that time were into tattoos.

"Tattoos were not in fashion on Long Island in 1982," recalls Paul. "My father didn't have them, but many of the criminals now living with us were covered in ugly jailhouse art, except for my favorite of my father's longtime friends, Billy the Kid who was with us before we were on Long Island. I'm sure he was older than he looked, hence the nick name."

It was Billy and his girlfriend who at would join him and his childhood pal Marko on vacations up in the Catskills. Stan knew that area perfectly because of his marriage to Amy, and there wasn't a lake or fishing hole that Stan didn't know.

"It was fabulous fun," recalls Marko. "And it is interesting the things our parents worried about with us kids—don't run, don't run—my father always said that, not because he feared us falling and getting hurt. But because when he was a kid, if you ran, there was a good chance the Nazis would shoot you."

One time Marko and Little Paul were running wildly on the dock and Marko ran too close to the slippery edge and fell into the lake.

"I didn't panic," remembers Marko. "I didn't thrash. Calm as can be, I sank to the bottom and just sat there, relaxed, holding my breath with ease, waiting for Dad to reach in and scoop me out."

"Yes," says Paul with a wry grin, "that is exactly what Marko's father did: he pulled him out in a very matter of fact way. Both Marko and his dad were perfectly calm and collected."

To this day, Marko avoids getting in over his head, respects the potential dangers, yet always remains calm and collected and under all conditions.

"That's being even-tempered," remarks Paul. "I didn't acquire that trait, or maybe I was born missing the even-tempered chip. I was always emotionally committed to whatever mood I was in. I get that from my father. I got plenty from my father—beatings and instructions."

Little Paul, even as a child of seven, was taught how to steal things.

"Billy the Kid constantly encouraged me to steal from the convenience stores we frequented. It didn't matter what I stole, Billy just wanted me good at it."

In truth, Billy didn't really have Little Paul steal anything. While Paul was pocketing items, Billy was paying for them at the cash register.

"I saw Billy paying for everything," says Paul. "Later I understood. It was wrong to shoplift, to rob this man of his profit and merchandise. There would be no insurance claim filed for the ink pen I pocketed or the purloined pack of Corn Nuts. "

Billy (real name: Velja Stajić) manifested all the traits and attributes that a child raised with gangsters would admire—hot cars, sleek women, fancy guns, and tattoos on his chest of a tiger and a black panther.

Billy was doing the biggest jobs with Stan in the seventies and his brother, Jovo Stajić, was an integral part of Mr. Stan's Paint Company.

"My father always had younger more capable guys that began as punk thieves," says Paul. "He transformed them from thugs into true gentlemen just like in the Alexander Dumas book, The Count of Monte Cristo."

Dumas remains Paul's favorite author, eclipsing even your current narrator. "My father gave me that book for my twelfth birthday and I treasure it to this day."

Stan's favorite was Oliver Twist, and he would regale Little Paul with stories about guys like Skagen, the old man who finds boys to steal for him,

"No wonder my father loved that story," says Paul with a laugh, "In all the Social Clubs around the Tri State area, wannabe thieves were planning heists and scores, but they were common criminals while the brilliant Mr. Stan was uncommon by all standards."

Paul becomes joyously animated when speaking of his father's incredibly cool approach to heists.

"Picture this: the alarms are going off like crazy, someone is trying to rob the vault! The cops come screaming up, sirens wailing, and in a matter of minutes the police and the security guard are searching every inch of the place to catch the intruder. He could not be found because he was inside the vault waiting for them to go home! Of course, they didn't look in the vault because they couldn't get in the vault. It never occurred to them that the criminal was locked inside. Did you see the movie, *The Inside Man*? That was no doubt inspired by Mr. Stan because that was his favorite vanishing act—hide inside the vault until everyone leaves. They won't be back till morning when they will stare drop jawed into an empty vault. Yes, my father is the Tesla of Gentleman Thieves, and he took young guys such as Billy the Kid and made real men of them."

Young Paul was easily impressed; Branka, less so.

"Billy the Kid was just another one of Stan's social experiments in whom Stan attempted elevating through exposure to a higher lifestyle and greater opportunity and wealth," says Branka. "I can see how his looks and behavior could impress a young boy, but an experienced adult would see him differently. I used to teach Art Appreciation, it was one thing for a student to pass the exam, but another to honestly have an appreciation for art. What's that expression? You can lead a horse to the Preakness, but you can't make it race? No, I'm making my own joke. I will give Billy credit, however, for being a far better person at heart than Moma, who was just plain disgusting."

The body art adorned object of Stan's tutelage and Paul's admiration were well trained by the ultimate role model, and his future as a sophisticated practitioner of artistic heists seemed assured until Billy went to prison for a false rape charge in 1979.

There was no DNA testing then, and Billy was never a rapist.

Everyone knew who really did it. The rapist was another Milan from Titograd Montenegro, and he did it when he was staying in one of Billy's apartments.

When they arrested Billy, he had a kilo of coke and a half a million dollars in diamonds and gold. The cops stole everything that glittered, including the shimmering 97% pure cocaine.

"Billy was remarkably kind and fun, as was his wife, a stunning Australian model," recalls Paul. "I can still see him in my mind's eye, his curly blond hair all tousled, and his face wreathed in smiles taking me for a boat ride on a beautiful lake in upstate New York. Billy got 16 years in upstate New York, but in prison instead of on a lake," says Paul. "Prison was not good to Billy, and when we spoke, he warned me."

"This place is no joke, Paul. Don't ever come here. Never go to prison, especially not upstate New York."

Billy was released from prison a broken man deported to the Dominican Republic where he died of cancer a few years later. Stan had big plans for Billy, but those plans ended with the fake rape charge.

"My father also had big plans for me which, at the age of ten, I couldn't imagine. I just didn't want him hitting me anymore. By this time, my mother was progressively falling out of love with my father."

The criminal entourage overtaking their home, coupled with Stan's workaholic nature and preference for male bonding over home and hearth had taken its toll on her romantic feelings towards her handsome husband,

"Stan should have been a priest or in prison," says Branka. "He always wanted to be around his male friends. He never cheated on me with other women, but it felt as if he cheated on me because he enjoyed the company of his friends more than his own family."

Branka, fearful of reprisals directed against her son if she were to divorce Stan, continued to endure living the high life surrounded by lowlife recalcitrant characters of diverse backgrounds and motivations. Some were devoted to Mr. Stan because he gave them a path to the American Dream. Others had the same goal of self-directed success but seeing themselves as the center of their universe left no room in their heart or mind for true respect and admiration.

John Gotti, by all accounts, honestly respected Mr. Stan. Simply put, Gotti didn't put Stan on a pedestal; Gotti recognized that Stan was already on one. Mafia crime families were not famed for their restraint and dedication to non-violence, refinement, sophistication, and manifest charm.

While there were some undeniably bright minds scattered throughout the Mafia families, the number of thugs, sociopaths, and psychopaths far exceeded those with a comprehensive education in the liberal arts. Some observers have voiced that Gotti wanted to be just like Stan to the point of dressing like him. Indeed, there is a rumor, denied by Branka, that she personally ordered the high fashion suits that earned Gotti the unofficial title of The Dapper Don.

"Stan's camaraderie with John Gotti," comments Fred Wolfson, internationally known security expert, "may have been motivated by assuring protection and admiration. It was undoubtedly not mere socializing. In terms of standards of behavior and criminal enterprise, Stan was one hundred percent non-violent, and he planned what he believed were victimless crimes. Gotti, however, was a gangster who had people murdered. No doubt Stan was in an arrangement with the mob whereby he did heists that they brought to him, and in return they assured his safety and position. In a relationship such as that—and it is a common one in organized crime—the only way out is to retire and leave the country."

In the late 1970s and early 1980s, Stan was not yet interested in retirement. He was at the top of his game. Little Paul was growing into the most conflicted pre-teen on Long Island. Both craving his father's attention and fearing it, his personal rebellion was in full force.

"I knew the day would come when my father would no longer raise his hands to me," says Paul. "I remember the last great beating he gave me—it was the one about Michael Jackson's jacket. You know the one I mean—red with all those zippers."

Paul was so enthusiastic about the jacket that he told Stan that he wanted one just like it. Stan seemed equally enthusiastic about the idea, and that should have been Paul's first clue to shut up about it.

"You want a jacket exactly like Michael Jackson's?"

"Yes, Dad I really do!"

"Would you like a glove like Michael Jackson's too?"

"Oh, yes, Dad! Yes!"

WHAM!

"He said he was going to beat the gay out of me. That was the last beating I ever got from my father. What I got from him next was a surprise that altered my life forever, every time my father completed a heist, we went on vacation. Sometimes Europe, sometimes the Virgin Islands, and every year we went to Yugoslavia, too. This time we went to Switzerland, and my parents came home without me."

Chapter Ten
Swiss Education

Neither Paul nor Branka knew that Stan enrolled Paul in the world's most elite and expensive international boarding school: Le Ecole International Crans Montana & Le Chaperon Rouge. This was the brilliant idea of Radomir Kovacevic, bronze medalist in the 1980 Moscow Olympics who also competed in the 1976 and 1984 Olympic games as a formidable Judo competitor. He oversaw the physical education program at the Dwight School in Manhattan until his sudden passing in 2006.

Founded in 1872, with campuses in New York, London, Seoul, and Shanghai, Dwight provides an international independent school education dedicated to igniting the spark of genius in every child.

"I started attending the Dwight School where Radomir became my mentor," explains Paul, "after my gym teacher at Saint Joseph's in Astoria physically abused me because I didn't have color-coordinated clothes for gym. My father had no qualms about beating me, but some gym Nazi at a Catholic school had no right to beat anyone's son other than his own."

"Radomir was the most positive, empowering, and humble man—he never talked down; he always lifted up," remembers Paul with a tinge of sentimental emotion, "literally, as well. He could lift me in the air with one hand."

Paul's new mentor was a man of intense purpose and dedication, and he shared most generously his view of life. Working with Radomir was a spiritual second birth for young Paul. He was more than simply influenced by Radomir, he was under the brilliant man's wing.

Radomir picked up Paul every day from home, took him to school, and brought him back. In that process of personal and professional interaction, Radomir rightly perceived the peculiar and possibly toxic nature of Paul's home environment.

The personal problems with which his students wrestled, Radomir believed, had their origin in family dynamics, roles within the family, and influences within the home. He rightly figured that a home full of criminals and frequent Mafia visitors, was not an ideal environment for Paul, especially with the unfortunate influence of Moma.

"Radomir and Moma are two extremes," says Paul. "All good in my life comes from my family and Radomir; all the evil comes from my own selfishness and self-perpetuated resentments. There is a distorted sense of security in familiar pain and I was investing significant emotional energy watering my judgmental attitude towards my loving father."

Radomir changed Paul's life by convincing Mr. Stan to spend over one hundred thousand dollars a year to send his young son to the famous Swiss boarding school, Ecole International Crans Montana & Le Chaperon Rouge.

"I felt awkward when I first arrived. I was only ten years old and had no idea I would be going there—and neither did my mother. Even though I wasn't a baby, to her it was as if I were ripped out of her arms."

Before the family arrived in Switzerland, Stan was surprisingly jovial and generous to Little Paul, buying him a brand-new wardrobe and numerous practical gifts.

"I was happily mystified by the way my father was treating me. I had never witnessed him in quite this mood before—and buying me everything you could think of in terms of clothing and accessories. Of course, once they left me there, I understood."

Initially, Paul viewed his surprise enrollment at this exclusive boarding school as punishment, but soon regarded it as a most welcome blessing.

"It was the most wonderful experience of my life," says Paul. "At first, I thought I would miss my video games. They didn't have them at the school, but they had so much more. For the first time in my life, I wasn't the outsider with the strange last name."

Paul thrived in that glorious environment, surrounded by rich kids from all over the world. He loved all the sports, and at long last the welcoming companionship of people his own age.

"Paul and I were in the same class," remembers Karla Morizzo. "He was really appreciated at the school. The teacher loved him, and his friends were fond of him. The girls found him most interesting because he was an attractive young man, plus there was something about him that gave him that added 'bad boy' element that girls find compelling."

There was indeed that element, although his fellow students were reticent to ask him what his father did for a living. After all, some of the other students had parents who were in the CIA or involved in other foreign government affairs. The students had their own affairs—with each other—and even with teachers.

"At that early teen age," confirms Karla, "it is the stage of discovery, of feeling attracted to the opposite sex or, for some, even for the same sex. Holding hands, first kiss, and more. I remember that there were stories about who was sleeping with whom but was not sure what was true or not."

"Karla is correct," confirms Paul. "It was a co-ed boarding school, and the fifteen to seventeen-year-old students were fucking their brains out like crazy. A perfect example was Marcelo and Guendalina who got caught sleeping in the same bed so many times they just let them have their own room. Her parents gave permission when she turned sixteen, and I was in the room next to them and admired their stamina and dedication to having what seemed well earned and perpetual orgasms. As for me, I had typical teenage crushes on several local girls, and one Arabian girl who drove me crazy, but my true glory was sports."

Karla and Paul were among the few students who played tennis, and it was immediately apparent that Paul was gifted when it came to wielding a racket.

"Paul was very good and very competitive," says Karla, "but we were all a bit competitive. He also really excelled at skiing. He and I could probably ski those slopes with our eyes closed, we knew them so well because we were racing twice a week. We wanted always to do our best and win the medals we got for the top spots."

"Karla is a very bright and kind person," says Paul. "We started skiing together, and after four years we were winning all the races and I had a lot of medals. I have an entire room of Medals from Princess Marcela Borgessie," says Paul proudly. "We all had Monsignor Jean Claud as our instructor—quite the ladies' man was Jean Claud."

Paul learned to behave like a perfect young gentleman in his Lacoste shirts, thick white cotton sweater, and white slacks. Benetton was the style then, and Paul became transformed.

"It was my life renewed, reinvented and vastly improved. It was as if the boy inside was being unleashed, yet refined and redefined," says Paul seriously. "It didn't cross my mind at the time, but today I think that for my father, it was as if he were investing money in a custom-built son, or like when you order a car to your specifications from the factory.

For me, it was like heaven in this beautiful skiing village. Movie stars lived there; sports stars retreated there. It was incredible. I skied with Roger Moore. There I was, downhill side by side with the Saint and James Bond. Imagine that!"

Wealth and prestige do not always equal ethics, and Paul encountered a few sterling examples of childish thievery in this rarified atmosphere.

"My friend Reza took my American Express card, treating himself to a fancy 35mm camera, a Rolex, and other pricey items. I don't mean he took it just for one day, he used it with consistency and bravado until my mother got the bill and I got the merchandise. I still have the camera. If we were not all rich kids that would have been a major issue. But not for us—the few, the proud the over-saturated with material things."

Paul adjusted to his new world and a new sense of identity severed from the overt and overly Serbian trappings of his parents' Long Island home.

"Just as I got comfortable in boarding school, I discovered that all the kitchen workers were Yugoslavian. As they take care of their own, they made sure that I ate well. They also were laughingly looking over my shoulder and peering into my private life. I'm sure they were not reporting back about me to my parents, but I wanted more personal privacy—after all, I was in love with/had a massive schoolboy crush on, a stunning Arabian princess. The kitchen staff knew it, as did everyone else, and they made fun of me by calling me His Majesty, the American Prince. If I had never blushed before, I certainly blushed then. There was no way to escape where I came from and to whom I repeatedly returned."

Paul would fly home to see his parents every three months, and he was thrilled that the dynamic between his father and him was so different. It was as if the beatings and verbal abuse never happened. The young man also noticed an increase in his father's visible interaction with

New York's infamous crime families, and John Gotti in particular.

Stan and John had always enjoyed each other's company. Stan, however, was a gentleman thief orchestrating what were viewed as the ultimate victimless crimes—robbing cooperating establishments that were fully insured if not over-insured—while Gotti was far from that designation.

"When I came home during the Christmas break of 1985 John Gotti came to my father with an interesting request. He wanted to have a private meeting at our home during the daylight hours with some of his associates. A very quiet sit-down, not to be mentioned to anyone. My father agreed, and Gotti had his little meeting while we went about our lives."

It was a simple request for hospitality. They came, they quietly met, they left. Paul Castellano, boss of the Gambino crime family, was killed, making John Gotti the Boss of Bosses.

Prior to the assassination of Castellano, Paul saw Moma, Bosko and a few others of the more dangerous members of Stan's entourage acting as if they were preparing for something, but Paul could tell it wasn't a heist.

"I was living in two worlds," recalls Paul. "One was the beautiful world of the most glorious, inclusive, and spectacular boarding school, and the other was my father's world. The problem with his world that I couldn't yet perceive is that illness is more contagious than health. When you're a criminal you associate with other criminals. That association brings you attention from law enforcement."

Mr. Stan had, for the most part, stayed below the radar of New York's Major Crime force. After all, his sphere of activity was very specific and exclusive: The Diamond District, New York's financial equivalent of Amsterdam's Red-Light District. Behaviors never tolerated elsewhere were basic facts of life in the Diamond District, a hotbed of illegality and deception responsible for a fortune in the city's coffers. The Diamond District was its own manifestation of the Containment Theory of law enforcement: keep all undesirable yet inevitable criminal activity contained to one easily monitored area. Add to that a Tolerance Policy in the Containment Zone. Hence the Diamond District became the nation's wealthiest ghetto of contained and tolerated criminality.

There were, of course, rules one must abide by to be tolerated. A perfect example was the NYPD's insistence, unofficial of course, that everyone in Mr. Stan's gem heist crews have regular full-time jobs and pay their taxes like all other good citizens. The upper-level NYPD protection of Mr. Stan will surprise no one familiar with the corruption in ever higher and ever widening circles at that time in New York's history.

"I was out to dinner with my father when the Chief of Police came to our table, shook my father's hand, and bought him a drink. Yes, crime had to be the crew's lucrative hobby, not their career."

Mr. Stan, America's most admired non-violent criminal was untouchable. Law enforcement shook his hand, bought him drinks, and admired him as if a local hero. For most of the crew, one heist was enough to secure their financial future.

"After that one heist, they took their slice of the pie and invested mostly in real estate," Paul explained. "I can look up at the New York skyline and tell you what heist financed the real estate company that put up that skyscraper. Yes, my father financed the New York skyline by stealing Manhattan."

Paul and puberty intersected between the ages of ten and fifteen—the exact years spent for the most part, in the rarified atmosphere of Switzerland. Each time Paul returned home for vacation he was taller, more sophisticated, and accomplished. He also was now being groomed by his father for a more active role in the family business beyond that of being Mr. Stan's designated driver when Stan was too hooched to drive.

"Yes," confirms Paul, "I was driving my father home in his Fleetwood Caddy when I was twelve years old. I would get good at it when I was driving him home from Panarella's at four in the morning. Dad would give me the wrong directions and I would wind up in Harlem or the South Bronx. Imagine the trust he had in me, or how messed up he was, to put his life in the hands of a twelve-year-old."

Stan prepared Paul for this task from an early age, teaching him how to drive when the boy was only five years old.

"Driving that Caddy at 4 a.m. wasn't as scary as it sounds," says Paul with a wide smile. "I would get back on the right streets and highways somehow remembering Long Island Expressway, exit 56." On the nights Stan didn't get drunk until he was in Harlem, a parade of Superfly Pimpmobiles stuffed with coke-sniffing scantily clad sex workers happily assured his safe return home.

"Dad gave them enough hundred dollar bills to make sure he was safely homebound, and they never harmed him. It was quite a sight seeing these Harlem nocturnals arriving in our driveway at the break of dawn, and two or three hot women helping my father to the front door."

Stan's excessive alcohol consumption during his recreational hours had seemingly no effect on his daily business activities, whether meeting with leaders of industry, politics, or organized crime—often the same thing—Mr. Stan was rock solid sober and charmingly professional. And although Young Paul was not yet a teenager, Stan took him everywhere, including a meeting with John Gotti.

Chapter Eleven
The Gotti Heist

"I was home on break when my father took me to a meeting with John Gotti. Dad wanted me to see everything, know everybody, and be able to pick locks behind my back at an early age. I remember that it was at that meeting that my father invited Mr. Gotti to go fishing with him."

Stan and Gotti sneaked away from the city and went fishing upstate. While concentrating on capturing trout, the two men planned a heist bigger than the Lufthansa—eleven million dollars. They were going to rob a prestigious place such as the Diamond Dealers Club located on 47th Street. The anchor of New York's Diamond District, the DDC is the largest and oldest diamond dealer organization active in the U.S.

"As I recall," says Branka, "they had this elaborate plan to rob the place from underneath. It would have been a most spectacular heist, and I don't recall which place was the final target, but I remember them mentioning the DDC. Regardless, Stan only selected those insured to the maximum."

According to Stan's good friend and former crew member, there were two heists planned by John Gotti and Mr. Stan, but neither of them were at the DDC, and Gotti only participated in one of them.

Gotti, via the Gambino crime family, arranged for two garbage trucks to block off the street. Arriving with Gotti were two men previously unknown to Mr. Stan: Malek Lacka and Joe Coffee.

Lacka, co-owner of the Lacka Safe Company, was on the payroll of both the Gambino's and the FBI. Joe Coffee claimed to be an alarm system expert but was an NYPD undercover cop allegedly also on Gotti's payroll. That allegation is hotly discounted by NYPD detectives who insist those allegations derive from his undercover persona, and not his authentic self. It has not been determined which of his selves spent the money paid to him by Gotti and the Gambinos.

When Stan and his cohort, Alek, showed up in the building's basement, Alek immediately discerned that Coffee had no idea what he was doing.

"He was a cop. I could tell," says Alek, "and I tried to tell Mr. Stan, but he didn't want to believe me. I said to him, 'you want to get arrested? Get out of here!' I was only there to let them into the building. I had keys. This Coffee had sold himself as an alarm expert, but he knew nothing, nothing at all. Coffee was supposed to cut the phone lines to the alarm system," recalls Alek, "and Stan was looking at me as if to say, 'what's with this jerk?' Coffee fucked up the entire heist. Instead of disabling the alarm he cut all the phone lines to the Federal Building. That caused absolute chaos and pandemonium. We got the hell out of there all in one piece, Gotti advised us to go on vacation while he cooled things off. Then, one day, I see this Joe Coffee on TV and he arrested Gotti three times. Gotti told us that Coffee was taken care of, so Gotti was either giving us false assurances, or he was telling the truth because the NYPD Task Force that Coffee was part of was obsessed with mobsters who murdered or ordered murders. If they were after Mafia guys, especially Gotti, they didn't give a rat's ass about us because, when you get right down it, we were committing burglary in the third degree—unarmed, no human contact—a wrist slap felony that will get you probation on the first conviction. In New York City, third degree burglaries are so common, they might name an intersection 3rd and Burglary."

Joe Coffee showed up at Alek's Long Island home unannounced saying that he just happened to be in the neighborhood. Gracious and hospitable, Alek offered him a beer and listened with feigned disinterest as Coffee pretended to call his wife to tell her where he was.

"I never saw Coffee again, thank God," says Alek. "He was so obviously a cop; it couldn't have been more obvious if he had his badge number engraved on his forehead."

The great admiration and respect shown to Mr. Stan by Gotti was graciously accepted.

"Oh, he was respectful, of course," remembers Alek. "Stan is a man of class and distinction. He was always number one. No one else even came close."

Paul clearly recalls overhearing his father telling Branka that after that Gotti failed heist, "two guys got whacked."

"On top of that," says Paul, "Sal Stagnitta committed suicide. That hit my father hard. He and Sal were very close."

Stan and Branka were now more than a bit overwhelmed. They had made millions looting the vaults of their willing victims, had vast property holdings and five offices in the Diamond District. They didn't need more money, and they certainly didn't need the attention of law enforcement.

"But sometimes," Stan said, "someone makes an offer you can't refuse—either out of fear for your life or greed for more than you need or deserve."

The offer was the brainchild of Carmine Lombardozzi, and it was a variation on the plot of Godfather III where the Mafia makes a legitimate deal with the Vatican Bank.

Chapter Twelve
The Big Deal

In this deal, one hundred percent legit, Stan would be elevated to the top of the jewelry business empire as the elected/selected President of Rolex to represent the Gambino Family.

The Gambinos sent Stan to Switzerland on this project where he took time to visit his beloved son with whom he was well pleased.

"I remember him showing up in a Mercedes 560 SEL," Paul fondly recalls, "and with him was his good friend from Australia, Cucak, the 'down under Simon Templar.' He really was the closest thing in real life to The Saint. He tried to convince my father to come to Australia, and my father was trying to convince him to get in on this Rolex deal as it was insanely prestigious and lucrative beyond imagination."

Stan considered buying an entire building in Manhattan and pairing it with the one across the street: Rolex 5th Avenue. His deal had the Lombardozzi family set up for life. It was written in stone that Stan had 47th Street—all of it—in his pocket. Any crime at any time had to go through Mr. Stan.

Law enforcement was focused on John Gotti and the mob, and. Stan believed that he was protected and almost invisible.

"My Father and Gotti were out enjoying a drink where they thought their privacy was assured. They were mistaken," recalls Paul. "Walking right up to John Gotti was a Federal Agent who handed Gotti a business card and advised him that there was a hit out on him and to watch his back. The Agent then turned to Mr. Stan and offered him one of his business cards."

The message to Stan was clear—the Feds knew exactly who he was, what he did, and it would only be a matter of time before he would be deserving of more concentrated attention.

Mr. Stan was prudent when it came to self-preservation. It was a desire to get out while the getting was good; you know, take the money and run or maybe Stan feared the Feds were concentrating on him unlike before.

"Nonsense!" exclaims Branka. "Even Stan has no idea of why he does some of his crazy things. In this case, he just suddenly announced that we were moving back to Yugoslavia! And as fast as you can imagine, he sold everything—every building, every home except one and every business. He sold everything for cash, and against my protests, we got the hell out of the USA and returned to a home country that I never considered home."

Paul was equally stunned by his father's sudden desire for relocation coinciding with Paul's graduation, and Paul was thrilled that his father gave every indication of being honestly proud of his son's accomplishments.

"Accomplished is an understatement," says Paul. "I was rapidly advancing in skill and precision as a tennis champion. My self-determined career trajectory was to go from graduation to Nick Bollettieri Tennis academy."

Stan had other ideas.

Chapter Thirteen
Custom Built Son

The next phase in "build your own adult offspring" was to buy off the most famous exclusive and expensive specialty school in Yugoslavia. Paul's former classmates were going to Le Rousey, which was the next level, but Stan insisted on Paul going to Sremski Karlovac Gymnasium—a strict and demanding institution founded in a previous century—a haunted school attended by Paul's grandfather, but not by Stan.

"He didn't qualify scholastically. I didn't either," Paul explains, "but my father's money did. I understood completely that my life was not my own, but of he who sent me. My father was not done building a son. It wasn't easy because I couldn't read Cyrillic, and that made everything difficult. but I soon added that skill to my list of mastered languages."

"I also mastered the art of being repeatedly poisoned by my host family. Is it not strange that I had constantly had severe food poisoning but no one else in the household suffered the same? My mother finally rescued me when I was found unconscious on a bridge, clad only in my underwear. I was taken to the hospital where a fight for my life ensued. I won."

Branka took her son home to her birthplace where he regained his strength.

"Over a period of six months, I built Mom a beautiful new home, one for her parents, and one for myself. Those homes exist to this day. Next came a period of further rejuvenation and self-examination."

Paul set about on a landlocked voyage of self-discovery.

"I spent six months on our family yacht in the Adriatic—the luxury of being raised in vast material wealth, contemplating what in my life was most important, and who was writing my future. I'll give you a hint. The most handsome suave and debonair gentleman thief in the history of America. The erudite, dynamic, and most admired of all immigrants. Lucky Stan. Stan the Man. Stan Silver, Mr. Stan the Diamond Man."

Looking back, Paul clearly perceived his father's child-raising strategy: accustom the child to pain—hunger, beatings—pain of every kind—during his earliest days and strongest period of development. Then, as he approaches puberty, cover that troubled haunted broken and bruised interior with a gleaming streamlined polished veneer of multi-lingual and multi-talented sophistication.

Mr. Stan may have built an updated version of himself, but Paul was making aftermarket modifications and customizations. He was now a bright teen who could speak several languages, excelled in science and the arts, savvy with modern technology, strong, fast, and an accomplished athlete.

"I excelled at every martial art and every form of self-defense. I had Mr. Stan's gift of strategy and my mother's love of the arts. I was fifteen years old, and I was invincible. War was breaking out—just our luck. We came to Yugoslavia just in time for violent upheaval. All Americans were told to get the hell out, which we did but not before our yacht was confiscated and the government placed a 50-caliber machine gun on it. We lost one million dollars when my father shipped gold, finished pieces for a Jewelry mall. He took a three million dollar loss two times."

Corruption was rampant before and during the war, and Mr. Stan got caught up in what is technically termed "serious shit" on the border.

The family survived financially because everybody had a stash. Branka had one, and Mr. Stan also started over again back in the USA on 47th Street.

Chapter Fourteen
Back to the Diamond District

"In 1989 my mother moved back first and set everything up for my father and I to come back," says Paul. "Uncle Paul and Aunt Rada rented us a house in Hackensack. My mother put me back in high school. I was advanced, and they really couldn't teach me anything other than English. I wanted college, so I enrolled in Bergen Community College in New Jersey where I joined the tennis team. I was soon team captain, playing tennis all the time and working on a tennis scholarship. I wanted to get it on my own to show my dad."

Once again, Paul was the kid that other boys decided to pick on and bully.

Why?

He seemed to be a sissy—a cultured, multi-lingual, super courteous, over-educated, elitist—a refined tennis boy. They picked on the wrong young man.

"The first two guys who made that mistake got handed their asses in a high hat, and that ended that. I got fed up with a bully and this fellow needed some attitude re-adjustment via the 'nice little tennis boy.'

"Perhaps I overdid the adjustment as they had to wire his jaw together. Meanwhile, my mom was having a true romance with the kind and one hundred percent legal Albert

DiGangi. My father didn't care about that at all. He had nothing but respect for Mr. DiGangi."

Stan filed for divorce in Yugoslavia, and Branka gave him power of attorney to sell the Long Island home which they still owned.

"Stan sold it and kept the money—the last good screw he gave her," quips Paul. "Now, this might surprise you: my mom and dad remained business partners and close friends. We soon all worked together out of an office in the Diamond District."

Branka confirms this fact, commenting, "Stan was wonderful as a businessperson, a friend, a co-worker, whatever, but he never understood being a husband or a father. If you weren't married to him, you never knew the other aspects of his personality. Consider yourself fortunate."

Her personal fortune was diminished during the divorce, but Branka had enough to pay the rent on the South Hackensack New Jersey house for Paul and her. Stan came back from Yugoslavia and Branka let him stay there, too.

"I told Stan he could stay for a while, but I was not sharing my bed. That did not bother him because Stan could always get women. He was as handsome and charming as ever. He was, what's the expression? A magnetic babe? Oh, babe magnet. So, there we all were together in, of all places, New Jersey. What a sight to see. Mr. Stan and Son. For Stan, it was as if had merely gone on vacation for a few months. It was as if he had never left. He still had the money, the prestige, the close friends, and the tight crews. And there was my little Paul growing into a man... a man who is Son of Stan. I could see my son's destiny as clearly as one sees a diamond while using a loupe. Paul—the world's second greatest gentleman diamond thief. My handsome boy was born and raised to be a diamond thief. Plain and simple."

"Yes," confirms Paul, "I am Mr. Stan's son, and my father is the greatest gentleman thief who ever existed, and who never spent a day in prison. As for my tennis scholarship, who was I kidding? No matter what, I wasn't going to win Mr. Stan's heart with a tennis racket. In my inmost heart of hearts, I knew exactly what he wanted from me. You know it too. I was a young man on a mission. I was going to super impress my father with my brains, bravado, and technique. If precise placement of tennis balls didn't do it for him, perhaps showing him balls of another kind would clinch the deal."

Yes, the boy was back in town, the wild overconfident cowboy who was still sowing his wild oats while planning his first "take the bull by the horns" rodeo.

Paul's childhood pal, Marko, was eager to see his old friend, but his father intervened. "It was as if my father could see the future," said Marko. "He told me that things were not going to go well when Paul returned and united with his dad. He was very firm on this, that as much as I like Paul and Mr. Stan, I must keep my distance. My father was a very sharp man, and I knew if he was emphatic about something, he knew what he was talking about. He told me that Paul following in his father's path was not going to end well no matter how impressive it would be at first."

Impressive indeed. How well Paul recalls sitting in the Manhattan movie theater watching *Batman*, starring Michael Keaton and Jack Nicholson.

"When the movie was over, I pulled my first multi-million-dollar heist. Stepping out into the crisp night air of October Manhattan, I couldn't resist quoting Nicholson's line as the Joker: Wait 'til they get a load of me."

Chapter Fifteen
Paul's First Heist

"I was fifteen years old—almost sixteen, in fact—when I planned and executed my first heist. My mother took me to a place to buy rubies for a ring, and I immediately saw the entire set-up and the shocking lack of security."

This heist would be 20 million dollars easy, and for anyone else on earth, it would be a retirement job. Paul wasn't planning retirement. He didn't do it for the money, and he didn't bring this job to his father so dear old dad could retire. He brought it to his father because he wanted his dad to be proud of him.

"If I were to win his heart and respect, I would have to steal it in the midnight hour, under the cover of darkness illumined only by light from Rockefeller Center reflected off cloud cover and cast into the depths of 47th Street where one misstep or ill-calculated leap leaves you dead or dying, mangled in barbed wire atop an air conditioning vent."

Entering the back of 47th Street transports you to a surreal darkness splashed with neon colors, steam, gas and water dripping like a nagging rain. The air conditioning units provide the aural ambiance and emotion charged soundtrack: a constant whirring hum as if some spacecraft is crouched in the dank darkness waiting to erupt from the asphalt and blast towards the diamond sky.

"It was 1:30 a.m. when we did it," Paul happily recounts. "The very first heist was a piece of cake—The Indian Star Trading Corp. I used a small crew called '2 plus 2'. The lookouts were my father and Mali Dragi outside on 5th Avenue in Dragi's red 911 Porsche tucked smartly away from the streetlight."

"Collaborating with me on the inside was Mali's first cousin, Peko, a soccer player for Syracuse University. This kid was lightning fast, and the cops would never catch him. What a night to remember. I took everything they had, I even opened my first vault and took thousands of carats of semi-precious and precious gems that were in the vault. The rest of the gems were in a locked steel cabinet inside what looked like strong boxes but not strong enough against a crowbar and a big screwdriver."

They opened with little resistance, revealing astonishing treasures, including a stunning emerald necklace worth $175 thousand, plus another two thousand carats of the finest emeralds.

"We loaded the boodle into eight black canvas bags, and they were incredibly heavy," recalls Paul. "We managed to get all eight bags out due to our combined physical strength and the added boost of adrenaline. With the job well done, I returned through an open window to take a last look and was casually walking towards the office when all a sudden, a side door pops open and in comes the NYPD."

"I ran like hell with the cops close behind, leaped out the window and went flying over the exterior air conditioning units like I was a jaguar. The first cop attempted to do the same but fell behind me in the dark hole of the New York night. I could hear the yelling and chaos echoing behind me as his fellow cops came to his rescue."

They made it back to Mr. Stan's quiet office on that cold electric night, lugging those eight full bags worth millions. All this merchandise could barely fit inside Mr. Stan's giant double door safes. The total take for one night's quick work and world class gymnastic moves over those air-conditioning units? Twenty million dollars. A true retirement heist, and enough to last a king for a lifetime.

And that is how you become a multi-millionaire at the age of fifteen.

"What did we do with all that merchandise? We opened Gemstones Trading 45 West 47th Street. We sold it slowly from out of our own store, under our own label, and in the process, became the biggest gemstone merchants and dealers in the world. Of course, we had paperwork that provided a believable paper trail of the gem's ownership."

With Paul now the executive sales manager and official vice president of Gemstones Trading, he had legitimate access deeper inside the diamond district as a professional. This was only the beginning of something amazing, unprecedented, and overwhelming in its daring, danger, and sophistication.

"The only thing I felt bad about," says Paul, "was that our cooperating victim was underinsured. He carried the required minimum insurance, instead of enough to make an immediate outlandish profit by being robbed. I made sure that never happened again. From that night on, I only hit manufacturing jewelers insured for one hundred million or more. The exceptions were few—other criminals who tried to screw us, or people against whom I held a grudge born of immaturity, anger, and opportunity."

Home base, and the nerve center of all the heists and operations, was an office on the top floor of the first modern white marble building in the Diamond District—the Modell Building.

Behind those large, blacked out windows was Mr. Stan, the most powerful and influential non-violent criminal in the history of New York.

"Our setup was foolproof, complex and incredibly lucrative although we weren't doing it for the money," Stan acknowledged. "We had more than enough to last several lifetimes. We did it because we loved doing it. It was a thrill better than any drug, no one was ever hurt, there were no victims, and everyone had a hell of a fun time."

The time Paul and his father shared together after that first heist is engraved in Paul's memory as if etched in chrysolite.

Chapter Sixteen
Mr. Stan and Son

"Everything changed. Dad and I would go together to Panarella's almost every night, or we would hit Atlantic City. He was a big shot there and always received the high roller amenities including his choice of a limo or helicopter picking him up in Manhattan and delivering him to a casino. He opted for a third option: drive with me so we could share more father/son time together."

While Stan and Paul invested energies in cross generation male bonding, Branka kept herself vastly entertained with Mr. DiGangi and her own brand of high level "micro-heists" that are immune from her minimizing.

She was, beyond a doubt, the largest purchaser of stolen high-fashion goods on the planet. She had her own army of gay thieves, remarkably loyal, who stole just for her. The most proficient ones made up to ten thousand dollars a week.

"They hit stores like Barneys, Bergdorf's, Sacks 5th Avenue, Bloomingdales, and every single culture shop on 5th Avenue and Madison Avenue up and down throughout Manhattan," says Paul. "When a Versace shirt was boosted, it was quickly brought to the top floor of our building."

To be more precise, let's have Paul walk us through the theft process:

"After it was stolen, it would find its way to our office in a manner that would make a fun opening of a movie. Just follow the silk Versace shirt—price tag two thousand dollars. The shirt gets passed off to another, and even a third thief, and within twenty minutes of getting taken off the rack, it's placed in a special shopping bag that blocks any alarm techniques. The shirt would get passed off in the coffee shop up the block and picked up by another person and would go through this Arcade and there would be so many thieves avoiding the cops and detectives. The cops knew the players of the game—it was a wide network of thieves, but the cops didn't know where the shirt was going. It was going to the same destination as countless other shirts, dresses, minks, sables of every hot label—our office desk where we would buy it. Remember my mom was a professional model. She would stand in front of that giant mirror, and model these incredible outfits in private for my father, Mr. Stan—the suave man in the shadows."

Branka had ten teams that visited the office starting at 9 a.m. bringing the hottest items in the windows of Barney's or Bergdorf Goodman. The men's navy cashmere long overcoats had a price tag of $10 thousand, and Branka paid 30% of retail.

"I had a few of those gorgeous coats," Paul says, "and it makes you feel important when you're wearing a slick Brioni suit with some Ferragamo Shoes. I always dressed to the nines because my father was always impeccably dressed."

Paul loved collecting ties, and the most expensive ones didn't have to be boosted because they were gifts from Barton G., the famed restauranteur via Aunt Rada.

"Barton wore a tie once, and then gave it to Rada. Lucky me," exclaims Paul, "getting hand me downs from the super wealthy, but it was all brand new. Rada used to bring an entire bag of clothing for me, all name brand, all styles only the best. Between Mom's booster crews and Barton G's hand me downs, I made out like a bandit."

Branka's bandits and their high fashion micro-heists were petty compared to what Stan and Paul's criminal crew were up to. They didn't steal single articles of clothing, but the entire store, complete.

"My father didn't participate in those store heists, although he would kindly offer planning advice when we stole the Entire Versace store, Banks, Hermes, Escada, Channel, and of course we robbed the Trump Crystal Palace. It was fabulous. I did that score with Alex Montenegro—we hit it from the empty store next door. It was locked, sealed, and perfect. We made a hole through the wall, and we filled twenty giant plastic five-milliliter asbestos bags with the finest leather and mink ... this was the best of the best and soon the entire NYC Underworld would have one of these coats. Hell, even John Gotti wanted one."

After hitting Hermes' store, Paul wore the brand so often they began calling him Pauly Hermes. George Carlin was delighted with the shirt Paul gave him, and Carlin wore a gifted Hermes tuxedo to the awards shows.

"I was young, it was fun and dangerous and exciting and every time I got closer to seeing the look in my father's eye that I so longed to see—one of complete admiration and acceptance."

It was, however, like running with scissors, or throwing lawn darts...it is all fun and games until someone trips, stumbles, or gets careless or too eager, and someone gets hurt, gets caught, and spends the best years of their life in the living hell of America's prison system.

"I could have retired after that first heist," admits Paul. "I should have retired—I had enough money to pursue any career. I wanted to open a pasta factory in the Balkans. At that time, all pasta was imported. Hell, what do you need besides flour, water, the world's best pasta making machines and the funds to back the enterprise?"

Paul researched all aspects of the pasta manufacturing industry and returned to normal life in New Jersey. No one suspected that this handsome, erudite teenager had just pulled off the gem heist of the century... over one hundred million carats.

"I even had an afterschool job working for Northern Electric and at Hackensack Athletic," Paul recalls, "and then I got in big trouble with the law when I was completely innocent of a stupid crime committed by classmates—a crime I knew nothing about until I was arrested."

Chapter Seventeen
Running from New Jersey

Two friends from South Hackensack asked Paul to let them into Hackensack Athletic so they could work out. They were lying. What they really wanted to do was rob people's lockers by using bolt cutters on the combination locks. They would replace the lock with a look-alike after riffling through the locker's contents, selectively removing one credit card from the victim's wallet.

It would take forever for the victim to get their locker open, and by that time, the credit card had been cashed out. That wouldn't work today, but back then it was far easier to commit credit card fraud.

Paul didn't know what his school chums were up to, but that misplaced trust changed the course of his life even if it didn't improve his selection of compatriots. The local park was the typical teenage hangout, and Paul cruised in to show off his new ride: a 1987 Callaway Greenwood Corvette with tan top and saddle interior.

"I'm just chatting with one of the boys and the next thing I know there are police all over us. The cops were wise to the locker thefts, and they just assumed I was one of the gang."

There is a sense of cosmic absurdity in Paul being arrested for a foolish high school theft in which he was not involved when he had recently committed the gem heist of the century.

The other boys got a slap on the wrist and sent home with juvenile probation. Paul, following his father's advice, never went back to the police station. "Hey, just stay out of New Jersey," said Stan.

Why would Stan advise his son to do something so reckless? Well, if you go back to the Fort Lee home invasion, it was Stan who never went back and somehow eluded any repercussions in New Jersey.

The cops were not going to let this slide. Failure to appear is no joke. Suddenly, Paul is a fugitive from justice. A teen on the run, with armed police at every frontier, knocking on doors with a fistful of warrants and no pity for a recalcitrant juvenile delinquent.

"They looked for me everywhere," Paul remembers. "They even went to the home of the girl I was dating. I was there when the cops showed up, but her mother bravely hid me in the basement and told the police she hadn't seen me and didn't know where I was. What a wonderful woman!"

Mr. Stan convinced his loyal friend Voja Kovacevic to give Paul an apartment in New York's alphabet city.

"Instead going back to Bergen Community College, I was on the run in New York City. You know what? It was easy. An absurdly wealthy teenager living in his very first apartment in the Big Apple. Hell, this was going to be fun."

Soon after young Paul's first heist, Paul and Mr. Stan were the lookouts as a hand-picked crew of well-trained professionals went inside Lucoral, a big pearl and watch place next door to Lacka's on 45th Street.

"This heist was the store's entire five floors, and the crew worked three days—Friday to Monday– and we took everything."

Paul had an affinity for pearls ever since he read the works of Jules Verne, author *Sixty Thousand Leagues Under the Sea*.

"I found a bunch of Pearl Companies in the Arcade and I passed them every morning when I went to get coffee. I asked my father to get ready to find a big buyer for pearls."

It wasn't long before Paul had millions of dollars in pearls, including a necklace alone worth one million dollars. "It looked like the necklace that Wilma Flintstone wore around her neck in the town of Bedrock," explains Paul. "Hell, Wilma loved that necklace so much, she wore it every day!"

The pearl heist was one that was done multiple times, and the first time was when Paul triumphantly opened a double door safe in sixteen seconds.

"At this point in my teenage years I had done one heist and was lookout on another. My second real heist was one I did with Ranko Mitckovic. My father was the lookout, and the target was Mr. Clasp Jewelry manufacturers on the tenth floor, two buildings away from our office."

As executive sales manager for Gemstones Trading, Paul had access to everyone, including those who ran Mr. Clasp.

"I had to come to the office every day and work because I had a real job selling gemstones," Paul recalls. "We had accumulated a collection of two million carats of semi-precious stones. We actually became the number one source for gemstone business all over the world. We had the highest quality, all the right sizes for the and we had the biggest inventory because I made sure that we stole it."

Finding potential gem heists was the other part of Paul's job.

"Finding those was easy: I would go into the Red Book, and I would come up with five brand new potential heists. The next move is to physically go and see what they have and how they are situated."

Paul would call and make an appointment to come in and do business in person. He would arrive in his two thousand dollar suit, thousand dollar shoes, a thirty thousand dollar watch, and a one hundred fifty thousand dollar pinky ring. Paul looked every inch the businessman with his expensive briefcase containing samples of the best diamonds and gemstones that only he could offer. "I called on everyone, including Mr. Clasp, who happily took me on a tour of their facility. I could see their entire layout," says Paul. "I saw how their security system was set up, what type of vault they had, where the security cameras and motion detectors were located... everything. I found this job, it was mine, and I brought it to my father and he and I agreed. That means everything from that point on was in motion and preparation. You know the process of successful completion: knowledge volition and action. Know what you want to accomplish, decide to accomplish it, and then do it."

What they did earned Paul his famous nickname.

Chapter Eighteen
Becoming Punch

"Ranko and I got prepared in my office, putting on our all-black heist outfits, then getting our gear and the bags. This heist was my favorite because it was that night that I got my nickname, Punch."

"From the top floor of our building, we make our way up the stairs to the roof top. I have the key to the emergency door where the alarm has been dismantled. From the rooftop, we cross over the fire escape and make a daring jump from our roof onto the building next to ours."

In the walkie talkie, Paul says in Serbian, "I am next to the club. I will go and check it out. How is everything out there?"

Mr. Stan, calmly smoking a cigarette, is on his walkie talkie on 5th Avenue. watching the side of the building where the guards come out of 580 5th Avenue; Alek Grbac is in a Lincoln Town Car just circling the 47th Street block with a police scanner and his walkie talkie.

"Everything is smooth," says Mr. Stan, giving Ranko and Paul the security they need: knowledge that no guards or police can catch them if they stick to the plan.

"We now have to climb up ten flights of jagged fire escape in the dark. When we get to the tenth floor Ranko is winded, and my mouth is dry. I take out my flashlight and point it through the window right on the vault. I immediately get on my walkie talkie. "Ok I'm at the door of the club and I am about to go in."

"I reach in my bag and take out the first tool I am going to use to stretch the bars on the window– a BMW carjack because they work the best. I put the jack in between the bars and start cranking. They bend as if they are made of string cheese. We immediately each take out a crowbar. "We're going in now."

Both lookouts, my father on 5th Avenue and Alex on 6th, respond, "Ok, clear."

Alex is in the Lincoln Town car picking up Mr. Stan and they will park further down the block and use binoculars. This is a Boombash job, meaning the alarms are running. The police and Holmes Security are going to come and come fast.

"I popped open the sealed window, and we know that in fifteen seconds the alarms will go off. Sure enough, the phone starts to ring as I go straight to the vault lightning fast and open my bag of tools.

"Ranko, turn on the lights," I said, "and fill the bags with the showcase items."

"Before he has a chance to fill the second bag, I punch the vault open and immediately started scooping diamonds and gold, filling up a total of five bags. Leaving the tools behind, I went into the nearby mini-fridge and found a Motts Apple juice. My refreshment break is interrupted by Mr. Stan on the walkie talkie: "Get Out! Get Out! They're coming!"

"I make it out the window and I tie two bags and send them down swiftly as Ranko is already making his way down the same fire escape and I strap my bag around my back and go down fast to make it through the back yard two buildings next to our building at 45 West 47th Street. Mr. Stan says that the police are in front of the place—two cop cars and they are waiting for the Holmes Security Guard,

Carlos Medina, to get there with the keys, Carlos was heavy set, slow moving and I bet he would love to make more money than what he was being paid by Holmes Security."

"Ranko is down now while I climb quickly up to our roof and throw the line down, I climb up with one full bag, take it off and pull up three heavy bags. Ranko struggles with his one bag and finally makes it up."

Mr. Stan on the walkie talkie, "Are you good? Are you good?

"Yeah, we're really good,"

"As I pull in the last bag inside, I peek over the ledge of the roof and see the cops shining their flashlights through the window, and plenty of gems dropped on the floor for them. Yes, they are filling their pockets. We make it to our secure office, and I look out of our window and see all the commotion: ten cop cars two, ESU Vans, and a SWAT team. They are looking for us, unaware that we are watching them."

"Ranko, thirsty in every, way asking me how much you think we got. I say back: *more than you can ever spend*. I was hooked forever with this. It was that good. Night after night we banged them out just like this."

After an initial series of successful heists, tension developed between Paul and his father for two easily defined reasons.

Chapter Nineteen
Tension in the Family

The tension was not only over the take allocated to Paul, but also because of Paul's adolescent tendency to overstatement.

"I had a girlfriend I met at the mall," recalls Paul. "Remember her mother protected me from the New Jersey cops. Well, I wanted to gift her a $175 thousand necklace from one of my first heists. My father threw a fit about that, insisting that was stupid and immature of me. In retrospect, he was right. But in my hyper-emotional mind, he was denying me the right to do what I wanted with my share of the boodle."

These father/son skirmishes didn't go unnoticed by Moma, a king mixer who simultaneously worked for Mr. Stan and robbed Mr. Stan at every opportunity. Moma realized his days with Mr. Stan were numbered with Paul taking on more responsibility.

Stan was also getting older, and although Moma had sworn loyalty to his benefactor, fidelity to the man who saved his life, Moma's psychopathic proclivities prohibited him from seeing beyond himself and his own advantage.

In the parable of the scorpion and the frog, Moma's stinger was always poised.

"It is sad," asserts Branka, "my son had so many years of resentment towards his father that even when his father embraced him and protected him—and my boy cannot deny that his father protected him– he was more comfortable fomenting arguments with him."

There is a distorted sense of security in familiar pain, and Paul's synapses were welded to a schematic of resentment that went from second nature to first nature.

For Moma, there was linkage to Paul, the energetic if high strung son. Looking back, Paul sees clearly what he then saw through a glass darkly, if at all.

"Moma was using divide and conquer—a tactic as old as selfishness and as destructive as a tornado… only slower, a creeping infection of disunity and suspicion. Naturally, Moma presented himself as my closest ally."

While Moma plotted his forays into deceptive division, Paul was forming exceptional personal alliances, including a close friendship with Rande Gerber, co-owner of the Whiskey with a fellow named Paul Montana who was briefly married to model Ashley Richardson. That Paul Montana is not Pavle Stanimirovic.

"I was not Rande's partner," explains our jewel thief. "I was his friend and helped him out. My dad and I conducted a lot of meetings at the Whiskey Bar. The real Paul Montana married Ashley, the marriage didn't work out, and Mr. Montana moved away to Europe to start a new life. I always needed new identities as I could never use my real name for anything because I was a wanted man. So, simply put, I became Paul Montana. I had an ID with that name on it, and the real guy and I looked similar, so I was able to get away with it. Ashley was a good sport about me pretending that I was her ex-husband and kept my identity a secret. I regard both Paul and Ashley as valued friends to this day."

The problem with history is that those living it, not knowing it is history, didn't always pay attention. Paul paid attention and rattles off names and associations as if this all transpired less than twenty-four hours ago.

"There is this great guy, John Scialpi, owner of the strip joint Goldfinger's, and we partnered together on some high yield banking projects," recalls Paul proudly." Everything seemed blessed and created for our own amusement and profit. John Dangelo, a loyal friend, had an entire truck filled with laptops one day. The next day he had Nike sneakers, and then it was a truckload of Fila and then Sergio Tachini. How he happened to acquire the abundance of such items was really none of my personal business but selecting the best of it for myself and my friends before passing it up the Mafia ladder was my business."

Mr. Stan had nothing to do with these criminal enterprises in terms of active participation. As Bret and Bart Maverick said, "Stick to your own game," and Stan could have adopted the Maverick motto as his mantra. America's undisputed master of the multi-million-dollar diamond heist had no interest in petty theft or even grand theft. He focused only on his specialty and not entirely for artistic reasons or matters of reputation.

He was not going to risk expansion into crimes that had actual victims. There was no reason for it. He didn't need the money, and he didn't need the risks. He had respect prestige wealth and seemingly everyone loved him. When you are a man of erudition education and strategic perception it is a tempting error to credit others with having your same level of ethics and altruistic attitude. Mr. Stan was not tempted. He knew exactly who he was, his specific sphere of expertise—the victimless heist—and he stayed true to his standards and stuck to his own game.

The brain behind Moma's activities—Moma's brain—was addled by a combination of abuse, head injury, and the constant ingestion of massive amounts of cocaine. He was a supreme manipulator, and he knew Paul's volatility and the surest wedge to play was one that would pit Paul against his father.

"Your father is ripping you off, Paul," Moma confided., "He's not giving you your full cut."

It was true and for a good reason. Paul, despite his skill, was still underage. Stan instituted his own version of the Coogan Law—protect Paul's money by setting aside much of it for when he was a mature adult.

Paul, in his immaturity, didn't see it that way. He railed against his father, venting years of pent-up resentment. Offended by Paul's verbal assault and demands for more money, Stan went on the offensive. "You must have forgotten how much I spent on your Swiss Boarding School!"

Paul, as headstrong as a young man as he was when a distraught ten-year-old, was too blinded by the dust storm of emotional content stirred up by. Moma to see the obvious: Moma wanted Paul away from Mr. Stan doing heists for him. Moma also wanted an easy manipulated scapegoat.

Branka, who always despised Moma, clearly saw what was happening and did her best to intervene, "I tried to clue my son in on what was really happening, but Moma had done everything he could to drive a wedge between all of us. He stirred up trouble between not only Stan and Paul but between Paul and me. Of course, I tried to reason with Paul, but he paid no attention to me when it came to such things. He only paid attention to me when I advised him on heists, but on the important matters of life and relationships, he ignores his mother."

"Yeah," agrees Paul, "I should have listened. Moma was playing all of us for his own sick ends. When I left my dad's crew, Moma left too, and it didn't take long to understand why."

By his own admission, Paul was self-centered and hot headed, but when it came to Moma, he wised up in a hurry when he realized that Moma delighted in viciousness. The Mafia would hire Moma to do collection jobs for them. They would send Moma and his boys in to get money from recalcitrant debtors.

Chapter Twenty
Off the Rails

It was on the first such assignment that Moma wanted Paul to come along in case they needed to open the safe.

"Moma, and I went to the Green House Cafe in uptown. His name was Mo, and he was resistant to making good on his debt. It was sold to Boa and Moma. They dragged me along and we pulled up in a big burgundy Lincoln Town Car."

"I had a huge crowbar in the trunk, and Moma took it and put his coat over it. This crowbar will be used as an intimidation tool. I am there to burn open the safe in case the target would not be able to open it. We arrived after lunch time and the place was empty like we knew it would be. As soon as we came through the front door this big giant Italian man with gruff voice came walking toward us saying that they were closed."

"Moma breaks his head open with his leather coat with my crowbar under it. This was a shock and a surprise to the Made Man we came to see. Mileta Miljanić pulled out a pistol and told everyone to relax and calm down. Moma takes Mo's hand and banged it with the sharp end of the crowbar piercing his hand twice so fast that Mo fell off his chair."

"Moma grabbed the tablecloth and wrapped it like a caring nurse to control the bleeding and slapped him again down the hall to the office to open the safe. Another smack to the head while Miljanić is controlling the room, I am looking at this like I'm watching *Goodfellas*. Now Mo is having a lot of problems because he can't open it with his left hand and is messing up. The next heavy-handed smack by Moma changed everything around and I emptied out the small safe that contained a kilo of coke, $120 thousand that did not belong to him, and $200 thousand in jewelry, a few guns and a three-carat diamond ring. All this is just for us to split. Moe still has to pay the $70 thousand cash plus interest and MM gave a taxi driver a $100 to take Moe to the Hospital to get his hand fixed and to be back at his restaurant because Moma wanted to have dinner here later. Guess who paid the bill that evening plus the $70 thousand plus interest and an apology for neglecting prompt payment—Mo with his bandaged hand."

"Now, why do you think they sent us to do this work? Because this was a made guy and no one can touch a made guy or you would get killed. They send in the Navy Seals. We were the Navy Seals. This was day one out of 47 days in gangster hell I spent with Moma."

Mr. Stan would never conscience such behavior, such violence, and to know that his son had sunk to such depths was more than disconcerting.

"At least he hasn't been infected with politics," Stan allegedly mused, knowing full well that partisan politics was by its very nature, divisive, corrupt, and deadly.

"After Moma and I got bagged from my father's crew, I experienced another side of life," says Paul. "I left and went with Moma to M.M and that's when I joined them, and Zoran and we did work for the Serbian Mafia. Bosko was the boss of The Westies, and we worked for Sammy the Bull. I took over his nightclub on the West side, ran Payroll for Marine Construction and Hawk from Englewood Cliffs,

New Jersey. There were decidedly violent and immoral aspects, and I had to make myself fit in."

He fit in all too well. Paul not only crossed the line, but he also took the street signs with him.

"Yes, looking back I'm ashamed of myself," Paul admits, "I did things that violated the standards of the Gentleman Thief."

His mother, hearing this, rolls her beautiful eyes as if hearing the understatement of the century. She opens her mouth to utter a sharp-tongued condemnation but allows whatever commentary to evaporate in a measured exhale.

"I wanted to spank him, but he was too big," she says, half seriously. "What was he doing with that damn Moma? For a true genius, sometimes my son is a complete idiot."

How crazy did it get? There is no way to exaggerate, and to site a few examples would be minimizing.

"Moma and my crew had an apartment on Hillside off Dykeman Street," explains Paul, neglecting to mention that the apartment was an entire floor with access to Moma's personal parking lot next door with every type of car from Porches to Caddies.

Moma owned horses in Arizona, and he took off for a work-play vacation in the great outdoors leaving Paul and "Money Mike," a male model for Bruce Webber Photography, with the run of the place for an entire month.

Unlike many male models, Mike wasn't gay or bisexual, but one hundred percent straight, and he scored his weight in women wanting a blue-eyed blond bad boy.

"Mike grew up in Brooklyn," says Paul. "His hustle was his incredible basketball skill. He was like a card shark or a pool hustler. If you ever saw the movie "White Guys Can't Jump," you get the idea. No one expected this "maybe gay" white kid to move and shoot like a love child of Michael Jordan and Larry Byrd."

Mike showed Paul how he made fast money; Paul showed Mike how he made faster money, and more of it. Money Mike quit his hustle and went to work for Paul.

"With Moma gone, Mike and I had a month to do what we wanted, and we accidently robbed a friendly acquaintance of over a million dollars."

Accidentally?

The friendly acquaintance was Supra, a powerful multi-millionaire drug dealer and member of the Latin Kings. Not to be confused with the Mambo Kings or Kings of Leon, the Latin Kings is not a 70mm cigarette—it is what some term "a Latino Heritage Fellowship" and others regard as a sick-ass gang of violent drug pushers and murderers.

Money Mike had just finished a photo shoot when he stumbled upon what was certainly a drug spot money counting room in the Dykeman district. Mike tells Paul, and the two go into action:

"We didn't have time to change into our authentic cop uniforms," Paul recalls "We did grab our cop badges and those lightweight jackets that have that Velcro thing you can pull down that reveals the word, police."

The two jumped into their black Ford Ltd, and raided the joint, tying up six money counters and making off with twenty hefty bags stuffed with cash.

"They were lucky that we were not real cops, we just looked like cops We also found ten kilos of cocaine," Paul remembers, "and we took that as an added bonus."

Soon, Paul and Money Mike had the entire block and all resident drug dealers outraged. Supra sent word throughout the 'hood that he wanted his coke back.

"We were already finding buyers for it," says Paul, "And here is the karmic irony—those million dollars in cash were all in fives and ones! No hundred-dollar bills, and very few twenties. Yes, almost a million one-dollar bills."

Telling the story, Paul begins laughing at his own absurd predicament.

"We had so much money we could not count it all. We stuffed it in a closet and there was still what seemed tons of it left. We filled entire bedrooms with cash. I even slept on a couch stuffed with it. There wasn't enough room to stash all of it, and it was exhausting work just trying to count it."

Paul gave up, but Mike started sniffing up the coke to stay up, and this is when Moma came back, cracked open a kilo and he stated sniffing coke more and more.

"He would then drive to Manhattan to do a heist whacked out of his mind," says Paul, and then rattles off an evening's agenda in a breathless staccato mimicking the frantic lifestyle of the over-amped Moma.

"And he asks Mike and me to drive him and he had to collect money and talk to the Mob in Brooklyn and then Speak to David Sanchez to make a meeting and sit down with Joe Sinatra in the Bronx with the Albanians and then go to NJ to pick up his girlfriend at her sister's and he would have to sell this swag on 47th Street so he can get $70 thousand and he would then sniff more and Kiro would call him complaining that he was robbed of over $200 thousand in jewels that he stashed in his fridge and we find out it was his roommate who is a waiter and not part of our crew. We got to go to Riverdale to Kiro Haki Murati place to question these fuck heads and find out who stole what they will feel the wrath of Moma and Moma would examine him, and he would either die or find religion."

Moma duct taped the guy with two rolls of duct tape and then he water- boarded the fellow. Moma claimed that his own father used to punish him with water boarding. Moma's victim confessed and revealed to whom he sold it. Of course, he would have confessed to assassinating Archduke Ferdinand under the circumstances."

That lifestyle of continual chaos, violence and duplicity wears thin on those who have known another life. Paul knew another, more refined and erudite life from which he now felt cut off.

When Mr. Stan cuts you off, you are cut off from everything and everyone, and that was Moma's exact situation. Angry and frustrated, Moma returned to the same Albanian gang that once wanted to kill him, the Mustafa crew. He convinced them that he could do infiltrating work against Mr. Stan to their financial advantage. All he needed was a strong pawn in the game.

"I was that pawn," admits Paul. "I stupidly hooked up with Moma and we pulled off between ten and fifteen heists before the infamous Miracle Watch debacle."

Pictures

All photos are courtesy of "The DiGangi Archive" and used with permission.

Call him "Mr. Stan."

Mr. Stan's passport photo.

Mr. Stan and his first-born son, Sasha Alexander.

Mr Stan contemplates the future.

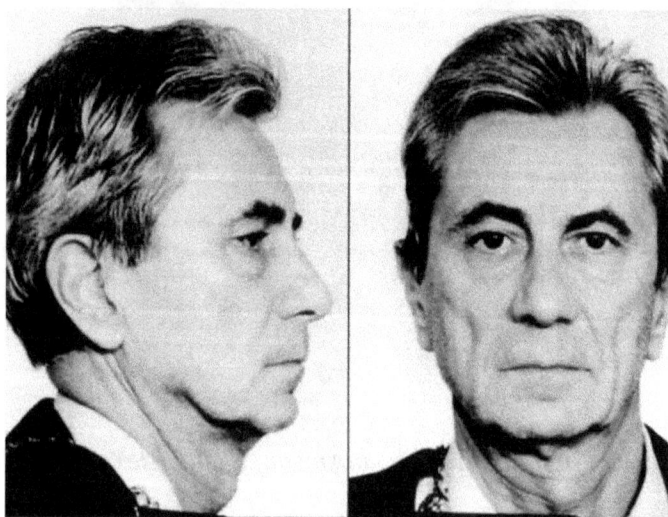

The Professor, Andre Montrose, Mr. Stan's best friend.

Branka Teofilovich, 18-year-old Serbian art student.

One of Branka's early modeling photos.

Branka in NYC the night she meets Mr. Stan.

Acrobatic burglars captured by police

NEW YORK (UPI)—A gang of acrobatic burglars who swung on ropes from building to building during a $1 million series of jewel thefts was stopped in the act Wednesday night by police using an electronic device developed for night fighting in Vietnam.

Police captured one man and recovered $240,000 worth of rings stolen from the offices of the Botell Ring Co., Inc., on Lower Broadway. They cordoned off a square block around the building in an unsuccessful attempt to trap four other men who fled.

"They were fantastic, real professionals, like something out of the movies," said Sgt. Thomas Connelly of the Police Safe and Loft Squad.

Police blamed the gang for about 40 burglary attempts on New York City jewelery dealers. James L. White, executive secretary of the Jewelers Security Alliance, estimated they had taken "in excess of $1 million" in jewels this year.

Connolly said the gang always followed the same pattern.

"They pick top floor offices," he said. "They either hide in the building or break in and chain the doors shut behind them.

"After they take an elevator to the floor they want, they throw off all power. They know all the alarms are going but they figure they can beat them.

"After they get into the vault, they don't try to go back down inside," he said. "They head for the roof and use ropes to get to other buildings. Usually while we are running up the inside they are passing us going outside."

Wednesday night was different, however, because police were patrolling the area of darkened office buildings where a number of jewelers have offices. And they were equipped with the owl eye night viewing system which, developed for use in Vietnam, magnifies available light more than 100 times.

When the burglar alarm sounded Connolly and two detectives sped to the building at Broadway and 20th Street, smashed through the plate glass of the chained front door and climbed 20 flights of stairs to the top of the building.

From there they trained the owl eye on a figure going down a wall in almost complete darkness.

Raymond Smith, 36, was nabbed as he dangled from a rope, over an inner courtyard, police said. Four other men hurled cases containing rings into the courtyard and fled, leaving police to an hour-long hunt on hands and knees for a cache of gold and diamond rings which spilled from one burst case.

Sidney Heller, president of Botell, said more than 2,000 rings worth $240,000 were recovered.

Who was "Raymond Smith?" The name was fake, and he vanished.

Layout of the Vizcaya Museum in Florida.

The foyer of Stan and Branka's apartment in Manhattan at the time of the Vizcaya post-heist shake-down by NYPD.

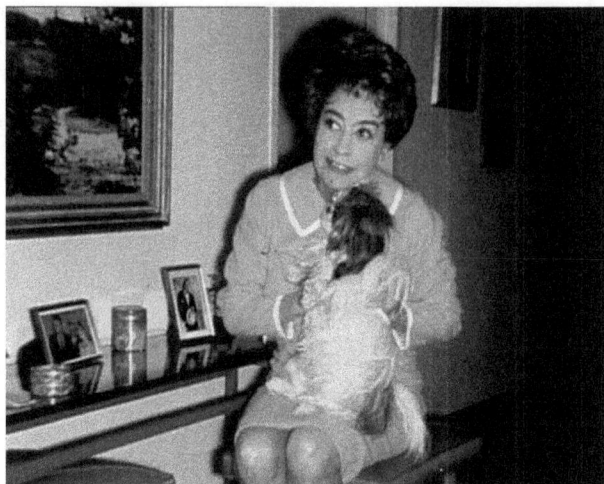

Joan Crawford with the dog, Princess, that she promised to Paul for his birthday.

Paul's birthday party at Joan Crawford's apartment.

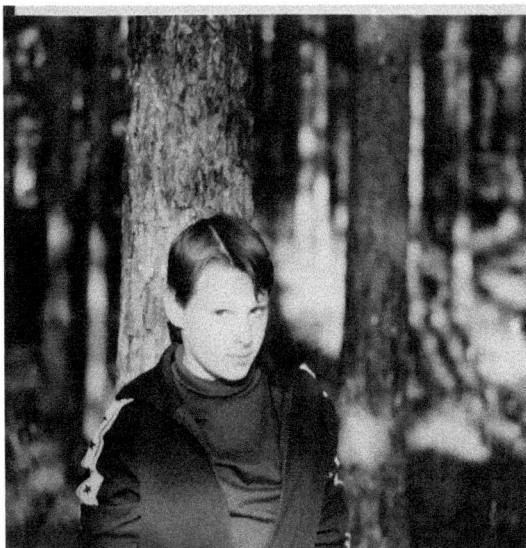

Paul in the woods behind the new house.

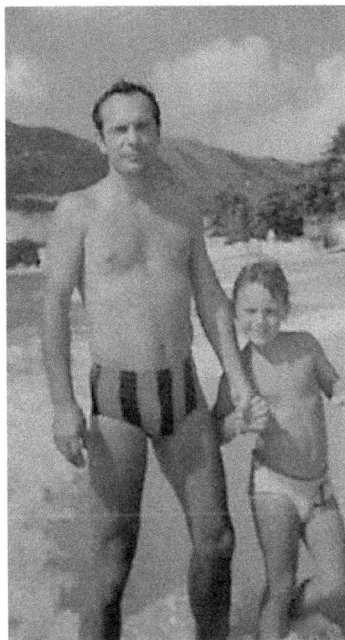

Stan and young Paul at the beach.

Branka and young Paul at the beach.

Mr. Stan and Alek, "the Moth" strategize a new heist.

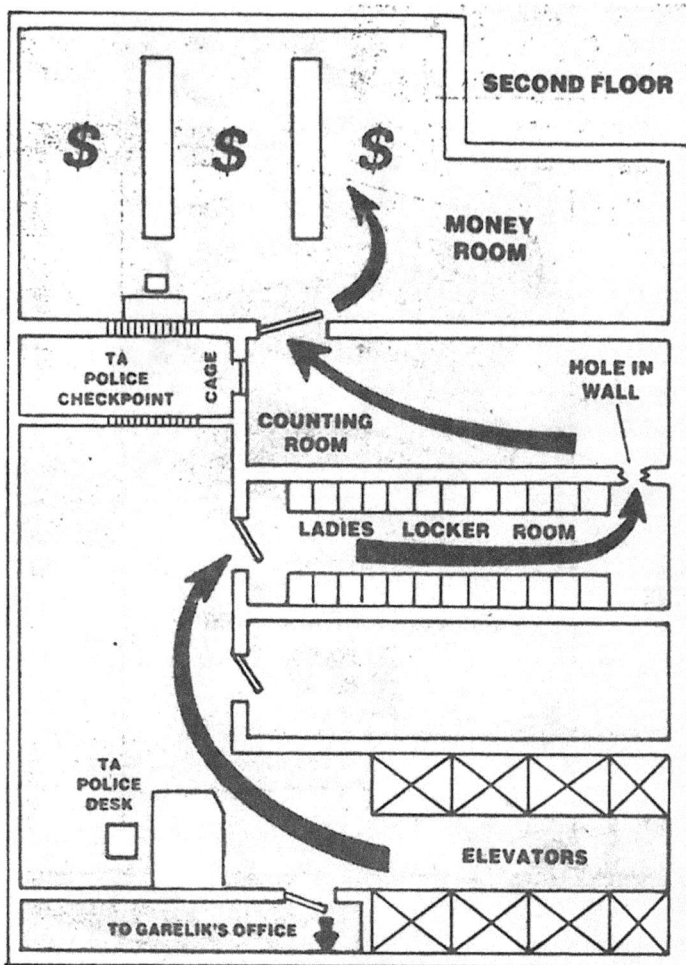

Diagram of how Stan and Alek stole
$600,0000 (insured of course).

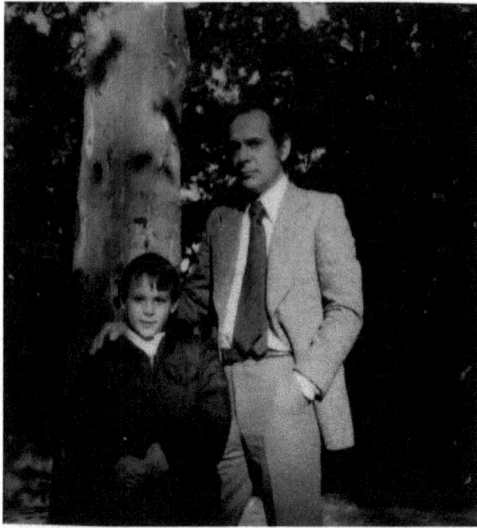

Stan and young Paul the day before
they leave for Switzerland.

Home from vacation in Switzerland, Paul
and his father relax together.

Branka and Paul at the time of his first heist at age fifteen.

Paul, the teenage diamond thief, and millionaire.

The top floor of the Modell Building belonged to Mr. Stan.

Mileta Miljanic, Nikola Kavaja, &
Westies Boss Boško Radonjić

Jamie Schafer, fourth from the left on the University of Washington Crew.

NYPD Detective Joseph Keenan.

Branka and her new husband, Al DiGangi.

Paul in high spirits despite facing thirty years in prison.

Paul beefed up in prison, often acting
as if a Puerto Rican gangster.

Paul marries Jessica and attempts going 100% legit.

When going legit doesn't work, Paul decides to go more bold and more outrageous. No longer a teenager, Punch is determined to knock NYC on its heels.

Chapter Twenty-One
The Warning

Mr. Stan could see his son's career arc clearly, and it wasn't a pleasant vision.

"You are going to wind up in prison," Stan stated succinctly, and did his best to reason with Paul. In this father and son meeting, it was pointed out that Paul was doing too much and doing it with criminal inferiors, Paul had nothing left to prove; he had reached the pinnacle of success and the only movement in his career was down, and down with a crash.

"Let's retire before it goes bad," suggested Stan in words such as these. "We can go back to the old country with our wealth and prestige where you can live like a king, have a luxurious home, cars, women, the best of everything. Travel the world, have fun, be free of any danger from gangs, cops, feds, anybody. If you keep going like you are, with the people you are associating with, it's only a matter of time before you are not only arrested but tried and convicted. I can't protect you except by warning you and inviting you to quit while you're ahead."

Remembering that conversation, Paul puts his head in his hands and takes a moment of silence before commenting.

"Why didn't I follow his advice? He talked retirement. He talked about stopping what I was doing, Retire? How can I even comprehend the concept when I am only twenty? Besides, I had an almost terminal case of criminal pride. My ego entered the room a half hour before I did. I was determined to be a billionaire. I'm not kidding. My life would have been so much different if I had listened to my father."

Paul turned down the offer and went off with Moma to pull a heist at the Miracle Watch Company. By sunrise, he was in police custody.

"If I had done this heist with my dad as lookout, I never would have been busted," laments Paul. "I had just been in this place with my mother when she sold them some watches. The owner was showing off some high-end Cartier watches that he had stashed above his bookshelf. I made a note of that. This was supposed to be an easy win-win job for everyone."

From the very beginning, things were not to Paul's liking.

First of all, Moma was so high on cocaine that he didn't know what planet he was on. Second, how they got into Miracle Watch was to first break into the women's restroom next door by going through the sheetrock, and then repositioning themselves above the showcases by making a hole in the ceiling.

"Moma was so whacked that the work was sloppy as hell, the ceiling was falling down on top of the showcases and there was dust and debris everywhere."

Paul immediately took command and started giving orders, determined to have the job go smooth.

"The crew, aside from Moma and the lookout, were guys that I knew were one hundred percent trustworthy. Zoran Jaksic and I were as brothers. He was smart as hell and had the kind of charisma that you associate with great success. Once we were in, I went right to the vault while Zoran attacked the showcases and filled up the bags, but one of the bags he filled was inside out, so we had to leave it behind. Five bags came out with us, and we dropped them off in the van.

Now, the question is, 'do we go back for the other bag or not?'"

Here is where criminal pride can override common sense. A basic rule of the successful heist is "Never go back—when you are out, stay out."

"As everything was quiet—no alerts from our lookout –I said that David Sanchez and another guy, Bato, and I would go back for the rest. Moma was so out of his mind that I didn't want him back on the inside, and there was no reason for Zoran to go with us because we were taking everything back to his apartment."

The reason everything was quiet with no alerts from the lookout is because the lookout left his post. He decided to take a walk around the block. Hence, he didn't see the cops show up. They were alerted by a custodian who found the giant hole in the next-door ladies' restroom wall.

Paul and his two pals retrieved the other bags and were on their way out when the lookout contacted them.

"Uh... there is a cop car out front, but I don't see any cops," he says. "The doors are open. What does that mean?"

"They're in the building, dammit," barks Paul and they race to the door, open it and three cops have guns drawn and pointed.

"All three of us were wearing Halloween masks," Paul explains, "and mine was the scariest—the Wolfman– so they all train their weapons on me."

Everyone froze as if someone hit pause on a DVD. David Sanchez, directly behind Paul, was the first to make a move: he threw the bag of watches at the cops. Struck by a fortune in designer timepieces, the cops stumbled back, and the door slammed shut.

Paul, David and Bada ran like hell.

"They chased us inside that building for over four hours without catching us. David ran one way, and we ran the other. Now, I had keys to every door in the building, and by the most remarkable of situations, I was able to get past them and opened a locked closet directly by the door out! Bada and I hid in there and waited. We could hear everything that was going on—the chaos of the SWAT team searching every floor, the choppers overhead—the works. I think they had David, but they had given up on finding Bada and me. We just sat there, waiting and listening. They were leaving, pulling everyone out. All we had to do was sit tight and wait."

The last man leaving was the man with the K-9. If the man and the dog made it past the closet and out the door, Paul and Bada would soon be up in Zoran's apartment counting the loot and preparing to bail out Sanchez.

No such luck.

"I was busted by the Swat Team called Emergency Service Unit ESU and they were all jacked up on steroids and they meant business. I will not lie, I was shaking. I did not want to go to jail. And I am with two guys who have never been arrested and didn't plan on being arrested that night: David Sanchez - his brother is a t pilot flying Mayor Dinkins around, and the other is Montenegrin Bato Kadovic, the brother of the legendary smash & grab thief."

The dog, Billion, was trotting its canine way past the closet when it suddenly went crazy barking and scratching at the door like Cujo on a mission to kill. Paul called out from inside, "Okay, we're opening the door. We give up."

"I opened the door, and there was a wooden stool between the dog and Bada. First the dog destroyed the stool, then it went after him, as did the cops. They beat the shit out of him probably because he was tall– over six-foot-six— before they took us all down to the precinct, rewarded the dog with a filet mignon steak and put us in a cage."

It was, according to Paul, like a scene from *Planet of the Apes*. Every cop in the precinct and beyond came in to gawk at the captives and help themselves to handfuls of watches.

"The cops were laughing and joking and asking each other 'what time is it?' as they took as many watches as they could. Only a fraction of what was in that bag ever made it into evidence. Of course, the charge was burglary in the third degree, and I gave my name as Reginald Mathews. I had ID in that name given me by Zoran and the address on my Reginald Mathews ID was Bosko's townhouse."

Moma was supposed to post bail for the unlucky trio, but he had other uses for the evening's income—a restaurant in which Paul discovered he shared a fifty-percent ownership. Paul eventually made money off the restaurant when they sold it, and the name was changed to Coyote Ugly.

"I went up in front of Judge Rene White and I had the famous Ronald Rubenstein as my lawyer. On the opposing team was none other than the partner of my attorney, Robert Wolf. People wonder how much money I've spent on attorneys," says Paul seriously. "Five million, but that's a good deal considering how many millions I made. When Reginald Mathews went before the judge, my lawyers told a version of the truth: I was a young man with a vast upscale education in Switzerland, I spoke numerous languages fluently and I was an accomplished skier."

The judge, fluent in French and equally adept in her knowledge of skiing and ski equipment, interrogated Paul in French regarding certain aspects of downhill ski racing. They had a delightful conversation."

Paul, alias Reginald Mathews, was simply put on probation and told to check in everyday at the police precinct just around the corner from his apartment. Once in the precinct, Paul would sign a logbook—the same process used by cops visiting from other precincts.

"When I realized that there was no perceived difference between other cops and me, I got an NYPD duffle bag and when I went in, I stayed in for hours hanging out with the cops who thought I was one of them from Metro. Hell, you know I had a perfectly authentic shield and other props.

I had original FBI, police, firefighter, and U.S. Marshall shields. I had access to passports like I was Jason Bourne, and many authentic DMV licenses. The first ones I had were from Rasha the Beard and Zoran Jakšic. My friend David Sanchez was great at getting them also."

"We would go to some little DMV and get as many licenses as possible," explains Paul. "I would be told to wait in line for that specific teller with the white headband or something and I would take a number and wait and I get called I take a test and they pass me and call me to take a photo and whatever name and address that I provided to the DMV was the one I would get back and it would be in the National Data Base wow. The cost? For you $2 thousand. For me, $300."

When Zoran Jaksic was arrested in Peru in 2018 for allegedly smuggling multiple tons of cocaine from South America to Europe via Freightliner, the press termed Zoran "The Man of a Thousand Names" due to his use of many aliases and false identities. On the list of names used by Zoran Jaksic is Peter Stanimirovic.

"Peter Stanimirovic was the name Zoran most often used in the USA," says Paul, "Zoran always like the idea of being my true brother."

Talking about the Department of Motor Vehicles reminds Paul of his pal David Sanchez who had a few car lots by Jerome Avenue. Paul and David used Sanchez's car dealer license to purchase cars at the auction at wholesale prices or less: Mercedes, Audi, Jaguar, Cadillac and, for work, a Lincoln.

"It's like I had the entire city in my back pocket," Paul says wistfully, "The days moved fast and as the day turned to night, we would be ready for a well-planned heist, and those take skill and some devious planning."

Paul made copies of every key he could get his hands on. This obsession with keys probably has some metaphoric meaning, but primarily it meant he could get in anywhere or more importantly, he couldn't be locked out or excluded, and that included pretending to be within a group sub-culture and pulling it off.

"It was fun getting away with daring stuff such as impersonating a police officer right there in a police precinct. I was pushing the envelope," admits Paul,." but I had to find something to do while the Albanians were outside waiting to kill me."

Excuse me?

Chapter Twenty-Two
Something Spectacular

"Moma told the Albanian's that I stole a truckload of silver—a complete lie. But Moma was pissed because... well... let me back up," says Paul. "When Moma didn't bail us out, I knew for sure that things had to change. Hell, when I finally caught up with him at our restaurant, he tossed me a plastic bag of watches and two thousand dollars. That's it. I asked him about a few specific ultra-valuable watches, the Rolexes and the Cartier, and he says that he sold them! I was pissed off, and I took Bato's and David's cuts in watches. And they have felonies to fight. This wasn't right. I had to find a way to get back with my father. I had to do something so astonishing that he would take me back with open arms, just being able to run a heist crew wasn't enough, not when you factor in how far down the ladder of ethics and altruism I had ignominiously descended. Okay, I admit it. I screwed up. I admit it. Moma and I would steal heists from my own father, the Mafia, Montenegro, Josip and the Professor, so you can understand that to counterbalance that, I had to come up with something spectacular."

All creative breakthroughs bein with "What if...?" Paul's breakthrough was, "What if we had the security companies, Holmes and ADT, working with us instead of against us?"

That was it. How could something so deliciously perfect be overlooked all these years? The Mob was already tied in with the insurance companies, why not have Diamond District security companies aligned with the Diamond District jewel thieves?

"I decided that was exactly what I was going to accomplish," asserts Paul, "and not as some wishful thinking in the future daydream. I didn't tell anyone of my plan. I simply immediately went to work to make it a reality by actively recruiting the slowest moving but quickest thinking Holmes Security employee, Mr. Carlos Medina, as part of our crew."

Medina worked five days a week as a Holmes Security armed guard in the Diamond District. His take home pay, after taxes wasn't a living wage, especially for a married man starting a family. His wife, an executive assistant at Playboy Enterprises, was the family breadwinner.

Much to Medina's delight, there had been a recent upturn in his personal fortunes. He found ten giant diamond cluster rings on the floor of a manufacturing jeweler whose alarms had gone off several minutes before. Carlos didn't have a long debate with himself over the wisdom of picking up those rings. He knew from experience that if he didn't pocket them, the soon-to-arrive boys in blue from the NYPD would certainly scoop them up.

"This was an anonymous gift from me to Carlos," admits Paul. "The price tag on each ring was twenty-seven to fifty thousand dollars. These were platinum cluster rings so gaudy that you would only wear them to the Oscars, the Tony Awards, or the Met Gala."

Carlos stashed the rings in his sock and down his pants, and soon he went to work with extra socks, so he would be prepared for more of these spectacular gifts. It became shockingly predictable because every time Charles went to work, there was another heist.

"The first time I saw those rings on the floor," Medina later recalled, "I thought to myself, 'who would do something like that, so stupid and careless?'"

It wasn't carelessness, it was intentional. After finishing his shift, the bulk of which was devoted to filling out his recounting of the night's activities, Carlos went to the Blarney Stone, an Irish Pub for a late-night beer or two.

Paul, dressed to the nines with a Rolex President on his wrist, sat down next to Carlos and struck up a conversation. The opening line of Paul's introduction left Mr. Medina dumbstruck.

"Did you find diamond rings on the floor tonight? I hope so, I put them there for you. I'm the guy that did the heist tonight, and I've been wanting to connect with you for some time."

Carlos was in shock, wide eyed and slack jawed in disbelief. After a couple more beers consumed in silence as Paul regaled him with captivating heist-based anecdotes, Paul handed him an envelope containing ten thousand dollars cash, the Rolex off his wrist and invited him to pay a quick visit to Paul's father in his plush apartment next door to the Ziegfeld theater.

"I came right out and told him that I was the guy who did it and then I convinced him that it was more lucrative to aid and abet rather than attempt to prevent. I gave that Rolex to him," Paul explains, "because he was eyeing it the entire time while I was speaking with my hands like I was a magician, and I am about to do a card trick or pull a rabbit out of Carlos' ass! He was mesmerized, and it was just us two talking over Heineken beers at the Blarney Stone."

Paul took Carlos to meet Mr. Stan at his incredibly impressive three- bedroom luxury apartment next to the Ziegfeld Theater.

"The lobby looked like the Pierre Hotel with the black & white marble tile," recounts Paul. "I pressed the buzzer and said, "It's Mali Paya." We went up a few floors. There were several doors, and one opened on the left leading us down a hallway past the kitchen into the dining room where we sit down around this huge mahogany table on chairs built for royalty. The place looked like a museum filled with paintings and old books. There is a statue of a big samurai soldier in the corner, and a heavy silver dragon in the other. Everywhere you turn there is wealth, and you know you that you are somewhere important."

This was a surprise visit because Paul and Stan had not been on the best of terms.

"My father was stunned to see Carlos in full Holmes Security attire, but he kept his composure. He knew immediately who Carlos was because my father looked out for us so many times. It was a most astonishing and impressive meeting. Carlos promised my father important printouts, keys and a system to copy them all. He even had ten heists in mind that he offered us."

Yes, Carlos Medina was Paul's ticket back into his father's crew.

"Dad took me back with a big fat smile. He was happy, incredibly happy. Not only was I welcomed back, but I was also back with more power and juice than ever before. It was a transformation. The next night, Carlos was my father's guest at the Whiskey Bar where Mr. Stan bedazzled him even further. Carlos was not bullshitted, because we never did that. We told him the truth. We were going to make him rich."

Ah, yes, the Whiskey Bar: laced in smooth marble, the entrance featured one thousand fresh cut roses every day. Large doors, lofty ceilings, and a whimsical staircase. Peter Stark designed the mirrored bathroom, and there was plenty of cocaine snorted in those luxurious stalls and more than a few sexual trysts as well.

"This was the spot to see famous people," insists Paul "This is where Robin Williams, George Carlin and I got stoned and laughed our asses off while Chris Rock is over in the corner having deep conversations with this girl he is working on. I recall the drummer from Nirvana and I on the maroon velvet couch. I'm drinking Corona; he's drinking Heineken."

New York actor/artist Laura Fay Lewis remembers it well, and the tight, one-piece cat suit she wore as a cocktail server.

"It was all gray," recalls Lewis, "with a thick black waistline looking like something out of *Blade Runner*. Those were great times. I recall the night that Paul, David Calderazzo, maybe Jamie Schafer came in and were throwing money around like I could not believe... they were almost giddy and tipping and spending like crazy."

Paul remembers that night perfectly and the reason for their unbridled jocularity.

"We were on our way to meet Mr. Stan at the Whiskey when we saw a safe in an open auto-shop garage. We slammed on the breaks, I jumped out of the car, popped the trunk, grabbed my tools, and in less than 30 seconds we were back on the road to the Whiskey with $40 thousand cash that we shared with everyone in the bar."

Ethical?

"That firm is well insured," says Paul, "although as a rule I only did manufacturing firms insured for $100 million. Sometimes," he admits, "even a gentleman thief yields to temptation."

Laura was tempting indeed in her custom crafted cat suit. The other model figure was the size of the tips from successful actors, musicians, entrepreneurs and, yes, jewel thieves as regular customers.

"I met Paul there when I was 32 and he was maybe 19 or 20," Laura recalls, "and he wasn't very forthcoming about himself other than he was from a wealthy family, and he was great fun and soon he started sending me gifts, wonderful gifts such as expensive jewelry. I met his parents, and they were both truly kind to me. The Whiskey was the kind of place where pop stars and pop star wannabees were in abundance, I recall boyish Mark Wahlberg having a thing for me. That was before he was an actor, and before he became as beefed up as he is now, he was still Marky Mark. I was constantly urged to go up to his room because he was living in the hotel, but I was not interested in going up to any guy's room who I didn't know just because he found me attractive."

"Believe me, there were plenty of other attractive women in The Whiskey. The place would get wild sometimes, famous people everywhere, people getting drunk or out of control, people high as kites and then Madonna couldn't get in one night because Rande Gerber told her that there was a private party which wasn't true, but it would give the place publicity on *Page Six*."

David Calderazzo worked the door with Jamie Shafer, and both became close friends and confidants of Paul who was using the alias, Paul Montana.

"Anytime Punch got in trouble, he simply changed his name and kept right on going."

"I couldn't be Reginald Mathews because there was a warrant out for his arrest for failure to appear," explains Paul, "and I couldn't be my real name because of that stupid bogus charge in New Jersey—also failure to appear. I looked enough like Paul Montana that a fake ID in his name worked fine."

This rarified showbiz fame pit where Stan and Paul would often plan their next heist was an alluring world for Carlos Medina who never thought of going to the Whiskey—he assumed it was a world beyond him, but in the presence of Mr. Stan and Paul, any imaginary walls of social role and status evaporated in the heat of infinite possibilities.

"We all even went on vacations together—Miami and the Keys fishing—and it was one of the best times we ever had, my father has a picture somewhere of all of us together.
"

After a week, Carlos brought all those rings back to Mr. Stan to sell them and not only that, but Carlos managed to bring over $350 thousand in stolen jewelry that he took since he had been working but was scared to ever sell it because he knew the Feds were watching him.

"It was always possible," says Paul, "that someone such as Moma could endanger our lives and freedom. We could only trust him to be irrational and violent. Carlos, however, was a man whom we could rely upon for quick thinking and professional dedication."

Paul's face brightens when recalling Medina's first heist experience.

Chapter Twenty-Three
Carlos and Alarms

"Carlos saved our ass for sure on his first heist with us," recalls Paul. "We had keys to all the glass doors, but we smashed them to look as if we broke in. We did this after we completed the heist. I forgot to close the safe, so when we smashed the glass door, the glass went inside the open safe, If the cops see the glass inside the safe, they will know something is fishy."

Carlos, thinking fast, said that he used his flashlight to break the remaining glass out, so he wouldn't get cut when he entered.

"We let the alarms run on that heist," recalls Paul. "It took Carlos ten minutes to respond to the alarm, get the keys, get his gun and flashlight and then take the stairs from 580 5th Avenue to 36 West 47th Street. Ten minutes was more than I needed. This type of heist is called the Boombash, meaning the alarms are running."

If you've watched any great heist movie, you probably think that security is incredibly high tech. It isn't. In fact, it is not much different now than it was thirty or even forty years ago.

"The way the alarms work is simple," Paul explains, "If the alarm is set off, it transmits a signal back to the security company through the telephone lines. It works on a zone system. Most companies have at least five zones. A zone is a specific place in the company. It could be the windows, the doors, inside the vault, different rooms and so forth. So, if all five zones light up you know something is going on because it will seem as if someone is running through the whole place."

If just one or two of the zones lights up, it could mean that someone is trying to break into the place, or it could be a false alarm caused by the weather, rodents, or some other reason.

"False alarms are more common than burglaries," says Paul, "but the security company must send a security guard to investigate. If more than one zone gets lit up, the police department must be notified. The cops usually get there fast, but that doesn't matter because they can't get in the place. They must wait for the security guard to show up. If the guard is slow, it can take fifteen to twenty minutes."

The dispatcher notifies the armed guard and gives him a printout that tells him where the company is located, and other relevant information. The guard then must go to a locked drawer and find keys to the place, break the seal, go to the gun rack and get a gun and a walkie talkie and make his way to the crime scene.

"Most security companies around 47th Street are in the basement," Paul explains. "For example, Holmes Security is in the basement of one of the most secure buildings in Manhattan—580 5th Avenue. This means that the guard makes his way to the elevator, then to the street level, walks to the scene that he's responding to and meets up with the cops. Then they go together into the building, up the elevator to the appropriate floor."

If the cops and the guard believe that there is indeed a crime in progress, the police will launch a full-scale takedown by calling for backup. That means SWAT teams surround the block, helicopters overhead and dogs sniffing every inch of the premises.

"Of course," comments Paul, "that's a lot of action, noise and excitement, the SWAT teams and helicopters would be too late because, with the exception of the Miracle Watch debacle, I would already be in my own office in the diamond district calculating how many hundreds of thousands or even millions of dollars I'd made off with."

Is it possible to disconnect the alarms in today's high-tech world of computer-controlled zone alarms? Hell, yes. In fact, it is easier than the old-fashioned method of using wire cutters—if you have someone working inside the security company who can either provide the computer codes or who will go on the computers and turn the alarms off for you.

"I am the first to infiltrate fully the new Holmes Security firm in 580 5th Avenue where their basement office was the nucleus for the Diamond District. I broke into Holmes Security branch offices and got to the main frame that was interlinked with every system. I had the passwords. If I were a bad guy, I could have thrown a bug into this and corrupted the entire Holmes Security network. What I did was turn off the alarms."

Paul didn't know it at the time, but he was captured on security tape recordings, but it was dark, and his face could not be seen. All that was clearly visible was a distinctive motorcycle vest.

"These gem heists guys were goddam brilliant," says famed international security expert Fred Wolfson. "They were a combination of cinematic staging, athletic prowess, and brilliant precision coordination. They were like the most complex and beautiful choreography you've ever seen played as performance art. Stunning. Absolutely stunning. And Joseph Keenan, the man who was supposed to catch them, felt the same way. He admired them one hundred percent."

Keenan wasn't as impressed by the sartorial selections in personal apparel worn by the unidentified fellow taking over the Holmes central computer and turning off the alarms. His face was unseen, but Keenan got a good look at the man's vest—one of a kind, it seemed, and Keenan would know it again instantly.

"I broke into the Holmes Security office in Queens, and with info provided by our inside man," boasts Paul. "I turned off the alarms for the location and duration of the heist, such as the one we did at Mr. Pearl."

Ten million dollars in pearls, diamonds and cash successfully pulled off by Paul and one accomplice, Eddy from New Jersey, who almost died trying to get away while carrying two eighty-pound bags.

"Eddy and I were making our getaway down a pole," Paul explains. "When Eddy swung one heavy bag to his back."

The weight ripped him off the pole and sent him and one hundred sixty pounds of diamonds and pearls arcing off into the abyss that promised painful death. Fifty feet of weighted fall crashed him into a bottom floor air conditioning vent.

"My God," exclaims Paul, "when I heard that awful sound, I thought Edo had died or if not dead, dying or crippled."

Paul called out to him, cautiously, and heard not cries of pain, but noises of mild discomfort and inconvenience followed by jovial laughter. Sometimes being alive is sufficient justification for jocularity.

"We became rich with the jewelry from Mr. Pearl," says Paul, as if he were not already rich by that time. "It was exceptional and abundant—another true retirement job. Mr. Pearl had another hidden safe of which we were initially unaware also filled with diamonds and cash. It was a very good safe, an Israeli SLS TL-30. I know how to open those faster than the owner could. It was if he were keeping it safe just for us because no one else could do what we did."

Paul began branching out, doing a three million dollar contract job in Philly with Izo and Joe, brothers with their own crew.

"We did Mr. Clasp twice," says Paul proudly, "and Oradan Gem Company, as well."

All of this was for one primary purpose—for Paul's father to not only approve of his son, but to get "that look" in his eye—the look of absolute delight Paul had seen on his father's face when crews would discuss great heists.

"At that time, I still hadn't achieved that goal, but my father's attitude towards me became far more accepting and encouraging."

While Paul was awash in father/son unification, two hundred agents, officials of the U.S customs and internal revenue agencies, were investigating money laundering in general with fifty of its agents dedicating their time just to 47th Street. This special task force was named Eldorado after the mythical South American city of Gold.

Chapter Twenty-Four
Operation El Dorado

"It is work that demands tremendous manpower," said Robert Van Attan, an Eldorado officer. "The target of the Eldorado agents is money and money alone. They are not interested in drug imports, drug deals or drug dealers."

They also were not interested in diamond heists targeting those they suspected of money laundering and watched with bemusement as Paul and his crew robbed a firm under Federal surveillance.

"We made off with $3 million in diamonds, but left behind $16 million in cash," admits Paul sheepishly. "There were these big canvas bags in the back that I kept bumping into. It never occurred to me to look inside. Who thinks that a bunch of canvas bags lying around are filled with money?'

The next morning, Paul sees the company he robbed being raided by the Feds. Eleven employees in handcuffs, and the Feds hauling out those canvas bags.

"The same bags I was kicking," laments Paul. "They were money laundering and the Feds had been watching them for some time. They even watched us rob them and didn't care. This raid made headlines, and my father playfully whacked me over the head with the newspaper after reading the story."

Eldorado captured sixty million dollars and arrested 120 launderers in the operation's first twenty-four months. In the overall scheme of things, which is next to nothing.

"That is not the point," say the Eldorado agents. "Obviously, it is impossible, with the existing legal restrictions, to put an end to the phenomenon. Our warfare is psychological".

There was one fact of criminal psychology and true crime reality that Paul and his father understood completely: being raided by the Feds was not going to stop the money laundering. All our altruistic outlaws had to do was patiently wait for eight or nine months—a year at most—and then hit them again, and this time they took the canvas bags of money.

"When someone does a heist, every other heist guy in the world knows about it within hours," explains Paul. "That's because we like to brag about our accomplishments, but because we stole the drug cartel's money, we had to keep quiet about it. Believe me, keeping quiet was more difficult that the heist."

The original job was brought to Stan and Paul by the Lacka Safe Company. Mr. Lacka had proposed selling the targeted company a new vault and new safes, but they turned down the offer. Now they would have no choice in the matter, and the insurance company would pay for it.

"Oh, didn't I make it clear," asks Paul rhetorically, "that it was from Lacka that I learned how to punch safes?"

Chapter Twenty-Five
Meet Mr. Lacka

Malek Lacka was a super burglar in Europe before he came to America as a legitimate businessperson and opened Lacka Safe Company, Malek designed his own line of excellent safes, held numerous patents, and was occasionally an expert witness for the Feds.

"The Albanian who walked through our doors at 45 West 47th Street was legitimate. His name was Lacka, and he came in wanting to sell us a safe," recalls Branka. "He looked sadly at the two massive older safes in the far-left corner of the office, and he laughed."

"I'll give you a good deal my friend," said Mr. Lacka. "I have two beautiful new safes up your alley. Just give me 30k and I will throw in the free pick-up delivery and removal of your old safes. You do know that there are tremendous amounts of burglaries—suddenly, it's spreading like wildfire. In fact, your neighbor next door was recently hit."

"Yes, I know," said Stan, looking directly at Paul. Stan knew it was Moma and Paul who violated standards of behavior by hitting Mr. Stan's own fence. "I appreciate the offer, but I think we are doing fine with these two old models."

"Well, here is my card. Call me if you change your mind."

Stan looked at the card and saw the name Lacka. It rang a distant bell, and as he was escorting Mr. Lacka out the door, he paused and asked, "Do you happen to have a brother?"

"Yes, my brother is Malek."

"Oh, I know him very well," Stan says. "Your brother is a real genius. A good friend of mine introduced us—me and an Italian guy."

"Who was that" asked Lacka.

"John Gotti. Carmine Lombardozzi wanted us to meet and work together and we did."

Lacka suddenly grasped to whom he was talking,

"Oh! You must be Mr. Stan!"

The next week, Stan, Alek the Moth, and Paul went to Lacka's primary office in Hoboken, NJ.

"There was a ten thousand square foot warehouse filled with the best safes in the world," recalls Paul. "As a team, we were going to learn how to open each and every one of them."

Paul practiced punching safes for eighteen grueling hours a day at Lacka's New Jersey headquarters, learning how to open anything they had.

"The Albanian Mafia eventually took over Lacka's safe company," alleges Paul. "The Lacka that I knew left to the EU with millions. It isn't even the same as it was before, back in the 1990s when Lacka joined forces with us."

Mr. Stan and son already had more than only Carlos Medina from Holmes Security working with them, they soon also had other guards, dispatchers and even an executive or two. And now the safe company was in on the deal.

"Not just any safe company," clarifies Branka, "but the best safe company. Malek Lacka was another genius added to Mr. Stan and Son's perfect team of gentleman bandits."

Stop for a moment and consider the astonishing combination of cooperating participants in what Stan, Branka and Paul believe are victimless crimes: We have the jewelry company, intentionally over insured in case they are ever robbed. Next, we have the security guard, Carlos Medina who was like an Amway devotee, selling this multi-level heist concept with missionary zeal. It was Carlos who brought "Monchy" into the mix—and extremely knowledgeable Puerto Rican with six toes on one foot who was, more importantly, a Holmes Security executive assuring access to the computer codes controlling every Holmes Security Alarm in Manhattan.

Finally, we have the strategic genius of Mr. Stan and the high-octane precision of young Paul that is manifested in crews that only Mr. Stan could have put together.

"It was then, with all the players in place, that we conceived the most daring and outrageous plan in the history of American crime: Ten jewelry manufacturing firms, each insured for over one hundred million dollars. We would do them all, one after another. The total value was over one billion dollars. These would be everyone's retirement heists. One billion. No one ever did a billion before but that is exactly what we planned in intricate detail. We saw no problems in doing so. My father has a supernatural ability to instill not only confidence and admiration, but absolute unflinching loyalty and devotion—and not out of fear but out of love and respect. I was the only American born in these crews," says Paul. "We had our own United Nations. Every country and culture from Croatians to Puerto Ricans, Ukrainians, and Dominicans."

Mr. Stan was the absolute ruler of this intricate victimless crime kingdom. He stole the old way—precision planning, diligence, intense rehearsals. and the absolute prohibition of weapons. No one must ever be in actual danger.

"I always knew my father kept me safe doing heists. Stan and the Professor were always the lookouts, and I was running the inside crew with an iron fist. Most crew members did one job, made their fortune, got away with it and then went one hundred percent legit."

"We were not the Mafia where you can't leave," Stan explained in a confidential interview, "We had no structure and no one compelling you to do things against your will. If you wanted out, fine. You were out. You must understand that we did not need the mob. They needed us. We knew how to open a safe and disconnect the alarms, and they didn't. We were like celebrities to the mob. If they wanted to do a heist in Manhattan, they called us."

"Another significant difference between the organized crime families and what we were doing," Stan explains, "is that everything with us was extremely easy going and laid back. We would meet outside cafés, sitting, talking, and watching. We would plan and then we would plan some more. It was all about precision, like a Swiss watch."

"Actually,' Paul interjects, "it is more like a Swiss ski race because a heist and a ski race are both about precision within a certain perception of time—a fraction of a second makes all the difference. I believe the most valuable preparation I had for doing heists was competitive skiing in Switzerland, damn! I loved every minute: No, make that every second and every fraction."

The ultimate heist finally gave Paul his long-awaited ultimate pleasure.

Chapter Twenty-Six
The Mega Heists

Nothing brings Paul more pleasure than recounting when he finally saw "that look" in his father's eyes when they perfectly pulled off the first of these ten mega-heists. He waited so many years, and it was as wonderful as he imagined.

"I could have died happy right then and there. That satisfied look I was seeking all my life was manifested in full. My heart leaped in my chest, and I was so filled with joy that I almost cried," Paul happily explains. "This wonderful moment followed the biggest heist of our career: Two full floors and a vault so huge that there were twelve high security Lacka safes inside."

As for the alarms, Paul personally disconnected them in the Holmes Security office in Queens. He took a sling shot and broke store windows to keep the guards on duty busy responding to that nonsense while he went into the office, got on the dispatcher's computer, and pulled up the companies that were on his heist list.

"I entered the addresses of these future scores and disconnected them one by one on specific dates a week apart. I prepared heist for major holidays, my father's birthday, Christmas, Memorial Day Weekend, and New Year's. This score, the one that thrilled my father, was a three-day job: Friday, Saturday, and Sunday."

"The first thing I hit was a small diamond safe. Inside was $2 million in stones that I stashed and would later split with my father. Then I hit two more diamond safes, and Monchie and I split them without delay. It was about $120 thousand in petty cash and four sleeves of diamonds. We were just getting started and I just knew that we had an unbelievable pay day not counting the gold and jewelry. There were barrels of gold dust lined up one after another, and there were forty tables for workers and casters in this gold factory on top of Pier One Imports. Honest to God, everywhere you looked there was another safe and more working tables. The first vault I opened was an entire room filled with gold, and we managed to take it out the first night—and we worked three nights on that heist."

"On the last night, I gave my father a plastic pail filled to the top with diamond rings, and it was all 18c and flooded with nice stones. That's when it happened, that's when I saw that look in his eyes. It was worth the wait: my happiness knew no bounds."

The very next week, they did another location that was the same layout, and both firms were in the Red Book as insured for over $100 million, and Lacka gave Paul all the information and the combinations to the safes.

"That was the week that we should have, could have retired, and never looked back, but the money was too good, and it was all so damn easy—and everyone was happy, including the firm that we are robbing. Remember, they are getting full retail value from the insurance company right away."

Paul and the crew took the insurance requirements into serious consideration when planning a heist. There was a recent requirement that to be insured, the firm had to have double secure safes and multiple alarm companies.

"We found the ones that did not meet the new standards but were still covered in full because they were in the process of getting in compliance. I had inside information about all these companies because I had the executives and dispatchers from Holmes Security working with me instead of against me."

On the heist following the one where Paul finally got the reaction from his father than he had waited for all his life, there was a vault with eight big safes inside.

"For some unknown reason, I received the wrong information, and we burned open a hole that led to the back of a safe—in other words, we burned our way inside a high security safe and burnt up the cash and certificates. This really threw us off. We are not getting in, and we must get out soon! There was only one solution—we needed a little kid, a midget, or someone with tiny hands to go inside and open things up from the inside. Otherwise, the owners would come to open and... well, it would be embarrassing. We had to go searching. Luckily, we found a very tiny twenty-one-year-old Puerto Rican kid who fit in just fine and opened it up from the inside so we could clean it out. It was a tense situation then, but it is amusing now."

A few entities were unamused by the astonishing number of incredible heists in the diamond district: the insurance companies, the FBI, and the NYPD's Major Case Squad's Joe Keenan.

There was always the link between organized crime and the insurance companies, and with jobs being brought to Mr. Stan from the Gambinos, you can rest assured that the mob infiltrated the very insurance companies that were compelled to make payouts.

"Hell, yes," confirms Paul. "The FBI was all over the insurance companies because they figured out that some or all of these were inside jobs. The insurance company employees had to take Polygraph tests, and yes, some of the employees of the insurance companies were collaborating with us, not against us. Face it, we infiltrated every security company, insurance company and of course we always left plenty of diamonds behind for the NYPD to put in their pockets. There were those in law enforcement whose job it was to catch us. There were also members of the NYPD who would be perfectly happy to never catch us at all but pick up what we left behind."

Federal Investigators begrudgingly acknowledged the expertise of the crews hitting the diamond district and the upscale Manhattan boutiques. The New York Daily News, in a feature story entitled *Smart and Dangerous* by Patrice O'Shaughnessy, gave extensive newsprint to inaccurate statements by the FBI regarding a crime organization called "YACS," attributing most heists to Albanians who also robbed supermarkets and ATMs.

"[they] deploy skills in everything from hack and whack jobs using 20-pound sledgehammers and splitting wedges, rappelling from a hole in the roof, to using 10 thousand-degree hot rods to penetrate a safe, to bypassing sophisticated alarms and motion detectors. In less than 10 minutes they chop in, get money and leave. The FBI has deemed them an emerging ethnic crime group calling them YACS, an acronym for Yugoslavians, Albanians, Croatians, and Serbians," noted the story., "Burglaries of safes in the Diamond District, ATMs in Banks and stores all over the U.S. have been attributed to the gang also."

This one big gang the FBI called the YACS existed only in their fevered Federal imaginations. All the sophisticated "athletic intensive" diamond heists in the heart of the jewelry world, on the four streets that comprise New York's Diamond District from the early 1970s and intensifying after 1988, were, with few exceptions, done by Mr. Stan and/or his son, Paul plus the Professor. Prior to 1988, it was simply Mr. Stan, the Professor and up to six rotating crews.

"Those ATM thefts were the work of a guy called Turbo. He personally took $50 million from ATM thefts,"

Paul explained. "That wasn't the YACS. That wasn't the American Serbian Mafia. That wasn't me. That was Turbo, and he was not affiliated with my crew although I did accompany him on a couple lucrative ATM thefts."

Capt. George Duke of the major case squad believed that this one big gang had two divisions: one high end and one lower end. One for diamond heists, and the other for grocery stores, gas stations, etc.

Capt. Duke was wrong. There were six distinct groups. Two were in Manhattan—Paul and Stan's, and four were Albanians from the Bronx.

"I did have some Albanians who collaborated with me from time to time," admits Paul, "but that doesn't make the non-violent Serbian gem heist group affiliated with the Albanians robbing grocery stores, or the violent punks who pistol whipped patrons when robbing a gas station or Jack in the Box. We never did that. In fact, our number one rule was 'No one gets hurt!'"

Paul insists that they were never violent, but there was a marked temptation for the violent aspects of the Serbian Mafia to become an operational reality in New York City by the proposed 1991 "official" launching of a New York franchise with the blessing of the famed criminal called Giška.

Chapter Twenty-Seven
The Serbian Mafia

The man's real name was Đorđe Mićković. He got the nickname Giška because of his resemblance to a famous bear by that name in the Belgrade Zoo. His childhood was one of poverty punctuated by the murder of his father who was himself guilty of murder.

Giška became a living legend in both the criminal and political worlds of former Yugoslavia. He had close ties with the Serbian Mafia in the old country, and an allegiance altering history as a secret agent assassin for the Serbian government. Giška fell out of government favor when he aborted an assassination assignment in Australia because he liked a speech given by his target. After that "failed" assignment, Giška became an outcast and radical political rebel creating his own armed insurrection.

On June 4, 1991, Giška formed the Serbian Guard paramilitary force along with (SPO) leader Vuk Drašković. It was not long after that Giška took a break, flying to New York where he sat down to talk business with an older, distinguished, and all-powerful man known simply as Mr. Stan. While their upbringings were vastly different, they both crossed into Italy illegally. Stan to find a new life, Giška to have a fistfight.

The reason for Giška's visit was not political, but criminal. Because of the large Serbian presence in New York, he wanted to scope things out. Giška then approached Stan about being the boss of the American Serbian Mafia.

The person who brought Giška to Panarella's was Sava the Boxer whose claim to medical fame was the successful re-attachment of his ear after it was cut off by an enraged Serbian White Tiger as punishment for having sex with the White Tiger's wife. It was Paul who had the ear in his lap, rushing it and the boxer to the hospital.

"When Giška arrived in New York he was brought over by Sava the Serbian, a pro boxer who knew everyone in the business. This was a great treat for me, and Giška and I had a mutual friend, Dugi Lajevi. They were best of friends."

Giška had all the respect in the world for Mr. Stan, and that was obvious in his demeanor and his approach when broaching the subject of there being another mob "family" in New York—a Serbian Mafia in America headed by Mr. Stan with Mileta Miljanić as underboss and muscle.

Stan had no desire to emulate the Mafia, extorting their neighbors and killing their own family and friends in a quest for illusory power. Stan declined the position, and the subject seemed stillborn when, one week after his visit to Mr. Stan, Giška was murdered in Serbia - killed by a sniper, allegedly because he had garnered too much personal power as demonstrated by his New York visit.

Mileta Miljanić, the most powerful Serbian in New Jersey, acted in 1993 to elevate himself, and take the position Giška offered to Stan two years earlier. One of his first orders of business was having Moma extort money from Panarella's by beating up Nikola Rebrecca, the establishment's owner/manager.

Moma beat Nikola bloody and demanded five thousand dollars per week to keep Panarella's safe from similar beatings and degradation.

Who are you going to call when the new mob in town shakes you down? There is only one man with enough power, prestige, and admiration—the man at the top of the world.

"Please. Mr. Stan," begged Nikola, "make them stop."

Stan didn't pick up a gun, a knife or a crowbar. He picked up the phone.

"One call is all it took," remembers Paul. "Dad picked up the telephone and called a private number that rang in a Belgrade nightclub owned by Bosko. The two bosses spoke to each other as gentlemen do. With that one call to Bosko, Stan put a stop to any attempt to have an American Serbian Mafia emulating the Sicilians. It was that simple. Mileta Miljanić was absolutely one hundred percent respectful of Bosko's wishes and would never cross him. I know that because when Bosko left America, shortly after the Miracle Watch Heist, Mileta, Zoran, and I took care of selling Bosko's townhouse and handing other aspects of his affairs for him, primarily collecting money that he had coming and making sure he got it."

It was on that telephone call that Bosko, over the din and frivolity of his nightclub, spoke from the heart to Mr. Stan. Although the two spoke in Serbian, the essence may be expressed in words such as these:

"Come here my dear friend," said Bosko, "and bring young Paul. You can live wonderfully here. I appreciate everything you have done for me over the years. It is not one hundred percent safe anywhere, but at least here you can live like a king– a small Balkan king, but a king nonetheless."

Paul recalls that conversation and its implications quite clearly.

"The FBI should have given my father a medal—a gold medal at that. He ended the American Serbian Mafia extortion racket with a phone call, not a gun or a crowbar. This was the quiet power of Mr. Stan. In the entire criminal world, the epitome of class is the victimless jewel heist. That means that those who comprehend this, admire and respect you for your brilliance. Those who have no class— sociopaths and psychopaths such as Moma and his ilk don't know the meaning of respect. Moma stole millions from my parents."

Mr. Stan shrugs his shoulders as if he didn't have the weight of his worldly accomplishments upon them, and simply says, "Easy come, easy go. Today it is yours, tomorrow it is someone else's. What you own is only yours temporarily. Consider it a gift entrusted to you for a little while, and it is light and refreshing. If you are attached to it, it owns you and becomes a burden. You can't travel light with a safe chained to your neck."

"If getting rich and staying rich in material things is the all-important thing in your life," says Branka, "you should have been planning and plotting on how to get it while you were still in the womb of your mother because that's when you were approaching this world and its treasure. But now, you are not approaching it. If you have material wealth, that's good because you can do good things with it. A good person in your life is more valuable than gold, even Olympic Gold Medals."

Paul laughs, agreeing with his mother. "I won plenty of medals in Switzerland, but in New York City I deserved the gold medal in nightlife."

Chapter Twenty-Eight
New York Nightlife

Paul hit all the best nightspots with the most popular promoters such as Michael Van Ault and his partner, Gordon Van Brock. Between them, they had a mailing list of over fifty thousand names and addresses. They kindly let Paul use it when he opened his own place, The Playground, with his good buddy Sal Linzalone.

"My son," says Branka with a sigh of fatalistic resignation, "was as impetuous, energetic, and emotionally conflicted as a young adult as he was as a ten-year-old and very protective of me almost to the point of absurdity. He almost punched Christopher Walken because that brilliant actor—and song and dance man—was flirting with me, to put it mildly, on the sidewalk in Manhattan. Paul threatened him., The only differences between Paul as a ten-year-old and the way he became a decade later were external and social—tall and handsome, artistic, and athletic, sophisticated and educated—and yet..."

According to his glamorous mother, Paul perceived himself as the chosen one of diamond heist theology, a 47th Street dispensationalist desirous of validating his exalted father while revealing a New Testament of miraculous innovation, expansion and consolidation. The self-crowned King of New York, he claimed the most luxurious suite in the Helmsley Palace and raced headlong into the abundant pleasures of New York nightlife by forming a solid friendship with an outgoing, innovative contemporary, Sal Linzalone. Both men loved the nightlife of the Big Apple, and it was perfectly appropriate for them to own a significant piece of it.

"When Sammy the Bull relinquished ownership of his ten thousand square foot, two story nightclubs on 50th Street, Sal and I took it over, and we knew exactly what to do with it. The fun we had was unbelievable, and the parties were unforgettable," Paul recalls with manifest delight, "We built a brand-new sound stage and elegant second Floor VIP art room where we had artist display their artwork inside the club was very cool, eclectic, and it felt like a place you can get lost and have fun."

Unaware of who owned the joint, the Mob came in to try extortion techniques. Paul stepped in and flipped the game on its head.

"I scared them with their own methods," says Paul with a laugh. "I used their own tactics on them. Ah, those were the days! It was big time, exciting, and we had great times."

The place was called The Playground, and the grand opening lasted seven nights featuring Madonna, Billy Idol, Beverly Peel, DJ Red Alert, and C+C Music Factory.

"I flew in an entire team of the best bartenders, and we also had exemplary security, it didn't get better than this— we were the absolute standard. All our friends and allies would meet us there, and we had the time of our lives. We thought it would never end."

Paul was also falling in ill-fated love with Therese Mersentes, the daughter of Alexis Constantine Mersentes, a clever social climber who married into the Chateaux Margot Empire. He and Paul got along famously, and the two men enjoyed dining with the elite of New York.

"I was sitting next to Donald Trump and Mayor David Dinkins in a place called Doubles in the Sheri Netherland,"

Paul remembers "and Alexis pulls up in a red Ferrari. *What class!* Trump used to hock his jewels with us when he needed cash. Yes, we also were a high-end pawn shop for the super-rich on paper who didn't have actual cash on hand. Trump was one of those. When he needed real money, he pawned stuff with us."

Trump was, according to Paul, a peculiar person.

"He sat by us at an Englebert Humperdink concert and spent the entire time staring at the ceiling. He may have had more net worth on paper than I did, but when it came to generosity, I had him beat by millions."

Paul not only contributed to reputable charities but personally devoted numerous hours and efforts to buying and delivering meals to New York's homeless.

"I think the hot meals meant more to them than the hundred bucks I gave each of them along with the food."

He also gave the hungry homeless their own Sony Watchmen, so they could be entertained and see the latest news.

"One of the homeless was a former Wall Street stockbroker who had some sort of breakdown, but he retained his grasp of the market and always told me what and when to buy and what and when to sell, He was always right. He had a gift for it. We all have gifts and I love giving gifts," admits Paul as if it were a social indiscretion. "And especially to girls that I like. One that I really liked was an alleged 23-year-old virgin named Therese Mersentes."

Therese, aka Palm Beach Terry, was also educated in the rarified high-cost atmosphere of Swiss Boarding Schools and projected a sense of style and identity so captivating that when Paul wasn't avoiding capture while raiding multi-million-dollar vaults, he was captivated by this mercurial and high-stylish international woman of mystery.

"She came from Greek background, and she totally did a number on me. I don't know what it was, but I developed strong feelings for this really cool chick who had a gun in her bag. Maybe she considered herself 'Jane Bond' because the gun she was lugging around was a Ram Line .22 marksman pistol. She probably liked the looks of it."

Terry was high class and had a remarkable sense of style allowing her to never look as if on her way to a costume ball.

"For example," says Paul, "it is winter in New York City and what is Terry wearing? Horseback riding pants with high top leather boots and a cashmere sweater. It's winter, for heaven's sake, and that is when she would wear to come out and play. She would break up with me in the summer citing complexes and insecurities as the motivation for separation."

Paul gave her gifts that she still wears today, including an 18k emerald cross.

"She was a 23-year-old virgin in 1991 when I meet her New Year's Eve. I started dating her on Valentine's Day. She lost her virginity to me at the Penthouse suite in the Empire Hotel, and I remember throwing out my Rolex and diamond ring out of the window to show her I don't care about money or wealth."

Branka remembers those days and her volatile son's romances with diamond-like clarity.

"He was very used to being rich every day. He could make a million at a turn of a head," Branka says with a light shrug. "He believed that he was the best thief in the world and he was going to prove it to everyone, but that was impossible for him to do because no matter what, his father is the greatest thief in the world and undoubtedly the greatest gentleman thief in history because he never got caught, and he never spent a day in prison for pulling a heist. Plus, he was an angel of generosity, and used Simon Templar, the Robin Hood of Modern Crime, as his altruistic role model."

"Yes, the son excelled his father in some brilliant and creative ways," said Branka, "but Stan remains the touchstone, the standard, the epitome of excellence in technique, artistry, and ethics. Just don't marry him! As for my son in the early 1990s, when he was not plundering a vault, he was plundering willing women, including Terry."

When Paul's crew saw that he was love-struck they began teasing him mercilessly and calling him "Terry."

"Terry was quite a mysterious person," Paul says, still a bit mystified, "and I was intrigued beyond my ability to understand. Equally mysterious if not as feminine was her father. And what was the story on her father? Was he another international criminal?"

As Therese's father appears felony free, accusations of criminality would obviously be metaphorical rather than historical. Paul and family hold the opinion that Terry's paternal unit had fallen into a giant vat of chicken fat— an expression meaning good fortune rather than anything unpleasant.

"I think he was a WWC—Wealthy Widow Chaser. He married into the Chateau Margot family. All sorts of allegations surfaced in the *Palm Beach Daily Times* and the *New York Times* about Mr. Mersentes, but I got the scoop on her father earlier than the newspaper."

Paul's scoops were spicy rumors courtesy of Mr. Stan's friend in Astoria, Spiro the Greek. According to gossip and innuendo, Spiro knew Terry's father back when Mersentes was driving taxi with more dreams in his head than gas in his tank.

Legend has it that he got a job working for a rich couple whose wife kept Mersentes' meter running. Both the wife and taxi were well lubed oiled and regularly serviced. The husband died, of erotic neglect, and the wife came into his fortune which was fortunate for Mersentes who came into everything when the widow went to her finances-free final reward.

After that, the taxi driver took on a new persona of gratuitous interest in the interest-bearing accounts of women well beyond any interest in bearing children.

"Social gossip comes with social status," remarks Branka, who is one well acquainted with the New York rumor mill. "But no one really cares or even remembers the gossip. Why? Because people don't spend their time thinking about other people. They spend 90% of their time thinking about themselves and ten percent wondering what people think about them."

Paul's father did not give his son significant support in pursuing Terry.

"My dad really discouraged me from being committed to Terry. He wanted me more focused on stealing diamonds than stealing her heart. Remember, we were on a quest to do the ultimate: One billion dollars. That is one stunning figure."

Another stunning figure was that of six-foot tall model Michelle Burka.

"She was indeed stunning and super beautiful. I invited her to my mother's to model a few Russian sables. I really loved her but treated her poorly. I made a serious mistake. She worked in the spot next door to Panarella's, and she was the hostess for *Sweetwater's*, and with high heels she was six-foot-six. She was originally from Ontario and her family was from Bulgaria. She had a huge add for Kenari in middle of 42nd Street and she was on my arm! Yes, the girl on that big billboard where they drop the ball on New Year's Eve."

It was Paul, however, who dropped the ball.

"She was stunning, I never should have broken up with her. I was an idiot."

Branka would never call her son an idiot, although she admits that he has done idiotic things. She does offer excellent advice regarding one's reaction to gossip about one's past transgressions. Simply put, the worst thing that you could do is only worth one night's dinner conversation in someone else's home.

As for the astonishing achievements in victimless criminality by Mr. Stan and Son, they were overshadowed in the New York news cycle by the Fed's quest to convict John Gotti, and the scandalous behavior of Michael Dowd and Ken Eurell of the NYPD.

"This was good for us in a way," says Paul. "Law enforcement was obsessed with getting John Gotti, and the press was obsessed with the 'cocaine cops,' Michael Dowd and Ken Eurell."

Ken Eurell finds Paul's comment mildly amusing.

"Hey, believe me, I would have been perfectly happy to have the headlines be about Paul instead of me. Who knows, maybe if I had been in a different precinct, with the mind set I had back then, I might have hooked up with Paul and Mr. Stan doing diamond heists instead of selling cocaine. Temptation is temptation."

From a criminal perspective, Paul had a different take on Ken's corruption.

"It was really a perfect storm—the right cops hooking up with the right drug dealer, Adam Diaz. He was to cocaine dealers what I was to gem heists. He was the best, and the most ethical and reliable. So, in a way, it was like the Holmes Security guards working for us instead of against us. The bottom line, other than financial, is that our diamond heists didn't get the level of press coverage that they would have otherwise because of Mike and Ken."

"Tell Paul I can relate," counters Eurell. "Amy Fisher came along two weeks later and knocked me off the front page."

Paul knew he didn't want to be on the front page for being taken away in a big sweep of Mafia thugs, hoods, and hitmen.

"I could read the precognitive clues. You are known by the company you keep, and by those with whom you socialize. Well, I stopped going to the Mob social clubs. No reason to be connected to those connected if I wanted to be king of 47th Street. I wanted my heists to be the headlines, not any affiliation directly with any of the families under heavy federal scrutiny. Sometimes you want the headlines, other times you want everything played on the downlow."

In 1992, there was minimal press coverage when Paul and his friends participated in the most lucrative and astonishing luxury hotel robbery in history, even outshining the famed Pierre Hotel robbery.

Chapter Twenty-Nine
The Regency Hotel Heist

"Dapper Thieves Startle a Posh Hotel" was the headline of the feature story in the *New York Times* by Steven Lee Myers who joined the Times only three years earlier. Myers told of the daring robbery of the Regency Hotel on Park Avenue by "well-mannered and well dressed" gentlemen wearing professional facial prosthetics to hide their true identities,

Capt. Michael Gardner of the Third Detective Division told reporters that the hotel's front door is usually locked at 3:45 a.m., "so it was not clear how the robbers got in, but once they did, they worked quickly and efficiently. only breaking into the [safe deposit boxes] ones they knew from a list of registered guests were full. It was a very smooth operation," he said. "I would classify it as a professional job. The sophisticated thieves worked with concentrated precision for ninety minutes to confiscate a fortune in spectacular jewelry from the hotel's safe deposit boxes."

This robbery, eclipsing that of the Pierre Hotel, didn't receive the same widespread publicity because the Regency put a lid on it immediately. Debra Kelman, a spokeswoman for the Loews Corporation, which owns the Regency, declined to discuss the incident, refusing to release the names of the guests held hostage or the names of the guests who were robbed.

The robbers fled about 5:15 a.m., and just before they left, they politely told their comfortable hostages that they were free to go, and that their kind cooperation was appreciated.

"We kept them amused and entertained," recalls Paul. "I was using at first a British accent, but I kept losing the accent, so I switched to a Scottish brogue in mid-sentence which cracked them up, then I figured why not go for more laughs? I went from being Scottish to speaking in a strong Hindustani accent as if I just came in from India for this job. They enjoyed themselves and despite their initial apprehension, they got a kick out of the experience."

"We don't know where they came from," said Capt. Michael Gardner. "We do not know details of how the bandits fled. We have no suspects at this time. We did, however, recover a large center punch and a rubber and metal mallet in the lobby."

Paul confesses he left that punch in the lobby as his calling card.

"Any job where they found a punch left behind was me telling them who did it: Punch. Now, on this job, I was called in to work it for a specific purpose: I was in charge of opening thirty-some safe deposit boxes from a list given to me ahead of time."

This lucrative robbery of the super-wealthy and over insured was the brainchild of Alex Vuckovic Montenegro with a valuable assist from hotel housekeeper, Desa, who had all the keys and information. Desa lived in the same apartment building as Paul, Money Mike, Sal Linzalone, and her lover, Ranko Mitckovic.

"Desa lived with Ranko," says Paul. "He was part of my crew in 1992, and currently had a café in Podgorica Montenegro until he passed away in late 2018. All the doormen were from Yugoslavia, and I had video surveillance set up and this is where we usually came to divide-up the money. On this particular job, however, we counted out the boodle at Mr. Stan's."

Based on Paul's recollection, the crew that robbed the Regency Hotel consisted of, in addition to Alex Vuckovic Montenegro, the Ax Man (Voya Kadovic), the Boxer (Sava Serbin), Mali Paja Amerikanac (Paul Stanimirovic), Zoran Jaksic, David Sanchez, and Money Mike Jones.

"We entered the hotel at exactly 3:45 a.m. through the side entrance that the workers use. We had keys and passcodes for doors. There was one person at the Concierge that was shocked to see us. The doors were locked, and we had to make the door attendant open the door for another few guests and workers and everyone was taken nicely to a secure area so that they would not be in the way. I went to work on the safe deposit boxes, and there was no one in the lobby—it was very quiet—then a guy and his girlfriend showed up, so we put everyone in a bigger room and told them to get comfortable, and that we apologize for the holdup and any inconvenience, but we'll be done soon, and no one would be hurt at all."

Was the loot from this robbery beyond the famed Pierre Hotel robbery? When asked that question, Paul laughs the laugh of a man victorious.

"Oh my God, you wouldn't believe how incredible this was—there were diamond earrings and a diamond necklace in each one of the first boxes and cash money and gold coins that looked like it was for a jewelry exhibition. Remember, this wasn't a bank vault. This was just a hotel safe and deposit boxes and it wasn't as if we were operating in the blind. Montenegro knew exactly which boxes to open first, and he was next to me emptying out and stacking the empty boxes to the side exactly the way it's in the picture in the NY Times."

The first few pieces alone would be worth between $40 - 75 million in insured value, or what they would sell for at auction, but you can't keep jewelry intact after a heist this big when each piece is famous, documented and individually insured by Lloyds of London.

"Each piece was exceptional and of the highest quality. There was gold a white gold cigarette case with a sapphire and diamonds that I wanted to keep but I was not allowed to because if anyone saw it or recognized it, I'd be finished. It was one of a kind. I did get to keep a pair of diamond earrings worth over $300 thousand that I gave to my mother."

"One piece I remember for the size of the diamonds: it was a brooch, and it was flooded with diamonds. Next was an emerald ring and necklace made of diamonds and emeralds, bracelets of rubies and diamonds—yes, this was my favorite score because it was so smooth and easy, and we got away with all the money and jewelry. Each piece was going to get broken down because of its importance. Significant pieces are known, and we don't want to ever to be connected to something this massive. It was the best jewelry we ever had, and it must have been for something important—no doubt an exhibition or a museum display. It was estate jewelry fit for royalty."

Mr. Stan was not even asked to be look out on this as he was against Paul participating in robberies because they had to be done with guns, even if the gun is only loaded with blanks or not loaded at all.

"But after it was over, everyone went to my father's apartment because he was going to buy everything from us including a diamond Chopard watch and a diamond ring that must have been fifteen carats. Most of the jewelry was in small leather pouches and boxes including a Cartier panther necklace and a South Sea pearl necklace work $500 thousand."

The robbers left the hotel the same way they arrived, in Paul's posh limo—a perfect cover and an ingenious part of the job.

"We were in my father's apartment by sunup," recalls Paul. "Unfortunately, all the jewelry was busted up, broken up, melted for scrap, we sold the stones, and that's the end of that. How much did I make personally for opening those safe deposit boxes at the hotel? One hundred fifty thousand dollars."

David Calderazzo remembers the Regency robbery quite clearly despite having no direct involvement.

"I walked in on Paul and friends when they had just finished robbing the Regency," recalls David, now an accomplished film and television actor. "Well, they trusted me and told me the truth. I was a bit taken aback but hey, they were so cool about it. I'll tell ya, Mr. Stan had balls of steel. And as for Paul, he had balls of molten lava."

"When David walked in on us," recalls Paul, "was after the Regency Heist when Montenegro and I brought the bags early in the morning to Mr. Stan's. at the same time that David was bringing coffee and donuts for Mr. Stan because they were going to 47th Street so David could get a good deal on a ring he was buying for his wife. When David saw me," Paul explains, "I acted like he was part of the crew. He is very perceptive. He knew what was going on."

The only added coverage or commentary on this robbery—one that the participants thought would get media attention at the level of the moon landing—came from former New York County assistant district attorney Kathy R. Perry in a letter to the editor published in the *New York Times*, Feb. 13, 1992. Ms. Perry chastised the Times for the language used in describing the crime and the perpetrators.

"Much of your reporting, as well as the reporting of news in other print and electronic media," wrote Perry, "subliminally instills fear and dread in the public when a minority member of society perpetrates a crime. In contrast, the tone of reports of a crime conducted by members of the majority culture attempts to assuage fears and trivialize the crime."

"Was this crime any less horrible and unsettling because the perpetrators were 'middle-aged white men'? Were these men armed with handguns," asked Perry, "because they had no intention of using the weapons to accomplish their end, or were the handguns brought along to accent their attire and complete the look?"

The absolute truth is that these men had no intention of using the weapons to accomplish their ends other than displaying them. The guns weren't loaded so no one could be harmed, even by accident.

"Had there been any problem, we would have got the hell out of there," acknowledges Paul. "Everything was preplanned to make everyone safe and at ease. Despite their first apprehension, the hotel guests quickly relaxed and enjoyed the experience because we were not threatening them aside from displaying our empty handguns."

Hotel robberies were nothing new in 1992 having had their highly publicized New York debut in the 1970s orchestrated by professional burglars Samuel Nalo and Robert Comfort.

On December 9, 1974, a team of five bandits took over the Sherry Netherland hotel for two hours and looted safety deposit boxes of more than $900 thousand in cash and valuables. Then, on October 10, 1977, four men walked into the Sherry Netherland's lobby and made off with cash and gems (some belonging to superstar Diana Ross) from the hotel vaults. The haul could have been worth up to $1 million.

"I can tell you where those gems went," says Paul as if he's unaware that people have speculated on that topic for decades. "My father purchased the gems from that 1977 robbery. He was also still buying from his longtime friends Bruno Sulak and Biki in France. In July of 1983, Sulak, tanned and dressed in a tennis outfit, stole an estimated $4.3 million worth of jewelry from a Cartier branch in the resort town of Cannes, France."

Alek Grbac brokered the last deal with Bruno—every item from the biggest Cartier heist ever. A resolute musician,

Alek retired from the world of heists and is not wanted for any crimes anywhere.

"You can friend him on Facebook," remarks Paul. "There is a statute of limitations on heists, and these were all done long ago when steam was still rising from the surface of the earth and dinosaurs roamed 47th Street."

Paul may portray these heists and robberies as ancient history, but they are top of mind pop-culture references to anyone who marvels at the bravado, class and derring-do of gentlemen thieves.

"Rakac the Pickpocket, Desa's brother," recounts Paul, "used to rob Tiffany every day and he only took singular items and he always worked alone. He sold the stuff to my father. Rakac was quite a character and very funny—a John Belushi type but always well dressed. He hung out at Panarella's all day but did not drink. He respected Mr. Stan so much. Ranko Mitckovic should get credit for Tiffany, but Mr. Stan had the biggest Tiffany heist—all silver."

The pinnacle of Stan's career, and that of his cohorts, was 1992.

Chapter Thirty
1992

The year 1992 was the pinnacle of Paul's Phase One superstardom, and the year that he grasped the full scope and range of his father's international reputation and admiration.

"I always knew that Mr. Stan was loved and admired," Paul says, "but it wasn't until he and I went together to Europe in 1992 that I realized how incredibly powerful and admired he was worldwide."

Paul and Mr. Stan went to Europe to purchase major lots of diamonds and other precious gems from their European counterparts. Mr. Stan was treated as if Royalty—a living legend of victimless crime, never captured never imprisoned, and never greedy or miserly. To those who came to see him, it was like seeing a mythic folk hero. There was no one else on Earth who carried such prestige as lightly and courteously as Mr. Stan.

For the first time in his life, Paul realized how vast was his father's fame.

"Every famous or infamous altruistic practitioner of the victimless crime came to pay their respects at the Intercontinental Hotel," Paul remembers. "I could not believe the gifts he was given."

It wasn't only Stan and Paul investing money in these diamond purchases—Paul, his mother and her new husband, and the New York Mafia each put up $1.5 million to purchase four lots of diamonds and precious gems.

Of course, when the famed Stan and "Punch" appeared in person, offers for future enterprises were abundant. As Paul was younger, and therefore deemed more approachable, he was repeatedly asked to lend his talents to spectacular heists in Europe and beyond.

"They also offered to come to America and be part of my crew, vowing loyalty and disciplined professionalism I could rely on."

Paul returned to New York City with a renewed sense of purpose and destiny, and an amplified appreciation of his father. The FBI chimed in with its own unintentional salute to Mr. Stan in 1992 when it launched a new effort as they explain on their website:

The FBI's Jewelry & Gem Theft program– created in 1992– offers investigative assistance and intelligence on theft groups to law enforcement and partners with the jewelry industry to create a unified and coordinated approach to this crime threat. The FBI is involved in these types of thefts for several reasons: The thefts usually cross state and even national boundaries—so they need a federal agency with offices across the nation and overseas to investigate these highly mobile jewelry thieves; these crimes are increasingly committed by organized criminal enterprises or theft groups that likewise require a federal agency with tough laws and with offices across the U.S. and overseas; and these groups are often involved in other kinds of organized crime activities already under scrutiny by the FBI.

Naturally, in deference to the FBI, Paul concluded the year with what the FBI would term one of the most lucrative armored car heists in history—minus the armored car.

"Armored cars are not really armored anyway," says Paul. "It is much smarter to rob the warehouse where they keep the money than the car they use to pick it up."

Brooklyn Theft Brings Robbers $8 Million Cash

"Robbers entered an armored car company's warehouse in Greenpoint, Brooklyn, late Sunday night and made off with more than $8 million in one of the largest cash thefts in the United States," said Federal investigators, "and the robbers left more than $30 million behind, probably because they could not carry any more."

Speaking on condition of anonymity, the investigators told the *New York Times* that the FBI was trying to determine whether the robbery was an inside job.

"Of course, it was an inside job," confirms Paul. "We did this one with Monchie who was a Holmes Security executive recruited into my crew by Carlos Medina. We were very tight, and this was one of his retirement jobs."

James M. Fox, the assistant director in charge of the FBI's Manhattan office admitted that they were looking into whether the robbers had help from within the company because they were able to bypass the company's sophisticated security system.

Neither the FBI nor the armored car company would identify the only security guard on duty who told a story seemingly adapted from the Vizcaya Heist Game Book,

"I was in the command center room about 11:30 p.m. I felt a gun at the back of my neck and heard a voice order me to the floor. My wrists and ankles were bound with wire, but I freed myself about 20 minutes after the robbers left, and then called the police."

That story had more holes in it than the wall next to the Miracle Watch Company. No one was ever charged with anything. And as for the armored car company, "the money was fully insured," said John Ryjacek, the operating manager of the Hudson Armored Car and Courier Service.

The robbers got away with $8,268,680.07 that was in four sacks in a company vault, the FBI said. The cash weighed about 120 pounds. Investigators found the vault door open, but officials would not say who had opened the door or how it had been opened.

"We just walked in easy as you please," said Paul. "We did several of the armored car company warehouses in this area of Brooklyn, and of course they were all inside jobs. You notice we didn't rob an armored car like in the movie *Heat*– why do that? Someone might get hurt. No, we took millions from the warehouse and left thirty million dollars. After all there is no need for greed. You notice they said that the stolen money was fully insured. That means they didn't lose a single cent. Another victimless crime where the money walked out the door, was replaced by the insurance company, and everyone was happy."

'Nobody's hurt," Mr. Ryjacek said. "We're all grateful for that."

"James M. Fox of the FBI went on to become exceptionally famous as the man who captured the WTC bombers," Paul notes, "and was significant in the case against John Gotti. Things didn't go well for Gotti after a while."

Chapter Thirty-One
The Winds of Change

Just when things couldn't get any better, they started to get worse. Burglaries turned to armed robberies, and the crews started turning on each other. The violence, according to Mr. Stan, was at an all-time high.

"New, violent and very hungry gangsters were coming from Europe," Stan recalls, "and things changed in many ways. Extortion, credit card fraud, fake documents, drug dealing, and other unsavory enterprises were in full swing."

"There was a great deal of double crossing going on," says Paul. "Robbing and kidnapping became the norm."

The kidnapping referred to is the grabbing of rival gang members and holding them for ransom. You might think that the cops wouldn't care about criminals kidnapping other criminals, but kidnapping is a crime no matter the perpetrator or the victim.

Unfortunately for Mr. Stan and family, nobody kidnapped Moma who plotted darkly against Paul and his father. Carlos Medina was let go from Holmes for alleged "poor performance."

His performances as a heist participant were highly valued as were the significant contributions of Holmes employees such as Edwin Villaneuva. Medina offered him ten thousand dollars to deactivate the alarms at Wasko Gold, a jewelry manufacturing firm on 5th Avenue in Manhattan. He agreed, and a security video captured him doing so.

He refused to testify against Carlos.

"Yes, Wasko Gold was one of our heists," confirms Paul. "We carried hundreds of pounds of equipment up three floors, sledgehammered our way into Wasko, burned a hole into the vault and made off with more than a million in jewelry down the freight elevator and left the tools behind as usual. Before doing the heist, we made sure that Wasko was fully insured. Perhaps they had a party to celebrate being robbed."

Carlos was arrested outside a heist in 1993 with fellow Holmes ex-employee, John Urena and two men from Eastern Europe. The following investigation into Holmes' employees cooperating with jewelry thieves uncovered decidedly detrimental alliances, at least as far as Holmes was concerned. Arrested Holmes Security personnel took advantage of being out on bail to participate in more heists.

"We did things in Long Island City, Queens, Astoria," Paul remarks, "Greenpoint Brooklyn, and around Glendale, Maspeth, Howard Beach, Ozone Park, Bushwick, ENY, Bedstuy, Bensenhurst, Brighton Beach, Coney Island. The Bronx, New Jersey, Philly, Connecticut, Florida, Chicago, Canada, and Europe."

Did someone say Europe?

Paul prefers to not go into detail of dates and locations because there are different statutes of limitations, or none in Europe. "Let's just say I often offered my advice on hypothetical heists that someone may or may have not performed."

Sticking to their New York accomplishments, Paul, Stan and Branka have enough true heist stories to fill volumes, and this time, despite describing the digging of underground tunnels, barely scratches the surface.

The real head-scratcher, as far as Joseph Keenan of the Major Case Squad was concerned, was who is the mastermind behind all these incredible heists? His answer, although inaccurate, was at least plausible: Mr. Stan's best friend, The Professor, whom Keenan pursued vigorously, hoping to catch him in the act.

Chapter Thirty-Two
The "head out the window" arrest

"Keenan was both obsessed with catching us, and obsessed with admiring us," says Paul. "He looked more like a sophisticated criminal than a NYPD cop, and I think he would have been an excellent guy to have on my crew."

"Detective Keenan was coming out of our building at 45 West 47th Street when we practically bump into each other. I was wearing that Diesel Daytona Florida vest; the same one I was wearing when I was captured on video tape messing with the computers at Holmes Security. I was with Money Mike.

That was the day that I wanted to buy a new BMW jack to use on the heists, and I was going to the office to get some petty cash for a major crime. Well, Keenan was after me from that moment—and I thought I would be safe in my father's office, but Keenan showed up and ever-so-politely asked my father if he could use the phone to call in to headquarters while he arrested me! I started to faint, honestly."

Mr. Stan told Paul to relax, that everything would be okay. Keenan told Paul to sit down and calm down before he fell down.

"Mike and I both get arrested and brought to Major Case Squad for about 18 hours of interrogation that got them nothing. I used all my best lines and routines to say nothing of value."

"Hey what do I know? I'm just a kid man! You probably have a son my age, come on do you have maybe a daughter? Let me see her picture."

Paul was being a wise guy, but Joseph Keenen was sharp, and Paul didn't fool him for a minute.

"That was the best performance I've seen in a long time," Keenan told Paul. "You really should become an actor after you get out of this, which you probably will. C'mon, let's get something to eat."

Kennan and his partner took Paul to get some pita and Greek cooked meat on a stick on the way to Central Booking.

"They had me on two warrants, one for Reginald Mathews and another for Paul Montana. Reginald Mathews was another failure to appear, and the Paul Montana arrest was the one where the crazy guy threw his father's head out the window."

Say what?

"This was Thanksgiving Eve, 1992. At the time, this was the biggest heist of my career: 55 West 47th Street, and everything was working out perfectly," Paul explains. "The person I chose to bring on this glamorous heist was a host at the Whiskey Bar, six-foot-six, from Canada and an all-around good guy, and one of the top varsity rowers for the University of Washington in Seattle."

"He had exactly what it took, except that he had no street in him which was a problem, and I didn't know how he would act if we got caught."

Just as Paul was contemplating that scenario, in bursts homicide – yes, homicide detectives with guns drawn. Why homicide detectives? Because a mentally ill man went completely homicidal, decapitating the family cat, bird, and his father. He threw his father's head out into the street. Soon the entire area was cordoned off while the cops pursued the killer. Paul and Jamie knew nothing about this, and the cops didn't know that there was a heist in progress.

"They stumbled upon us by accident," Paul recalls. "The police abused Jamie. This was his first brush with the law of any type, and he was in shock mentally and he didn't know what to do. Homicide beat his ass, and they threw him over the ledge, and he hurt himself bad. I saw his eyes give out as he fainted in agonizing pain. I felt bad but, I was in a messed-up position myself and thank God the two officers that had me were better towards me then the four who mistreated him."

Paul was arrested as Paul Montana, and Jamie was arrested as Rande Gerber. They insisted that they were simply looking for a place to smoke a joint and had no idea any sort of burglary had been going on.

"Jamie eventually decided to flee the country," Paul recalls, "and he packed up $300 thousand that he had left and got free passage to Serbia compliments of the Serbian Mafia, and they set him up very nicely from what I understand.

Jamie wanted to be on my crew, and he did that one heist that went bad through no fault of our own."

Paul has nothing but praise for Jamie and David Calderazzo, two friends who were first responders when there was an explosion in Mr. Stan's apartment. Paul shudders at the mere mention of the incident, blaming himself.

"It wasn't intentional," he explains. "It was carelessness on my part that caused Ms. Kim, my father's beautiful young Korean lover, to have her hand blown off during the height of the Christmas season."

There was a stick of dynamite tucked away in the back of a drawer in the dining room. It had been there for quite a while, and if you were not searching for it, you would never find it. Paul came searching for it.

"I intended to take half a stick of dynamite, but I changed my mind," recalls Paul. "And like a thoughtless idiot, I didn't return it to the back of the drawer but left it right in front when I went to use the toilet."

Ms. Kim enjoyed candlelight for romance and for creating ambiance in general. Looking for more candles, Kim opened the drawer, saw the object with a wick and assumed it was a type of candle. The wick was too long for her taste, and she carefully shortened it before lighting the sizzling fuse. Before she could comprehend the peculiar behavior of the wick, the dynamite exploded.

"David Calderazzo and Jamie were summoned to clean up the damage," explained an embarrassed Mr. Stan "I was speechless. Her entire hand was now in the sheetrock in the ceiling—not in one piece of course. Having dynamite accessible in your apartment is a direct violation of not only the apartment management's policies, but there are also city and county ordinances regarding high explosives. Adding eviction to injury, I had to vacate my Zeigfield adjacent apartment."

Meanwhile, Keenan of the NYPD was still obsessed with catching the Professor. His dream became something similar to reality in 1993.

Chapter Thirty-Three
The Professor

1993: The Professor got popped while doing lookout for the crafty Son of Stan. Blame that on Joseph Keenan of the NYPD. One of his anti-heist crew spotted our erudite criminal with a walkie talkie outside a building housing a prestigious jewelry manufacturing firm.

Paul was already out of the building when this happened, so he wasn't caught. When Keenan found out that the Professor was in custody, he raced as fast as he could to keep the Professor from being released. He was too late.

The Major Case Squad issued this press release:

April 5, 1994

Jewelry Burglar, 'The Professor,' Wanted by Police

Police are looking for the leader of a group of sophisticated burglars who prey on jewelry retailers and manufacturers. The suspect, dubbed "The Professor" because of his ability to speak seven languages, was arrested last October with three others while committing a burglary at a jewelry manufacturing building in New York, but then jumped bail. The Professor is thought to be Andre

Montrose (also known as Carl Martin, Andrzej Zalenski and Mark Conti.)

He is a white male, age 61, 5 foot 11 inches and weighs 174 lbs. Police have identified the burglars as being part of an organized criminal group of immigrants from Yugoslavia and Albania which may include as many as 100 members.

This burglary gang does extensive casing and are able to defeat state-of-the-art alarm systems. They may pose as construction workers and leave one lookout outside with a walkie-talkie and police scanner. They will take molds and models during burglaries from manufacturers. If you have any information about The Professor or his cohorts, contact the Jewelers Security Alliance at 1-800-537-0067 or Detective Joseph Keenan of the N.Y. Police Dept., (212) 374-6910.

The Professor's lawyer finally negotiated a deal with the Major Case Squad whereby he would turn himself in and be a cooperating witness.

"They had him in the Tombs—Manhattan detention, and I showed up courtesy of Joseph Kennan nabbing me at our building, I hear about this older guy being a snitch and a rat and then I find out it is my dear old friend the Professor! I manage to get to his cell and he's working the Rosary and praying and looks like shit, I mean, he aged decades since I last saw him. At first, he pretended that he didn't know who I was, but I spoke to him in his language, and he broke down in tears. Oh my God! Is he ratting out my father and mother? It was so tragic to see the Professor in that condition, a scared and broken man." Paul called his father to warn him that the Professor may be rolling over on everybody. Mr. Stan could not imagine that being true. The next morning it didn't really matter.

The official story is that the Professor killed himself in his cell by hanging himself with one of his socks. Alek Grbac says that his death was faked, and that the Professor and his wife were safely within the witness protection program. Alek also insists that the Professor didn't rat out Mr. Stan, Branka, Paul or any of their crew, and only provided essentially dated information regarding a couple of fences, now inactive.

The Professor never had a funeral, and his wife vanished the same time as the Professor, giving credence to Alek's version of events.

"I will never know for sure, unless I see the Professor again," says Paul "He was my father's closest friend. and we all worked together on some incredible heists that gave me an amazing personal collection of jewelry. I had the best collections of jewelry, the biggest private collection, under my bed. I had it all; Tiffany, Cartier, Bulgari, Graff, Buchaletti, Wempe, and names that I can't remember. So many of these gems were acquired with The Professor working lookout."

There was one item that Paul found in a heist that he didn't share with anyone—an old burgundy leather box with gold etching, and inside was a 9-carat diamond ring.

"I had it cut down to 8.55 and sold it to the same person who owned it originally," admits Paul. "That didn't bother him in the least as he had already been paid by the insurance company and used their money to pay for the replacement,"

Paul somehow always manages to justify stealing from his own father, not violently of course, and his father was incredibly perceptive, meaning that Paul never really stole anything. It was similar to when Billy the Kid paid for what Young Paul was "stealing" at the convenience store. Mr. Stan was above all, astute.

"I realize now that I didn't get away with anything, even when my dad was drunk. Looking back, I must wonder if he was always really as drunk as he seemed, or if it was a test to see who was going to rob him."

Paul and his father share a valuable trait: charm. Stan, it came naturally. For Paul, it was an acquired characteristic that opened as many doors of opportunity as it did vaults of precious gems. He could charm his way into a vault of safety deposit boxes with the same ease with which he punched a safe,

"I did it like I was a suave James Bond character—no weapons, just armed with an expensive suit. I looked like a million dollars, and I would get friendly with the guards in the basement of the Diamond District, and I was able to get inside my father's safe deposit box and make a $500 thousand switch in diamonds, convincing myself that I had it coming, and Dad would never notice. Okay, I was a punk kid with delusions of grandeur and a lack of appreciation, but those delusions were established upon a firm foundation of fact and a remarkable ability to justify my behavior based upon self-perpetuating resentments."

Paul invested in resentments, nurturing them, and stashing the dividends. Stan, Branka and Paul each had jewelry stashed all over the world, including Switzerland and Serbia.

"This was long ago," says Paul with a sigh. "That was before we were robbed by relatives and swindled by so called compatriots. Today we are normal people, you know, like the end of Goodfellas, where he comes out his front door in his bathrobe to get the morning paper and he feels like a real schmuck. To go from all action all day to no action any day is a shock to the system."

Nothing would please Paul more—at least in his imagination that comes complete with emotional revisions—than to return to those glory days of yesteryear when his mother was the mother of all panthers, and his father and the Professor were lookouts while Paul was stealing Manhattan.

"The Professor was a man I could always trust, and I never clashed with the Professor the way I clashed with my father."

A typical clash between Paul and Mr. Stan took place during one of the ten mega-heists and one that had true life-threatening repercussions and the loss of multi-millions of dollars.

"We were doing Carlos Medina's retirement heist; this one job would take care of him the rest of his life. It was one of those elaborate heists that took a huge crew and three full days and was one of our ten mega-heists. I only lasted one day before my father, and I had a falling out. He wanted to do it his way, I wanted to do it my way. Either way, we were blessing these Hassidic Jews with a tremendous increase in cash flow when the insurance company paid out."

The Hassids had solid silver and gold bars hidden behind the walls.

Naturally, our outlaws loaded up an entire truck with silver and stashed it in Rados Milojkovic's garage.

"Rados and his parents left the country to visit relatives," says Paul with a labored sigh, "and Moma shows up at night banging on the door and telling Rados' wife that Mr. Stan and Paul were arrested."

"The cops are on their way here," lied Moma. "We gotta get the stuff out of the garage before the cops show up."

She believed the lie and let Moma make off with the entire truck of silver. The story then circulated that it was Paul, upset over his clash with Mr. Stan, who then stole all the silver. In truth, Paul was the last to know and first to be accused. Moma, true to his scorpion nature, stole the silver and blamed it on Paul, and then got the Albanian gang involved to go after Paul,

"It was crazy," says Paul. "I didn't steal that truck load of silver—it was Moma as usual. So, I suddenly have these crazy blood lust Albanians after me wanting to kill me in addition to being on the run from the law."

This had to get worked out somehow, and Moma approached Mr. Stan saying he wanted a nice respectable sit-down with Paul at Panarella's. Paul wasn't crazy about the idea, but Mr. Stan convinced him to show up.

"I show up, proving there are times when I can do what my father asks of me," Paul recounts, "and right there in front of God and half the upper crust of New York low-lifes, Moma smashes me in the face—blood everywhere!"

This was Moma showing off for the Albanian's and validating that Paul stole the silver, which he absolutely did not.

"You think I wasn't under more pressure than an astronaut? I am on the run from the law, but not running that fast, honestly, and now I'm on the run from dangerous killer Albanians in NYC while putting together my own crew, including some excellent young talent I called Coco and Gorilla, plus two other Serbians, Ivan and Nenad, who begged me to let them do a heist with me."

Because they were Serbians begging him, Paul felt obligated to do what he could to help them get on their feet financially, and the three of them pulled off a perfectly rewarding heist for all involved, followed by duct tape and death threats.

Chapter Thirty-Four
Nightmare in a Bathtub

After the heist, Paul went to his new crew member's place to see where they were living in Jersey City. He hung out there socializing for a couple hours. then they asked him to stay because Nenad was going to pick them up Chinese take-out.

Nenad didn't bring back Mushu Pork. He brought back Moma.

"It had been four months since I last saw Moma at Panarella's when he punched me in the mouth to prove to the Albanians that I stole the truck of silver. Hell, I didn't steal it, Moma stole it, and I had to prove to my father and Monchie that I was not the one that robbed them for the silver from this huge heist that I was kicked out of after the first day working on it."

Everyone but Paul finished that heist—Jamie Schafer, Mike the Model, Monchie, Carlos Medina, Rados, and several others. Paul, hot-headed and over-opinionated, clashed with his father and was sent home to sulk.

Paul predictably put together a quick crew including the men he now refers to as "the two idiots."

"Ivan and Nenad," explains Paul, "were both models and martial artists. One was a kick boxer, and the other was into karate. I brought them on a few big heists after I was kicked out from my father's crew. I pulled ten nice heists on my own. And took these two knuckleheads along. At first, they listened, and they were fast and exceptional, but I soon found out that they were greedy and no good."

Paul tried looking nonchalant when Moma appeared, but suppressed resentment is always perceived—the atmosphere crackled with distrust and ill will.

"So, I hear you're doing heists on your own now," said Moma. "Good. I want you to do some with me."

This was an obvious set-up, but a set-up for what? Paul just wanted to get the hell out of there.

"Moma reached out to me in a gesture communicating that we should hug and let the past stay in the past. I wasn't crazy about the idea, but I went ahead and hugged him. That's when he grabbed me and put me in a choke hold.

"I'm strong, but Moma was not only stronger, but he had the element of surprise. No sooner does Moma start choking the life out of me than the two idiots slap handcuffs oh my wrists and start duct taping my legs, and then my entire body."

Paul fought like hell, but he was unable to break free. Moma then ripped the diamond rings off Paul's fingers and tore the Rolex from his wrist.

The idiots rolled out garbage bags on the floor while taking turns punching Paul in the gut while Moma continued crushing his windpipe, alternating pressure to keep Paul alive long enough to torture him some more.

"I could not breath," Paul remembers. "I was in a panic. I had a piece of appetizer lodged halfway down my windpipe, and Moma was constricting and squeezing as hard as he could. I thought that my eyes were going to pop out of my head."

Moma accompanied his physical assault with a nonstop diatribe of horror stories of what he had already done to Mr. Stan and Branka.

"He told me that my parents were dead," says Paul. "He said that my parents were murdered, and their bodies dismembered and stuffed in suitcases like the silver from the Vizcaya."

Moma ranted like a madman, bragging about all the money he made for Paul's family, money that paid for Paul's expensive Swiss education.

"I should have killed you when you were ten years old, that was my only mistake, but today is the day you die. Your folks are dead, and your friend Money Mike is in the trunk of your car. Too bad for him. You can't save him."

This was the beginning of three days of living hell. Encased in duct tape and repeatedly beaten, the next horrific assault was Moma shoving a hypodermic needle into the pulsing vein on Paul's hand, injecting him with Heroin and God only knows what else.

"He knew I had an aversion to needles, and eschewed all addictive drugs, so he was either going to kill me by overdose, make me a drug addict or use chemical coercion techniques. He was successful at number three because as long as I fed him the information he wanted, there was more to gain by keeping me alive."

Moma demanded the combination to Paul's safe, the one in his apartment in the city, and Paul provided it, groggily mentioning the three lucrative heists he had already planned out for Mr. Stan.

"He went to my apartment in the city, opened my safe and took my three and a half carat D flawless ring, my three-carat diamond pendant, and my Rolex, my Patek Philip and the $3 million in cash I had stashed in the safe, and all the incredible stuff in my walk-in closet. I kept telling him of greater and greater opportunities for more money to keep myself alive long enough to break free and kill all three of them."

Moma, cackling like a deranged film villain, gloated over taking everything from Paul.

"The entire time that he's doing this, I'm enraged and deciding that there is nothing left to do but kill him."

The only time Paul was alone in those three days was when Moma and the two idiots tossed their tape wrapped and close to overdosed prisoner into the bathtub where our durable desperado sank deeper into depression.

In that porcelain open air casket Paul did his best to maintain a sense of sane perspective. This clumsy melodrama of dishonor among thieves had a story arc with more high tension than the electric fence in Jurassic Park. Moma managed to momentarily convince Paul of numerous lies but when the shock wore off, Paul shifted his thinking.

"I looked at things exactly as I would a heist or a bank robbery. In that scenario, the getting in was done and the booty already bundled. All that remained was to escape."

While Paul marinated in his own opioid juices, Moma went on a heist bender, doing at least one and even two per night. These were heists planned for Mr. Stan's crew by Paul. Moma was determined to get to them well before his former benefactor.

Paul, even in his drugged and dazed condition knew that Moma made off with close to five million dollars from Paul's apartment and the keys to all of Mr. Stan's offices.

"Each office has at least one safe, and that safe could contain over a million dollars in cash and even more in precious stones. I knew that because of going after the offices, let alone murdering my parents, Moma would have to murder me as well. There was no other option: I had to escape."

On the third day, the handcuffs came off, and Moma admitted that Paul's folks weren't dead and that he had to do this to convince Paul to work with him, this obviously wasn't an evidence-based technique.

As drugged up as his prisoner, Moma babbled incoherently, alternating between animation and digression into stupor.

"Thank God for perspiration," says Paul. "After three days of sweating under that duct tape, it became loose and slippery. That never occurred to my captors, and when they took off to rob more of my father's offices, I broke loose from the tape, pulled myself out of the bathtub, fell to the floor, forced myself to get up, and I called Brasilia Restaurant because I knew that my mother and Albert were having dinner there that night."

Albert and Branka were still there, and Paul told them what had happened before getting the hell out of New Jersey.

"I jumped the turnstile on the Path train on the New Jersey side and took a cab from the Path to Brasilia. They took one look at me and could see all the pain and disorientation in my eyes. They covered the cab, and I went home with Mom to get my .357 and real bullets. I was seeing red and could only think of killing Moma. It was a simple deadly plan. I thought I knew which office he was hitting next, and I wasn't there to wait for him. He would break in and there I would be there waiting with a .357 and when he realized what was going to happen next, I would kill him."

Branka cries when recalling the sight of her drugged, dope-sick, sweat drenched and disheveled son pleading with her to give him that .357 so he could go after Moma.

"Thank God my son went to the wrong office," says Branka, wiping a tear from her eye. "If he killed someone, even someone as evil as Moma, he would be in prison forever."

It was fortunate for both Moma and Paul that our primary protagonist was waiting in the wrong office. Paul did not kill Moma, but that was the night that he killed Phase One of his brilliant career as gem heist king of New York.

"I really thought he would do 45 West 47th Street. but he hit our new office that had $5 million inside, three of it was inside the safe he destroyed and melted my guns that were in the safe and the bullets exploded. He and his two idiots spray painted in black: Don't steal from your Jewish neighbors, and he painted a big swastika."

"That was the second worst night of my life," asserts Paul. "The first, of course, was when Joan Crawford didn't give me that dog. Hey, some things are not easy for a kid to get over. Anyway, Moma was injecting me with heroin, and he wanted to make me into a Heroin addict. But this is why I couldn't even fight back and the same night that I tried to kill Moma was the night that I got arrested—not for a heist—but for trying to get $5 thousand out of a guy who owed me. I wasn't thinking clearly at all. I mean I was still really screwed up from all the drugs that jerk pumped into me. I was on a rampage, not thinking like a rational person."

Moma not only stole everything Paul had at home, and his keys, and what he took from several of Mr. Stan's offices, but he took off on the run and didn't pay those two idiots a single dime for helping him.

"I went to jail that night and I was so dope sick that I was violently ill. I thought I was going to die; I kept flashing back on John Lennon screaming on his hit song, "Cold Turkey," and how he screamed when he saw me shoot my thumb with a miniature gun at Anita's Chili when I was five years old. It's amazing what goes through your mind when you are delirious. I never told anyone about this before other than my mother. Now everyone knows."

The rental car used in the heist on which Nenad and the other idiot worked with Paul was rented by Branka and was in her name. The night Paul escaped was the night that Moma and the two idiots drove that rental car into Manhattan to further rob Mr. Stan.

"Now, get this," says Paul. "When they were done, and Moma ditched those two and ran off with the millions, Nenad actually returned the car to the rental company, and did so graciously so that my mother would not get any further charges."

Paul's antics following the Moma kidnapping episode had horrific repercussions:

"My original sentence was six months and then five years of probation. I messed it up by getting arrested for a fight in Tavern on the Green that culminated with a car chase, a car crash and my real ID jumping out of the glove box and waving at the transit police. "

Wait," says Paul, "There's more. I followed that with a stupid kidnapping charge trying to shake down some guy who owed me five thousand dollars. I had a .357 revolver, and the old New Jersey warrants are suddenly revealed. I thought it was over but once again Judge Rene White gave me the best sentence possible allowed by law: one to three years. I wind up doing seven years on that sentence. How crazy is that?"

Chapter Thirty-Five
Prison

Paul could have avoided prison completely. All he had to do was rat on his father, the Professor and all his closest friends.

"Yes," confirms Paul, "that's the kind of offer they made me. Tell them everything and everybody's names and I get to just go home. I'm not a rat. I never gave up anybody, never sent anybody to prison. I didn't give up any information, no names, not a one. I'm not Henry Hill who ratted out everybody and went into witness protection. If I had done that, I would have had a book, a movie, or a TV series long ago. But I didn't rat. I never would."

It is impossible for a young man such as Paul to prepare for prison, but there was no other young man quite like Paul—a combination of measured, reasoned strategy and hot-headed impulsiveness.

"I quickly figured out that a white kid from a rich family in Manhattan would be the lowest guy on the prison totem pole, the least respected and the most pushed around. Hell, I wasn't going to put up with that. Being as I could imitate any culture, do any accent, and speak almost any language, plus being a master at virtually all forms of self-defense from boxing to Judo, I went in as a Puerto Rican gangster. I only acted that role a few times and in a couple places, and strange as it may seem, I used all the awful things that Moma taught me to stay alive and become the most powerful and dangerous man behind bars."

All it took was for someone to try and beat him down or rough him up and they were immediately stunned and mortified to discover that this kid was light years ahead of them in speed, technique, and impact.

Fact: The kid was professionally trained by Olympic class mentors in martial arts, had the basics of boxing pounded into him from childhood and had the most extreme street fighting techniques taught him before he was eleven years old. The important prison principle involved: Don't be on the menu. Once you are food, you can't get off the menu no matter how fast you try to crawl off the plate.

"At first, I tried to explain to an entire unit where I was from and blah blah blah. I might as well be talking to a rock, because in prison all that fancy shit goes out the window, and you are food, meaning you are on the menu. I had to fight every day to survive just to eat. I was not going to be on the menu.

"The first people I connected with right away in the Manhattan tombs were Luis Felipe (a.k.a. King Blood, founder of the Bloodline Latin kings) and Hector 'King Tito' Rivera former of the Latin Kings' Sun Tribe."

Originally founded by Puerto Rican immigrants to mainland USA to counter racism and prejudice and unify immigrant voices in the face of rampant ignominious discrimination, the Latin Kings have evolved into an incredibly large and diverse organization accused of being a criminal gang whose purpose and function are solely and completely linked to criminal enterprises.

To portray this organization, whose roots are clearly humanitarian and essentially spiritual as a criminal enterprise is no different than calling Judaism and Christianity criminal gangs due to frequent arrests of Hassidic Jews in New York's Diamond District for money laundering, the mail bomb murders carried out by the terrorist Jewish Defense League, the reprehensible pedophiliac proclivities of particular Christian clergymen affiliated with the Roman Catholic Church, and the not as publicized, but even more deadly Christian Death Squads that slaughter entire villages of Muslim men women and children for the crime of not being members of the Church.

"When an organization is founded by convicted criminals behind bars, what sort of behavior do you expect? The best sign of future behavior is past behavior," says Paul. "They all knew where they came from, and they all knew what qualities and attributes they wanted to manifest, but the process of personal transformation is exactly that-personal, and time takes time."

Once it was obvious that picking on Paul was a big mistake, they found a more rewarding way to define their relationship with him.

"Hey, they wanted art, and I did excellent art—murals at Rikers and more men's bodies featured art by more than any other tattoo artists in the system."

If they gave the Oscar for the best actor in prison, the winner was Pavle Stanimirovic—he with the solid gold chain around his neck, the guards in his pockets, the powerful Latin Kings gang behind him one hundred percent and living in prison as if in the Helmsley Palace. A former inmate—one you would not use as a character witness nor would you want your sister to date him, met Paul in prison, and validates Paul's altered identity.

"I was terrified of him at first—everybody was. He was solid bulging muscle and had a hurricane attitude—you didn't dare cross him, although many tried. The story of Paul incarcerated is almost unbelievable, but I saw it with my own eyes. It's true, it's fascinating."

You never saw a prisoner with more power in your life, especially when you realize that he could have escaped any time he wanted—he could do everything, be anybody, and even within that most vile of environments he was a beacon of protection for the weak and a defender of the defenseless. The incarcerated mob bosses admired him, the convicted killers confided in him. He could win hearts and minds and win fights in the ring or in the yard. To everyone who encountered him, he was a true game changer.

"The first person I encountered worth mentioning was future celebrity 50 Cent."

Chapter Thirty-Six
The Incarceration Process

"Right off the bat," recalls Paul, "I'm sent to what they called Shock Camp with this other inmate, Curtis Jackson, known now as Fifty-Cent."

New York's Shock Incarceration program has two legislatively mandated goals:

- To treat and release selected State prisoners earlier than their court mandated minimum period of incarceration without endangering public safety.

- To reduce the need for prison bed space. The program emphasizes treatment as a means of promoting public safety. It seeks to build character, instill responsibility, and promote a positive self-image.

Paul's shock came when he was expelled from camp because he was busted with a .357. Curtis had a starter pistol; he got to stay.

"Back then Curtis wanted to be a boxer," says Paul, "so I got him all set up ahead of time with a gym, the trainer, the works. We would talk about big plans the way you do when you're in prison. Now that we are both out, we are both doing crime on screen or behind the scenes. In 2019, I was asked to be a consultant on his film, *Den of Thieves II*."

Despite being able to escape prison at any time, a promise made by his father and compatriots who visited him often. Paul didn't want to spend his life a fugitive. He did, however, plan a one hundred percent successful escape and sent another inmate to the freedom of being a fugitive.

"Why should I live like a fugitive, a refugee, when I can live like a king, or at least a prince behind bars because of my art talent, fighting prowess and beyond the wall connections, including, of course, my father?"

Mr. Stan continued doing what he always did, albeit without the added value of Paul's hands-on involvement, but free from Moma's underhanded duplicity.

"I was planning heists for my father while I was in prison, so we kept a close relationship in terms of the family business. Did you think my father would retire after a billion-dollar mega-heist? Of course not. Maybe if I had agreed to retire also, but with me in prison, what is he going to do with himself while I'm forming lucrative alliances within the prison system?"

The inmates with whom Paul shared time, space and cells reads like a "Who's Who" of notorious mob bosses, professional killers, political prisoners and missing in action wannabees surrounded by a surging sea of non-criminals: people whose crime was the medical condition of drug dependence or full drug addiction.

"So many prisoners are victims of the war on youth, war on minorities, war on behalf of corruption," says Paul. "They shouldn't be in prison unless they committed real crimes against people and property, not for their medical dependence. It's crazy. And the bad guys in prison were nothing of note on the outside, and the big shots on the outside who are now on the inside keep a low profile. They don't want attention. I wound up as cell mate with all manner of murderous and corrupt characters. I think ninety percent of my prison experiences belong in a different book because it detracts from the overarching story of what my father started in NYC that is now worldwide, if mutated."

Suffice it to say that Paul, himself mutated into a character created and manifested out of Paul's talent and imagination, survived, and thrived in America's broken prison system for the duration of his sentence.

"I had to survive, and I had to position myself as a force of nature. Meanwhile, things back in New York were changing as well. Mr. Stan was the world's greatest gentleman thief, a man renowned for his ethics. Sadly, he was a breed as rare as the Antelope Valley antelopes. In 1996, three years before I came home, former members of one of my final crews turned on my dad like vipers. They followed him and invaded his home. It was like the Fort Lee home invasion times ten. They held Ms. Kim hostage while they pistol whipped my father to the point of near death and stole over $3 million in cash, gems, and rare antiquities."

Outraged and impotent to do anything about this tragic assault, his anger could prompt no retribution, but lie there sizzling like a piece of bacon in a microwave oven.

"I was on fire from the inside out," Paul says of his desperation. "How could they have such little respect, be so selfish and brutal? Neither my father nor I, nor the Professor would ever violate the sanctity of anyone's home. Did Bruno Sulack, Biki or Stiv ever do such a thing? No. Never. Would Alek or Montenegro or my dear mother? My other crew members—Coco would never even think of such cruel behavior. That is the action of thugs, punks, and psychopaths such as Moma. Fearing for my father's safety, and not being able to personally protect him, weighed heavily on me those final thirty-six or so months in prison. He was robbed again in 1998, and it was arranged for former boxer, six-foot-six Joe Pudar to move into my father's house in Astoria, Queens."

When the prison doors swung wide on the day of his release in 1999, Paul anticipated some sort of media recognition when such an expectation derived solely from his personal grandiosity. Even more grand was the joy of freedom.

"My beautiful mother picked me up and took me to my dad before she returned to Florida where she was now Mrs. DiGangi. I found two former associates and an intermediary waiting for me at my father's new home back in Astoria, Queens—Nenad and Ivan and their negotiator, Ricky."

The men were not at Mr. Stan's to cause trouble. They were there to beg Paul's forgiveness.

"They have been living in fear," explained Stan. "Their only hope is for you to set them free from the guilt and shame they have been living with since your three days of hell."

Paul wasn't in a forgiving mood, and he headed for the kitchen to grab a butcher knife. Mr. Stan's bodyguard, Joe Pudar, intercepted him, pleading with him to calm down.

"What else could I do," asks Paul rhetorically. "I couldn't really kill them, and they were so pathetic and contrite that I forgave them."

With that bit of business resolved, there were a few things on Paul's agenda—new clothes, old friends and a fresh heist. With that bit of past business resolved, there were only two things to do: buy new clothes and pull a heist with old friend Alex Montenegro, the architect of the Regency Hotel job.

"It was a strange thrill to do it again after that time away," Paul explains. "I was back in the game, but it felt different. I wasn't exactly the same kid I was when they sent me away."

The target was Mascot, a five generation American luxury eyewear brand. It is one of the oldest local businesses in New York City.

"I teamed up with Alex Montenegro for this one. I went into the store during the day and cased the joint. I tied a shoelace around the push-handle that opens the side door and let it drop down outside the door. That night, all I had to do was pull the shoelace and the door opened. As this was not zone one on the alarm system, it would look like a false alarm to the security company. Sure, the alarms went off, but we were out of there with the alarms running and loaded the entire store—lenses, frames, and machines—into two Astro vans and drove away."

The year 1999 seemed decades away from 1992, and everything was changing.

Chapter Thirty-Seven
Everything is Altered

The year 1999 was a volatile and challenging time in the lives of Paul and his parents. Branka was happily married to the incredibly wealthy, honest, and fun-loving Albert DiGangi. They were living in Miami and Paul visited them often, spending time in the local nightclubs contemplating his personal evolution and life trajectory.

"I know my son well," Branka states flatly as if expecting Paul to jump out from behind the divan and contradict her. "There was always conflict within him. One minute he brags of being a great diamond thief, raised and taught by the best. The next minute he is complaining that he had no choice in his life, that he didn't want to be a thief, he wanted to be an artist, an entertainer—and he has natural talent for all of it. The same day that he praises his father, he lashes out at the way he was treated in childhood. He no doubt thinks that he is unique. Of course, he is, but so is everyone else on Earth. All people are blessed with gifts from their creator, but it is only a fortunate few who are in a position to follow their passion that leads to self-realization and personal fulfillment. He needed a good woman, a good vision of himself and the feeling that comes from knowing who you are."

It was in Miami nightspot that at least one piece of that personal potential puzzle fell into place because of a chance meeting and conversation that he started up with Ms. Jessica Perez. a street wise and ethical beauty with a sharp mind and a good heart. They danced and romanced and soon were an item.

"It was romantic, if not a bit outrageous explaining to Jessica what I did for a living. I stressed the point that it was all victimless crime, everyone was in on it, and that our number one rule was no one ever gets hurt. She was understandably concerned but she was street smart as well as accomplished, so certain aspects of illegality were not completely foreign to her. She got to meet all sorts of my compatriots when Dad threw me a giant party. No one can put on a party like Mr. Stan!"

Mr. Stan knows how to celebrate, and when it comes to parties, no one can equal him. He threw a party for Paul that, in all honesty, defies proper description. Everyone Paul worked with who wasn't behind bars or deep underground, literally or metaphorically, was there from Alek the keyman to Coco and Gorilla. If Mr. Stan could find them, they were all there including Paul's party pal, Sal Linzalone. Moma, of course, was not invited. He was first rumored as dead but was hiding out in Chicago.

"It was the ultimate party," confirms Paul. "What a scene! And of course, Henry the Horse dances the waltz!"

Wait, there is more: Paul went legit, although that wasn't his conscious intention at the time.

Paul, always well dressed and appearing the consummate professional, was casing the diamond district offices of Concord Enterprises when the owner, Haratch Kaprilian, asked Paul why he was there.

Thinking fast, Paul said he was seeking employment. After all, he had impeccable credentials as Vice President of Gemstones Trading.

"I managed to obtain a prestigious job with Franck Muller. I was just lucky to get this opportunity and it worked out like a dream come true. Living in a lovely Long Island home, making excellent, honest income, I was an incredibly happy man. I even married Jessica."

Paul's father was perfectly happy with Paul's union with Jessica, but Paul going legit was a disappointment.

"Of course, it was," explains Paul. "You must understand that heists were what we did and who we were. Heists are not simple things—you don't just run out and do an incredible heist. My dad planned heists that are works of art—complex, brilliantly planned and perfectly executed. We had warehouses of specialized tools, garages of vehicles—this was our life—a life of endless painstaking planning and re-planning, of constant rehearsals and making sure you had the right people for every aspect of the job. If my father needed a strong man, he called on Embrio. Later, if I needed a strong man, I called on Gorilla. If we needed a key person—a lock expert—we called Alek. You need people of discipline that you can train, trust, and rely on without a doubt. Coco is a good example of a bright guy who learned well. Acrobats? We can get them. Just look at the guys my dad had in the 1970s. This isn't a criminal enterprise; this isn't a gang or a mafia family. It is simply a genius such as my father—and I am the secret essence of my sire—planning a project down to the last detail, and then bringing in specialists for each and every aspect. Independent contractors, each and all. My father waited with great anticipation for my return, and when I came back it was Mr. Stan and Son all over again—but I turned my back on making millions overnight to making hundreds of thousands in a year. He was hurt that I wanted to not do heists, but to sell watches, not steal them. I believe that he could not fathom me doing anything other than what I was raised to do and do with him. In truth, I loved the job, I loved the company, the product and I especially loved being one hundred percent non-criminal. My mother was proud of me, but Dad was disappointed." The company, as with others "cased" by Paul as heist targets, was fully insured by Lloyds of London for a hundred million dollars. Lloyds ran a check on Paul's social security number and promptly cancelled the firm's insurance.

"How do they expect convicted felons to be respectable and successful if they can't get an honest job? And guess what security company practically dragged me out of there in handcuffs—Holmes Security. The person that was Haratch's number two man looked at me as if I had been caught in the act of sodomizing his favorite gerbil or something—he would have shot me on the spot if it were allowed."

"My son was heartbroken beyond belief," recalls Branka. "He cried like a baby."

"That's true," confirms Paul. "I broke down in tears and sobbed. The only person happy about the situation was my father."

Branka, a woman as known for her long-suffering sighs as she is for her brilliance and beauty, has a well-formed opinion of what happened next.

"I think losing that job triggered something like a crisis of identity just when he was building a new self-image," says his mother. "Ironically, his father and he got along better than ever when planning and doing heists. But this was a new era, a new decade, and my son, brilliant and as wound up as ever, launched into a series of astonishing escapades that knocked New York on its ear."

Paul told Jessica what he was going to do, and the sheer audacity of it both enthralled and amused her. Her response was one of loving support with a rock-solid admonition, "I'll stand by my man, Paulie, but remember the number one rule: No one gets hurt."

"I was going to keep doing heists, but I was going to do so much more, and do it as it had never been done before. Did I go too far? Well, you will see for yourself. The world was alive with innovative technology, and while that would make some things more difficult, it also offered astonishing new opportunities for entirely new dimension in so-called victimless crimes. As usual, the insurance companies would pay, no individual would be hurt, and I could gloriously justify everything. I had an attitude that while daring and audacious, was also one of self-exaltation and supreme grandiosity. Oh, I was going to prove to the world that there is no other name under heaven or Earth that knows more about the creative redistribution of wealth for the sake of adrenalin than the man called Punch."

"If this were the season finale of a TV show," comments Paul, "it would end with me standing in the heart of Manhattan, looking as if I own this town at night, a look of glorious victorious anticipation on my face, and blasting on the soundtrack comes Bachman-Turner Overdrive: *You Ain't Seen Nothin' Yet!*"

For More News About Burl Barer and Punch Stanimirovic, Signup For Our Newsletter:

http://wbp.bz/newsletter

Word-of-mouth is critical to an author's long-term success. If you appreciated this book please leave a review on the Amazon sales page:

http://wbp.bz/manhattan

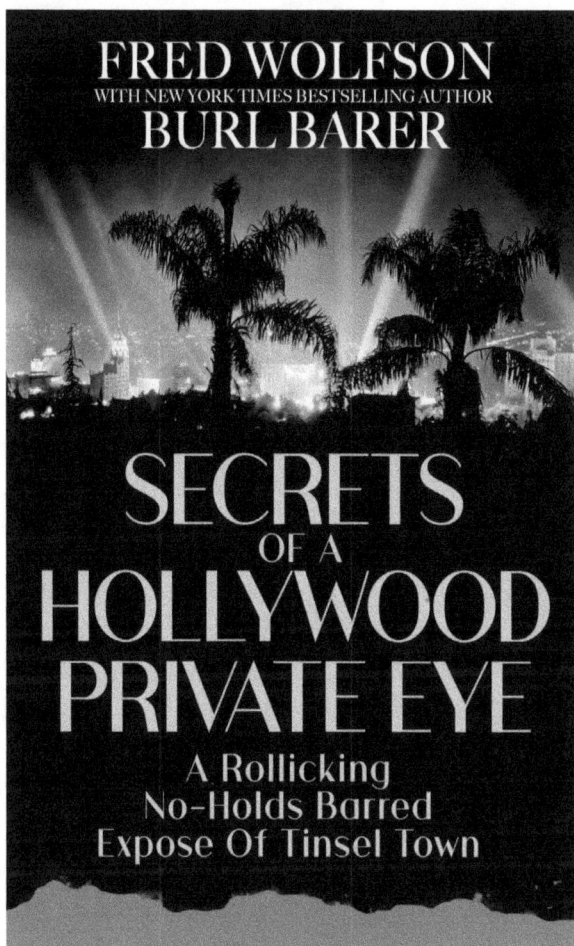

INTRODUCTION

The world is not full of crooks and criminals. In truth, you are surrounded by kind, honest, decent people who will never lie, cheat, or steal without first failing the dual temptations of opportunity and justification.

The world is not full of crooks and criminals. In truth, you are surrounded by kind, honest, decent people who will never lie, cheat, or steal without first failing the dual temptations of opportunity and justification.

Before a person can lie, thus beginning the progression that includes cheating and stealing, they must convince themselves that the deception is justified.

Some lies *are* justified. A doctor assuring a dying patient that they are on the path to recovery may be the positive deciding factor in life or death. When Nazis ask you if you have seen any Jews, and you have a family of four hiding in your attic, telling the truth would be an egregious sin. Malicious lying—giving false information with evil intent—is another matter.

Malicious liars steal the truth first, and then they steal possessions. Once you cross the line between truth and lies, the distinction between "yours" and "mine" is the next border breached.

Integrity erodes quickly or slowly depending upon the efficacy of justification, and this was tested by an interesting sociological experiment. A group of researchers entrusted people with one million dollars to hold safely for someone supposedly going out of the country for five years.

Only ten percent of the study's participants safeguarded the funds as agreed. The money, plus interest earned, returned untouched.

The majority—a whopping eighty percent—occasionally used some of the funds for financial emergencies or for granting themselves short-term loans. They justified these indiscretions because, at the end of the five years, they returned the full million.

The final ten percent stole all the money.

In another study, researchers set up a candy display in the middle of a supermarket. A hidden video camera allowed them to watch people help themselves without paying. The next day, they placed a guard in front of the display. The number of people helping themselves to candy dropped from six per hour to only one per hour. The one was the guard.

Conclusion: a primary characteristic of temptation is its ability to tempt. It is no coincidence that the Lord's Prayer says, "Lead us not into temptation, but deliver us from evil," acknowledging that most people, once tempted, lower their behavioral standards.

Theft is not always money. Sometimes it is time and/or emotions. When a spouse or lover cheats on you and then loots your bank account, the broken heart hurts more than the negative bank balance.

The number-one business loss is employee theft; the fastest-rising crime in America is identity theft. If you have money, someone wants to steal it or cheat you out of it.

It does not matter if you are poor or rich, famous or unknown. Actress Kate Beckinsale had her purse snatched while Christmas shopping in London; three men robbed an Amish family at gunpoint as they rode their horse-drawn buggy along a country road in northern Indiana.

When it comes to financial scams, people are most vulnerable when ignorant, and that includes Hollywood stars, producers, directors, and network executives. Rich and famous is not synonymous with investment savvy, nor does an absurdly large investment portfolio assure immunity to emotional and financial predators.

Former network news commentator Greta Van Susteren, actor Peter Coyote, and movie producer Armyan Bernstein (whose films include *Spy Game*, starring Robert Redford and Brad Pitt, and *Air Force One*, starring Harrison Ford) were among those entangled in an investment swindled by conman clergyman Reed Slatkin of the Church of Scientology.

"I wish I'd never met him," Bernstein told the *Los Angeles Times*. "He preyed on good people who were trusting."

"We were all stupid," said Greta Van Susteren's husband John Coale, a prominent Washington attorney. "I'm not a dummy. I went to school, but he got me on this one. Plus, I paid the asshole fees." Coale sympathized with the people who lost their life savings—he talked to a quadriplegic who gave Mr. Slatkin all her money. "I was ripped off too. I'm getting whooped at home, if you know what I mean," he said. "I'm not even allowed out of the house to buy cigarettes anymore. For a couple of years, I looked like an investment genius. Now I'm just a dope."

Catching and revealing a lying thief who takes advantage of people's trust and swindles them out of their life savings is one of the great joys of my career. A crooked executive in Los Angeles stole millions of dollars from investors, flew to Switzerland, and deposited the funds. His outraged victims confronted him with their accurate accusations; he insisted that he never went to Switzerland and he could prove it. They hired me to prove him wrong.

I had no idea what kind of proof he would offer, or how I would counter it. We sat down at a conference table, and he produced his proof—his passport.

"I never went to Switzerland," he insisted. "If I had, there would be an official Swiss stamp on a page in my passport. Go ahead. Look."

He handed me his passport. Sure enough, there was no Swiss stamp. Then, I silently counted the pages.

"Does anyone else in this room have a passport?" I asked. One of the other men had one. "Please be so kind," I asked, "to tell us how many pages are in a passport."

He carefully counted them. "Twenty-five," was his accurate response.

"*All* passports are twenty-five pages," I confirmed. "Yours, sir," I said to the crooked executive, "has only twenty-four pages. One page is missing—the page you removed because it had a Swiss stamp."

It was like a scene out of *Perry Mason*. He was drop-jawed. I got up, collected my fee of three thousand dollars, and walked away knowing I had exposed a criminal. He was guilty as hell and thought he could get away with it by tearing a page out of his passport. He was charged and convicted in a court of law. While it was comforting to his victims, they never recovered all their funds or their self-respect.

All of his victims were supposedly smart people. If it can happen to them, it can happen to you, especially if you are greedy.

The principal factor in any scam is greed. Without greed, you won't have a victim. When people get greedy, they throw caution to the wind and proceed without thinking. Sometimes greed is the very factor that the scam artists down. Some people think they can get away with anything, and they walk away with nothing. A perfect example is the unscrupulous fellow who attempted to use his minority status as a ticket to free rent for himself and several undocumented immigrants. Here's the story.

A landlord had a tenant who used his residence as a "home base" for almost twenty people, all of whom were in this country in violation of immigration policy. The landlord wanted these people out, but the tenant threatened to portray his landlord as a xenophobe, prejudiced against immigrant minorities. Believing he held the upper hand by threat, the tenant had not paid a cent in rent for a solid year.

Not wanting this false and damaging publicity, the landlord finally hired me to take care of the situation. Promising that I would get this undesirable pack of cohorts off his property, I went to the home in disguise and claimed to represent a major real estate developer who owned an exclusive residential high-rise in Century City.

I told the tenant that the developer was in serious trouble with the Department of Fair Housing for not renting to minorities, and was about to be hit with a substantial fine.

"The developer is offering free rent for a year," I lied, "if you will move in immediately." The tenant was understandably disbelieving, so I took him to a five-million-dollar penthouse and let him have a look around.

Needless to say, the tenant was rather impressed. He agreed to move in under three conditions: he wanted the keys to the condo immediately, an electronic key to the underground garage, and sixty dollars for moving expenses.

I agreed to all three conditions and gave the man sixty dollars. The greedy tenant couldn't believe his luck. He immediately packed the truck with his belongings, loaded up eighteen of his friends, and headed off to his new home in Century City.

When he arrived, he found his luck had changed. The doorman had never heard of the real estate developer, the keys didn't fit the lock, and the electronic key for the underground garage was an expired Shell credit card that had been painted black.

Heading back to his old home didn't help either. Armed guards were now stationed outside, and the locks had been changed. According to California law, once the premises are vacated, all renter's rights are relinquished.

I kept my promise to the landlord—his greedy tenant was gone, as was the threat of slander and libel. Yes, it all starts and ends with greed.

A client whose friends were taken by a conman to the tune of eight million dollars contacted me. It was a typical con. He approached his marks by offering them twenty or thirty percent on their money in a very short time. With his first victims, the conman invested fifty thousand dollars of theirs in a motion picture deal. Within two months, he returned seventy-eight thousand dollars, a profit of twenty-eight thousand dollars. His first victims were thrilled, returned the check for seventy-eight thousand dollars, and asked if it could be reinvested.

The conman agreed to invest the money in the next deal coming up in a couple of weeks, but he had to hold on to the money, as he would need it at a moment's notice. They agreed to let him hold the money. They received the check for seventy-eight thousand dollars but never cashed it. In truth, that check would have bounced: the account only had four thousand dollars in it at the time.

The victims couldn't wait to get their friends involved. They told all their wealthy pals about their new investment counselor. They extolled virtues by showing their friends a copy of his bogus check. It soon snowballed. Everyone was calling the conman to invest, and the returns were great. Only one person pulled out early after investing one hundred thousand dollars. He received a check for one hundred sixty-nine thousand dollars.

In only three months, the conman had a bankroll and was wheeling and dealing. He actually turned down some people he didn't like; their investment was too small. He was now only dealing with people who would be willing to invest at least one hundred thousand dollars. This went on for about eighteen months until the conman had accumulated over eight million dollars. This was safely put away overseas in numerous motion picture deals, or so they all thought. To add credibility to his operation, he rented a large swanky office and furniture to match. It was an impressive operation. But it was all a façade.

The problem with investing with conmen is that the return on your investment is limited to the length of time he continues to operate. Once he has accumulated his money, the deal somehow falls apart. The crook suddenly either has a problem with the company he invested in overseas or the overseas market has fallen—neither of which, he sadly laments, he has any control over.

My client and his friends hired me to find any assets so that they could recoup at least some of their money. My contract said that I would receive twenty-five percent of all monies found, plus a three-thousand-dollar retainer to cover expenses. The client would also have forty-eight hours from the time I found the assets to tie them up, or to execute on their judgment. After forty-eight hours, if they did not get the money, they still owed me my fee. In the interim, they must place half of the money owed to me in a bank trust account. That money would be released to me after verification of the assets. I then obtained a lien on the second half of the money, so I am first paid. They agreed to my terms and conditions, and signed the contract.

After five months of tracking the money, I found three million of eight million dollars. He had a very elaborate scheme: He had deposited the money in a local bank. Then he would transfer the money to a bogus motion picture company in Italy. A second investment company in France invoiced the Italian company for services rendered.

The money was transferred to France, where it was then transferred via wire to a third company in England.

A company in New York owned by the conman's brother and mother would then invoice the English company. They would in turn invest the money in CDs, stocks, bonds, and real property under a corporate name. It was the best-planned and thought-out scheme I had ever encountered. The total assets of their investments, minus their living expenses, were substantial. I had found two million dollars in liquid assets and the rest tied up in worldwide investments.

I contacted my client, telling him that I was able to locate three million in assets, and requested that he place half my fee in trust. He wanted to know where the assets were before he would deposit the money. I explained to him that this was not the deal. I would divulge the fruits of my five-month investigation only after he deposited the money. He begged and pleaded with me to tell him the location of the assets.

After two weeks, it was obvious that he had no intention of living up to his end of the agreement. He contacted his lawyer, who was also a victim of the con, who tried to intimidate me into revealing the whereabouts of the conman's assets.

I realized that any further involvement with these greedy people would be fruitless. To buy myself time, I gave them worthless information that was in direct proportion to what they had paid me for my five months' work. But it bought me enough time to sell the information to the IRS, who would guarantee me in writing ten percent of all taxes collected by them. Since the total worth of the income that they had received was twelve million dollars, the tax liability would be about six million, plus interest and penalties that had accrued on the money for the last four years.

I estimated my ten percent was worth in the neighborhood of about nine hundred thousand dollars and was backed by the treasury of the US government. After my client couldn't find the money, they asked for a refund of the money they advanced me for expenses. I gladly returned their three thousand dollars and cashed a check from Uncle Sam for close to one million dollars. Greed doesn't pay.

One look at showbusiness lawsuits reveals that having a hit TV series or a price tag of twenty million dollars per film will not protect you from a cheating spouse, a burgled house, or a "good friend" swindling you out of your hard-earned cash.

Average folks sit and watch their clothes at public laundromats because if they don't keep an eye on their belongings, someone will steal their jeans and T-shirts. The rich and famous do not sit at laundromats, but the same concern prevails.

The Rolling Stones' guitarist Ron Woods had his jeans stolen—jeans studded with diamonds. His response, of course, was not to simply say, "Darn it, I should have kept an eye on them." Instead, he hired me to find the impressive, if impractical, Levi's and get them back. I did.

Of course, I am a real private detective. Not only that, but I've played one in the movies—Raymond Chandler's Phillip Marlowe in the private eye classic *Chandler Creates Marlowe*. You don't have to be a real private detective to act like Phillip Marlowe, Sam Spade, Jim Rockford, or Mike Hammer, and you don't need to learn from tragic mistakes before you "wise up."

Sad but true, even I had to wise up. I was famous for protecting others, but I left myself vulnerable. If I had hired me to protect me, I wouldn't have been poisoned, drugged, and robbed of over sixteen million dollars.

Of course, when the poison was out of my system and the drugs wore off, I promptly hired myself to get it back.

You are about to learn how to stop dishonest people from hurting you—be they so-called friends or loyal employees. I will show you how to know for sure if your lover or spouse is cheating on you, or if you are getting involved with someone who is hiding something.

Using the secrets I've used for years as a Hollywood private detective, you will increase your odds of finding missing persons, runaway kids, or stolen clothing. If you want to:

- track down money that has been stolen from you
- find and secure assets that your spouse is trying to hide in a divorce case
- prevent others from finding out things about you that you don't want them to know.

All you must do is keep reading, and put what you learn to work for you. I promise you; it is all here in *Secrets of a Hollywood Private Eye*.

Fred Wolfson, PI

Chapter One

Cheating Spouses

There is an old Arab proverb, "When a man gets an erection, he loses seventy-five percent of his religion." That may be an understatement. Often, the man loses one hundred percent of his marriage and fifty percent of his assets.

Men can't have an affair alone, and married women are almost equally unfaithful. The Hite Report on Male Sexuality (1981) found that seventy-two percent of men married two years or more had had an extramarital affair; the Hite survey of women (1976) found that seventy percent of women married five years or more had had an extramarital affair.

Sadly, having an affair can become a behavior pattern for both sexes. According to recent research, approximately fifteen percent of women and twenty-five percent of men have more than four affairs during their married lives.

You may already be familiar with the ten telltale signs of cheating. If you are not aware of them, you should be.

1. He claims he is working late and then doesn't pick up the phone.

2. You check the car odometer after she has driven to and from work, knowing the mileage is fourteen miles... and she is, on some nights, putting on sixty-four miles.

3. You go through her phonebook and find names and phone numbers in code.

4. You go through his phonebook and find numbers that appear on your phone bill. You run those numbers through the phone company to find out Carl Cummings is really Carol Johnson.

5. You run a marriage check on him through the local state and find three marriages and one divorce you didn't know about.

6. You go through her purse or wallet and find names and phone numbers hidden away in a secret compartment.

7. You find women's panties in the glovebox of the car, and you don't have a teenage son who borrows the car.

8. You go through the credit card bills and find restaurant charges on nights he was working. You call the restaurant and find out from the receipt number that it was dinner for two.

9. You go through her checkbook and find checks for clothing for the opposite sex that you never received.

Around Christmas and birthdays, you should wait for the occasion to pass before the confrontation.

10. He has condoms; you are on the pill.

There are other so-called danger signals. Beware, all of these can have innocent explanations.

1. He suddenly starts losing weight, wearing different cologne, and changes his hairstyle.

2. She closes down your joint bank account and opens a new one in her name only.

4. He cancels his life insurance policy.

5. After years of being affectionate, he tells you that you are smothering him.

6. Your sex life appears on the endangered species list.

7. Her sexual technique changes dramatically.

8. He asks you to do things sexually he never asked for previously.

9. She calls out someone else's name during a climax.

10. Your friends tell you that they saw your loved one with someone else in a restaurant holding hands.

11. He claims he must go on a business trip and won't tell you where he is going.

12. She tells you she is leaving on a business trip to Cleveland on United Airlines, but no such reservation exists.

13. When she returns from a business trip, you find a hotel receipt under the names of a Mr. and Mrs.

14. He joins a social club with meetings every Thursday night. His car, however, is never in the parking lot of the social club on Thursday nights.

15. She joins a bowling league and you can never find her in those alleys.

Yes, those all seem suspicious. Before you embarrass yourself with false accusations, make sure you are not projecting your own insecurities or personal guilt. Allow me to give you a few illuminating examples from my own files.

Back before American travelers experienced Soviet Union-style restrictions, a clothing store chain hired a Washington state television director to shoot some commercials in Hawaii. Part of the deal included the use of his favorite cinematographer and one attractive female model with whom he previously worked.

To save money, the client took advantage of a "family fare" promotion with the airlines and booked all three under the director's last name. This was also done at the hotel, where the three were given a suite under his name. The model actually had her own hotel room, although it was located inside the suite. The two men shared #410; the woman was in #410-A.

The director, unaware of the hotel reservation peculiarities until his arrival, gave his wife the hotel phone number before leaving town. She estimated the time of his arrival and called the hotel.

When she asked if her husband was registered there, she was informed, "Yes, the three of them checked in to suite 410 just a few minutes ago."

The wife, assuming the worst, accused her husband and the cameraman of having a wild tryst with the young lady. No amount of reassurance from the cameraman, the model, or the client would convince her otherwise. Her erroneous conclusion-jumping did not help their marriage, and her continual accusatory phone calls to all concerned disrupted the project and damaged the creative atmosphere.

"Not only that," recalled the director, "but this was in August, and it was hotter than hell. We were working long, tedious hours. I think we had one afternoon to ourselves, during which I stewed over my home situation while the woman I was supposedly having the affair with was gift shopping for her real-life lover and kids back home. The idea of having an affair hadn't occurred to me at all—by the end of the trip, it was sounding more and more like something I could easily justify if the opportunity dropped in my lap."

Indeed, the business traveler, male or female, is most vulnerable to an extramarital affair. Anyone who travels extensively as part of their employment knows that the glamour and fun of traveling is short-lived when it is a constant occurrence. Baggage claim becomes a nightmare, flight attendants appear hostile, and fellow passengers seem agents of fate sent to repay you for every bad deed in your life. You land at airports in the middle of summer that have lost their air conditioning; you land at airports not on your itinerary because of weather conditions in winter. Hotels give you the wrong keys for the right room, or the right keys for the wrong room. Outside your window is a vehicle whose car alarm wails incessantly; you hear sexual participants in the next room going for the gold in the erotic Olympics.

From tardy room service to rental cars with faulty ignitions, business travel can be one stressful event after another, especially when it is part of your life on a regular basis. Consider the following true-life example, an example that is a perfect set-up for an affair.

You are on a multi-city business trip. It is winter in Denver, ice and snow. Some freeway off-ramps are closed. After dropping off your rental car, you have to hustle like hell to make the flight. You can make it if you run, and pray you are not "randomly selected" at security for a full body search and in-depth investigation.

You make it just in time to experience one of these two dispiriting events: your plane pulling back from the gate, or the flight is canceled. You sleep in the airport, waiting for the next flight out. After several hours, you feel like a POW.

Then she (or he) catches your eye. This person is in the same situation and shares your destination. What happens next is a perfectly natural phenomenon investigated by scientists as far back as the 1960s. A person under emotional stress will immediately bond with, and be sexually attracted to, the first decent-looking person of the opposite sex they talk to. It has something to do with the survival of the species.

In some primitive part of the human brain, stress is associated with threat to life. Threat to life sends a signal to propagate the species—in other words, SEX.

None of the above-mentioned process is conscious. From the business traveler's perspective, travel just became more pleasurable because of attractive company: a companion who, like you, will gladly exchange pulling out their hair in dismay for clawing the sheets in delight.

You don't even notice the flight since you are in a first-date mode—charming, talkative, and very important. Life's little problems fade away. The flight attendants seem pleasant again. The food is a good excuse to have dinner with your new traveling partner. When you arrive at your destination, you find out where your new friend is staying, and make plans to meet later that evening for a drink, maybe dinner.

The evening turns out great. You return to your room, date in hand, and spend the next three days missing meetings at the convention you were scheduled to attend. The person in the next room goes home talking about the sexual Olympics that occurred all night in the adjoining room.

So it starts: the beginning of the end of the relationship that you developed back home. It wasn't planned, it "just happened."

Most first affairs are cases of accidental infidelity, unplanned acts completely out of character with the person's self-image. "The most startling dynamic behind accidental infidelity," says noted expert Frank Pittman, "is misplaced politeness, the feeling that it would be rude to turn down a needy friend's sexual advances. In the debonair gallantry of the moment, the brazen discourtesy to the marriage partner is overlooked altogether."

Once someone has an affair, he or she makes one of four decisions.

1. Decide that it was a stupid thing to do, and resolve not to do it again.

2. Decide that the infidelity is because your spouse let you down, and then go home and make your marriage fail.

3. Decide that this is a new, fun, and inexpensive hobby.

4. Decide you must be married to the wrong person, and declare your love to your new bed partner.

All but the first are tragic errors of judgment. Fewer than ten percent of people having affairs divorce their spouse and marry their lover. Seventy-five percent of these marriages end in divorce.

In most crimes, be they legal crimes or crimes of the heart, the perpetrator does not want to suffer the humiliation accompanying the revelation of impropriety, but fear of punishment is the world's worst motivator.

No man, or woman, lives happily ever after in a fear-based relationship. In fact, as our television commercial director noted, the continual assumption that he was cheating provided possible justification for doing exactly that should the opportunity arise.

The vice president of one of the big three television networks contacted us. "My wife is having an affair," he insisted. "I've hired three other firms to catch her, but they have all failed."

The reason they failed was simple: she would always look in her rear-view mirror and if she suspected that she was being followed, she would not show up for her rendezvous. This went on for about three days. We told our client the only way to tail his wife would be by helicopter, but it would be quite costly. He said that money wasn't an issue. He had to know.

We rented a helicopter from a local airport at a cost of two hundred dollars per hour. The helicopter served as a command post that coordinated the activities of four investigators in rental cars on the ground.

We started tracking her when she left her place of employment at about 11:30 a.m. She drove around Westwood for about thirty minutes before entering a local hotel. Our ground units were in hot pursuit. She didn't check in, but went right to the elevator with a female operative following. She knocked on door 532 and was let in by a man wearing a bathrobe.

Our operative contacted the helicopter via radio, and the message was relayed to our client via cellular telephone. He was about fifteen minutes away; he drove over and waited by her car in the below-ground garage, hidden about three cars away. Within the hour, the post-coital couple walked over to her car, embraced, and kissed passionately.

As you may imagine, our client was displeased with his wife's behavior, and even more irked at the actions of her paramour. In fact, he punched her lover in the mouth, broke some teeth, and more punching and hitting continued until the police arrived.

Our client was first charged with battery, but the case was dismissed as mutual combat. His cheating wife moved to Cleveland the same day. He filed for divorce. It was uncontested. He was a rich television executive; the lover (no, he didn't go to Cleveland with the wife) had nothing special to offer except infidelity. Being rich and semi-famous did not protect my television executive client from heartbreak and deception.

I've been hired by famous people, worked with them on television and in motion pictures, and I've also investigated famous people. Some of them are wacky as rabbits; others are emotionally insecure individuals who pay a high price for high income and front-page fame. A perfect example is the peculiar romantic coupling of comic Roseanne Barr with comedy writer/actor Tom Arnold.

Tom Arnold, despite his personal peculiarities—or perhaps because of them—is an incredible talent. That does not mean his particular talent is obvious to everyone or appeals to me personally. As a writer, producer, and actor, Arnold has established himself with both television and film audiences worldwide, having won such awards as the Peabody Award for writing and a Golden Globe for writing and producing.

His introduction to Hollywood began after he moved to Los Angeles as a writer on the first run of the highly successful television series *Roseanne* before eventually serving as executive producer of the sitcom. Of course, he married the show's star, Roseanne Barr, and that is where I come into the story.

Before they were married, Arnold wrote intimate love letters to Barr. Somehow, this highly personal correspondence wound up published in the *National Enquirer*. "Someone stole these letters," said Arnold, "and obviously sold them for a hell of a lot of money. I want you to find the love letters, and find out who sold them to the *National Enquirer*."

I have worked for the *National Enquirer*. They were a little slow in paying but have a high degree of integrity compared to other tabloids. Before they publish any story about a major celebrity, they do extensive fact checking, and actually require independent sources to verify virtually every detail.

Most people think that celebrity stories come from some secondary source, such as a talkative house cleaner or a bought-off limo driver. The majority of the stories actually come from the celebrities themselves or their publicists.

In Hollywood, the old adage, "there is no bad publicity as long as they spell your name right" still applies. If a publicist goes to the *LA Times* and tells them that their client's marriage is on the rocks, the chances of that story ever seeing publication are remote. The publicist's choices are limited because most of the time, there is nothing happening in a celebrity's life that is very newsworthy. So, they do the next best thing; they run to the *National Enquirer*, planting a story that gets their client's name in front of readers.

The relationship between your favorite stars and the *National Enquirer* is very much one of love-hate. The stars say they hate the *Enquirer*, yet when things are slow, they use the *Enquirer* and in return, the *Enquirer* uses them to sell to their dedicated readers.

The cases I worked on for the *Enquirer* involved verifying stories about celebrities prior to publication. I knew most of the reporters in the L.A. office and the editors back in Lantana, Florida. All of them were very nice to me. The only reason I stopped working for them was that my price became too high; I left on good terms and we were still friendly.

When fellow private detective Bob Frasco approached me on the Roseanne Barr love letters case, I had severed my relationship with the *Enquirer* so there was no conflict of interest.

The first thing Bob wanted was a polygraph test of all the employees working in the Arnold/Barr residence. Most likely, the purloined letter caper was an inside job.

Barr and Arnold lived in a thirty-five hundred square foot home in Beverly Hills. The "office" was formerly the garage, converted for business purposes.

I showed up with a secretary/assistant from the Frasco Agency. Tom Arnold, clad only in boxer shorts and flip-flops, met us at the door. The head of his flaccid penis peeked out of his shorts. I was a bit taken aback; the woman averted her eyes.

After an equally short introduction, Arnold said, "I'm not taking that test. You know that, don't you?"

"You're the client, Tom," I replied. "I'll test whomever you want tested."

"I don't like the whole testing idea but it's something that has to be done, just not to me."

He introduced me to his executive assistant, a young fellow named Chris. The two men met at a photo store where Chris was an employee. Eager to work for a star, Chris' persistence in pursuing his goal convinced Arnold to bring the fellow on board as his own form of personal security.

Chris was the first employee I selected for polygraph testing, and the first person subjected to an in-depth interview. Some people with certain medical histories are exempt, as results can be inaccurate. Then again, polygraph results are, in the final analysis, unreliable in general.

I also wanted to find out as much as possible about his involvement in the case. During the interview, Chris offered me his telephone bills for the previous three months. "I can prove I didn't make any calls to the *Enquirer*," he said. "I'll even show you my bank statements. The only money I've deposited is my paycheck."

"Wonderful, Chris," I responded. "In fact, I'll drive you home right now and we can get that stuff."

As we were leaving, Arnold asked us where we were going. I told him that Chris was willing to produce his phone records and bank statements.

"Okay," said Tom with a scowl. "Get right back. I have other things to do besides test people all day. I have a company to run and a show to get out." As we were leaving, Roseanne came out of her bedroom and headed for her Jeep. Chris and I said hello to her, and we took off.

Chris lived with his girlfriend in an apartment in the Valley. We arrived at the apartment and started looking through the records. The phone rang. It was Arnold.

"I don't like you getting so personal," he said. "Looking through Chris' records and stuff."

"Well, I assure you, Mr. Arnold," I told him evenly, "that Chris volunteered to show me the records, and he hasn't been coerced in any way." That seemed to settle it.

Not more than two minutes later, the phone rang again. Chris handed me the phone. "It's Roseanne," he said.

"Yes, may I help you?"

"This is Roseanne Barr," she barked, "and I want this whole investigation to stop. I want you to leave Chris alone right now. We love him and trust him and I do not want him going through this. Do you understand me?"

"You are the client," I told her, "and I'll respect your wishes." As I did with her husband, I assured her of Chris' voluntary cooperation.

"I don't care," she said emphatically. "I want this thing to stop right now. I have had enough of this. Take him home, and leave us alone. Do you understand me?"

"Yes, I understand you."

I drove back to Roseanne's home, dropped off Chris, packed my polygraph, and my assistant and I left the house. On the way back to the office, my assistant told me that while Chris and I were gone, Tom Arnold paced back and forth like a caged lion.

"The entire time you were gone," she told me, "he kept harping at me, saying stuff such as, 'Is this what I'm paying you for, to just sit around?' I explained that he wasn't getting charged anything extra for my time. He seemed very uptight. What's his problem?"

"He's got a lot on his mind, probably," I answered, figuring it is always easier to excuse than accuse. "I'm sure famous people in his position are under more pressure than an astronaut."

In truth, it was a wasted day. Nothing accomplished. Roseanne and Tom hired us, yet both blocked the most basic aspects of the investigation. Investigator Bob Frasco and I decided to take another approach—instead of finding out who sold the letters, we would find out from whom the *Enquirer* bought them. Different question; same answer. Our new approach: penetrate the *Enquirer*.

Step One: The Diversion

I contacted an honest, ethical *Enquirer* reporter named Lyita Enisastas, and made her an offer I knew she would refuse. "Lyita," I said in conspiratorial tones, "I'll give you five thousand dollars if you reveal your source on the Roseanne Barr story."

She went ballistic. "I wouldn't sell a source for a million dollars," she insisted angrily. "I can't believe that you would even ask me to do such a thing." She then hung up on me and immediately contacted corporate headquarters, informing them of my unethical offer. This was exactly what I wanted.

I then contacted *Enquirer* assistant editor John South, another loyal employee. "John, I'm in tight with Roseanne Barr," I lied. "I'll give you exclusive stories about Roseanne for the next year if you'll reveal your source on the love letters." He denied my request, as did the *Enquirer*'s president, Ian Calder. This was perfect. The *Enquirer* now felt one hundred percent secure that I would *not* be getting information about the love letters from them. As I had gone all the way to the top with an offer to buy the information and been refused, the matter was settled. The *National Enquirer* felt secure that I would not obtain the information; the matter was closed. Their image of me as an ethical reporter was certainly damaged, but that could be repaired when the truth came out.

Step Two: The Con

Because the *Enquirer* was notoriously a slow paying organization, I was on first-name basis with the much-harassed folks in accounts payable. I called in, disguised my voice, and pretended I was a reporter from their Los Angeles office.

"Hey, I need your help," I said. "One of my sources insists they didn't get paid for a story, and I'm sure they did. Please pull the Roseanne file and read off the names of all the sources that we paid on Roseanne Barr stories." She pulled the file, giving me the names, the amounts, the check numbers, the dates of the checks, the banks on which they were drawn, and the reference number of each story, and where the checks were mailed.

"Do me one more quick favor," I asked politely, "just fax me a copy of the front and back of the cleared checks." I gave her the number of a fax machine at Quick Copy print shop on the other side of the city.

Next, I sent one of my people, dressed as a messenger, to pick up the fax. Even hotshot private eyes make mistakes, and here's where I made mine: I neglected informing Quick Copy of the incoming fax and that a messenger was on his way to pick it up under my assumed name.

The print shop was not expecting anything from the *National Enquirer*, so they called and asked for whom they should hold the fax. The *National Enquirer* ordered them not to release the fax. The *Enquirer* would send an employee, with credentials, to get the documents. If Quick Copy released that fax to anyone else, the *Enquirer* would sue.

Not knowing any of this at the time, I called Quick Copy under my assumed name and asked if I received anything from the *National Enquirer*. The next thing I knew, Quick Copy's manager was reading me the riot act, not the fax information. I was semi-screwed: I had all the information, but not that hardcopy proof that would crack the case.

I had every name of every person who sold a Roseanne story to the *Enquirer*. Reading over the list, my attitude towards Roseanne Barr softened considerably. Selling chunks of her private life were many of her so-called trusted friends and confidants. People she had treated as family used her as nothing more than an exploitable cash cow.

One of the checks was payable only to a social security number as added secrecy. The one story meriting that degree of secrecy was the love letters. Once I researched the social security number, I knew who sold Tom Arnold's love letters to the *National Enquirer*. It was Tom Arnold.

Here, apparently, is what happened. Tom Arnold and Roseanne Barr were engaged to be married, but he had a drug problem that Roseanne wouldn't tolerate. She called it off, telling him he had to choose between his "domestic goddess" (Roseanne) and his "white lady" (cocaine).

Tom, resentful, sold the love letters to the *National Enquirer*. Roseanne took Tom back; they were married in January. The letters hit the newsstand in February. There was no way for Tom to save face. He continued his charade all the way through, making a false police report to the LAPD and the FBI, and then going along with the federal litigation against the *Enquirer*.

I gave my report to Bob Frasco, and he gave the report to Roseanne and Tom. They paid the bill in full. The litigation, of course, came to an abrupt halt.

The Tom Arnold/Roseanne Barr relationship was not destined to be the great love story of the twentieth century. Their union, sadly doomed, ended in divorce. Sometimes it is hard to tell the victims from the perpetrators.

I am sure it broke Roseanne's heart to discover that Tom sold the letters. It was painful enough to learn how many of her so-called close friends and co-workers sold pieces of her life to the tabloids. To them, she wasn't a real person, she was an exploitable oddity.

At least Tom Arnold didn't try to kill her, drive her insane, or turn her into a drooling incompetent so he could gain control of her fortune. That is exactly what I believe Erin Fleming attempted against famed comic Groucho Marx.

Fleming appeared in minor roles in five films from 1965 through 1976, during which time she became acquainted with Groucho Marx and became his secretary, assistant, promoter, cheerleader, and perhaps his number one exploiter.

Her influence on Groucho was controversial, with Groucho's son, Arthur Marx, describing her in Svengali-esque terms. In the years leading up to Groucho's death in 1977, his heirs filed several lawsuits against her.

Groucho was, in his later years, a pathetic figure unable to care for himself or act in his own best interests. Erin Fleming hired me to protect Groucho from alleged attempts on his life. Fleming claimed that Groucho's son, Arthur, was trying to kill his father in eagerness to inherit Groucho's millions.

It was no secret that Groucho wasn't Arthur's nominee for Father of the Year, and Fleming was credited with getting Groucho his recent special recognition at the Academy Awards and revitalizing interest in all things involving the famed Marx Brothers. I considered it an honor to have Erin Fleming as a client and to be of service to Groucho Marx.

Arthur Marx and Erin Fleming were disputants in an upcoming hearing regarding the conservatorship of Groucho and his assets. Since the conservatorship hearing was less than a week away, she claimed that in case there was an attempt on his life, she wanted a reliable witness who could come forward and testify on her behalf.

As she was the client, I took her at her word and assigned two armed off-duty police officers to the residence. The first day they both quit, claiming they didn't want any part of this woman—she was, they claimed, "the bitch from hell."

I immediately hired new men, but their response was the same. Every time I hired agents to work at Groucho's house, they would resign that same day. Obviously, this case demanded my on-scene personal attention.

I arrived at the house at 8 a.m. on a Tuesday, just as my last shift was walking off the job, claiming that they didn't need money that badly. Located on Hillcrest Drive in Trousdale Estate next to Beverly Hills, it was a large house filled with old memories. There were pictures of Groucho with every big celebrity in Hollywood on all of the walls. I am not easily impressed, but this was impressive. This was the home of a showbusiness legend.

I wasn't in the house for five minutes when I heard loud screaming coming from the back bedroom. Following the insults to their source, I found Erin standing over Groucho, yelling, "Sign the check. Sign the check, you fucking old bastard. Sign the fucking check."

"Excuse me," I interjected, "what exactly is going on here?"

Erin, outraged at my presence, replied angrily, "As far as you're concerned, I am Mrs. Groucho Marx, do you understand? What's going on here is none of your damn business."

I bit my tongue, nodded, and left the room. Insulted and pissed off, I decided to walk outside and check the perimeter. Perhaps the fresh air would help me calm down.

As I walked past the storm drain in front of the house, something unusual caught my attention—a brown paper bag stuffed in the drain. Kneeling down, I reached in and pulled the bag out onto the lawn. Inside the bag were used syringes and medication with Groucho Marx's name it.

I brought the bag back into the house and asked a nurse if Groucho was receiving any type of injectables. The nurse said that Groucho was a diabetic and they were injecting him with insulin. I asked about the yellow capsules and the nurse claimed she had never seen them before. I took one of the capsules and a syringe and placed them in my car.

I confronted Erin with my discovery. She said that Groucho had suffered a stroke and was under medication by his doctor. I asked what the doctor had prescribed and she claimed that she didn't know specifically what the doctor prescribed, but whatever it was, it was none of my business.

I asked her about the yellow capsules that I had found in the storm drain. She said that they were placebos. She said Groucho had become addicted to some medication and that the doctor had prescribed placebos until he could be weaned off the medication. I asked her why the "placebos" had a number written on the side. Most placebos I have seen don't have any identifying marks. She had no explanation for the yellow pills. She said, "Give them to me and I'll take care of them." She then asked me where I had found them. I told her I found them in the storm drain. She didn't believe me and told me to leave her alone.

That night, I took the syringes, pills, and other medications to an independent lab to have them analyzed. The chemist found the yellow pills contained a barbiturate. The syringes also contained traces of the same barbiturate, as did the injectable solution.

The next day, I asked the private duty nurse if Groucho was on any type of barbiturate. She claimed that he wasn't. I asked how the trace elements of barbiturates got into the solution they were injecting every day. She had no explanation.

That same day, much to my surprise, I was invited to join Groucho and Erin for lunch. Groucho was at the head of the table, Erin was at his left side, and I was sitting at his right side. The family cook served the meal, and did so as if absolutely terrified of Fleming. I soon understood the reason for her fearful demeanor.

Since Groucho had a stroke, he had lost some control of his muscular system. He had trouble eating, and sometimes, he would miss his mouth completely. When this happened, Erin yelled, "Groucho, you fucking pig. Don't drop your food like a dog or I will make you eat off the floor like a dog."

Once again, Groucho started to drool and miss his mouth. Erin took his plate, threw it on the floor, and yelled at the top of her lungs, "You stupid fucking dog. Eat off the floor like a stupid dog should, you old fucking dog!"

I could not sit there and pretend such rude, abusive behavior was tolerable. I had to say something. "He is an old man with physical problems; there is no reason to treat him so rudely."

"Why the fuck is anything that goes on in this house any of your business," she snapped. "Where the fuck do you get off questioning anything I do? Don't you realize who I am? I am Mrs. Groucho Marx and you are a fucking idiot who I don't want in my house. Now get the fuck out of here before I kill you or have you killed."

Obviously, I needn't save room for dessert.

"Do you understand how dangerous someone like me can be?" she ranted. "Do you? Do you? I could have you killed by the time I snap my fingers, as I could have anyone killed who crosses me. Killed now. You understand who I am, don't you?"

I politely set aside my cutlery before responding, lest inadvertent gesturing be mistaken for assault with a culinary weapon. "No, I really don't," I responded evenly. "All that I can see is an old man being abused by some angry, manipulative, gold-digging has-been actress who will pay for what she has done, either in a court of law or in hell."

I got up from the table and walked out the door. She was still threatening to have me killed when I closed the door behind me. She hired me to protect Groucho and that was exactly what I was going to do.

I made an appointment with Detective Brooks of the Beverly Hills Police Department, and showed him the evidence found in the storm drain. I also advised him of the abusive behavior.

Next, I consulted my attorney to see how I could prevent this crazed woman from getting conservatorship of Groucho. He instructed me to attend the upcoming conservatorship hearing as *amicus curiae*—a friend of the court.

Launching a full-scale investigation at my own expense, I found nurses formerly employed in the Marx home whose testimony verified and validated my allegations of abuse. In the investigative process, I also found a cook, living in Canada, whom Erin had allegedly offered ten thousand dollars to poison Groucho.

The first day of the trial was a three-ring circus. Erin Fleming walked into court believing her claim was uncontested. Groucho's son, Arthur, had given up; she knew of no legal reason why she should not become Groucho's conservator. Then I showed up.

It became a madhouse of surprises, allegations, and reporters clamoring for interviews. Erin Fleming went ballistic. Before I could get home that night, Erin was banging on my front door. My fiancée called the police, and I arrived about the same time as the cops.

Erin was with a group of people yelling and screaming outside my home. They were chanting and yelling death threats to everyone who came in their path. As the police arrived, she yelled to them to watch out, saying I had a gun.

The police drew their service revolvers and instructed me to interlock my fingers behind my head and not to move. One of the officers patted me down as the other pointed his gun at me. The officer who was patting me down asked me where the gun was. I told him that I didn't have a gun but to go ahead and check for himself. When he didn't find any gun, he asked Erin where she had seen one. She replied that I always carry a gun.

The focus of their attention switched to her. They asked who lived here and I replied that I did. They asked Erin what she was doing there with her group of friends yelling and chanting.

She told them a story of how I had gone into court and perjured myself by lying about her, and that she wanted me arrested for perjury.

The police officers instructed the group to disperse and to stay away from my house and me. As she walked away, she yelled, "Death to the pigs!" They both looked at me in disgust and told me if she came back to call them and they would arrest her for disturbing the peace.

That night, the phone calls started. At first, they would just call and hang up. But as it got later, the calls became more aggressive. They started telling me that Manson had nothing on them and that I would pay for what I had done. Then they came out with actual death threats. They told me that I would be killed when I least expected it. I took the phone off the hook and waited for anything else that might occur. I knew this woman was crazy. But just how crazy, I had no idea. The trial went on for a long time.

Erin lost the conservatorship battle and so did Arthur. It was given to an old-time friend of the family, Nat Perrin. Groucho lived for three more years.

I don't dispute any good things Fleming may have done for Groucho early on. I wasn't there to see it, so I won't contradict it. I do know what I saw, what I heard, and I would not keep silent.

After Groucho's death, Bank of America sued Fleming for $472,000, claiming she coerced him to give her money and gifts above and beyond her earned salary as his secretary. She didn't have the money. "All I have in my checking account is thirty dollars," said Fleming. She passed away on April 15, 2003.

People asked me for an exclusive interview, giving them the in-depth story on what went on inside the Marx home. According to the reporter, I was the true centerpiece of the story. I gently refused their kind offer, content that simple, accurate reporting would sufficiently portray the depth of my involvement.

One week later, I was discontent; *People*'s story on the Marx fracas, despite acknowledging the important testimony of the nurses and caregivers I brought forward, left me out of the story altogether.

People, in a dazzling display of insufficient fact checking, reported that Erin hired two private detectives to find out if Arthur Marx was bugging his father's house. The two gumshoes allegedly turned against her, claiming she threatened to kill them, and were "now trying to peddle paperback rights to their story."

Disgusted with the distortion of truth, and appalled by the now proven disingenuous pitch of *People*'s reporter, I promptly cancelled my subscription. I'm sure they are still reeling from the shock of this sudden financial embargo.

Arthur Marx graciously expressed his gratitude, and assured me that he would send enough work my way to make up for whatever this altruistic act cost me in time and lost fees. "Expect my call, Fred," said Arthur. That was 1977. It was nice of him to say, although I did not really expect his call then, and I certainly do not expect it now.

Expectations, be they good or bad, are often the undoing of both the cheater and the cheated. Consider the story of multi-millionaire real-estate tycoon, Harry, and beautiful movie actress, Sally.

Harry, one of the most eligible wealthy bachelors in Beverly Hills, attended an exclusive black-tie event—the fiftieth birthday party of a Hollywood mogul. Harry arrived at the party about 8 p.m. and soon after met Sally, a lovely twenty-eight-year-old up-and-coming actress. Sally was bright, charming, and well dressed. He found no fault with her, but the attraction did not seem mutual. He tried all night to form some sort of conversational bond, but one diversion or another interrupted every attempt.

By night's end, Harry was almost obsessed. Finally, as she was leaving the event, he wrote down her license plate number. The next day, Harry called his attorney and inquired as to the best way of finding Sally's home address and phone number. The attorney contacted our firm, and by the next day, we had Sally's personal information. We were not going to hand it over, of course, without making sure Harry wasn't some psychotic stalker.

Our requirements for obtaining this information are quite strict. We must have a working relationship with the attorney and we must know the client and his intentions to avoid obsessed fans.

Harry was pleased with our findings and started sending Sally large baskets of exotic and beautiful flowers. Enclosed in basket was a card from Harry. The first one read, "I hope you don't find this too forward, but we met at a party last night and I would really like to spend some more time with you." Harry provided his name and number. The flowers were in her vestibule, and the ball was in her court.

Two weeks went by with no reply. Finally, Harry got up the nerve to call Sally. When the phone rang, a woman with a foreign accent answered it. Harry asked for Sally. The voice on the other end explained that Sally had been out of the country for the last two weeks, but was expected back that evening. Harry asked if she had received the flowers, and the voice assured him of daily delivery.

Returning home, Sally encountered a remarkable display of half-dead flowers. She asked her secretary what was happening, and after listening to the story, Sally called Harry. She thanked him profusely, and explained that she had been working on a motion picture for the last two weeks. They got along famously in the phone, and made a lunch date for the following afternoon.

From that lunch forward, it was a whirlwind courtship—romantic trips to Paris and cruising aboard private yachts in the Mediterranean. Three months later, Harry asked Sally for her hand in marriage and presented her with a four-karat engagement ring. Soon married, the happy couple moved into a lovely beach home.

As part of Sally's dedication to health and fitness, she worked out every morning with Burt, her personal trainer and a dear trusted friend. Harry noticed that Burt was also exceptionally handsome and athletic, a man most women would find hard to resist. It was also clear that Sally and Burt shared a special relationship.

Rather than rejoicing that his wife had such a good friend, Harry expressed jealousy. At length, Harry asked Sally to get a new trainer. Taken aback by her husband's request, Sally was hurt and insulted. She was a loyal wife; Burt was a trusted pal.

Rather than embrace reassurance, Harry first threw a temper tantrum, then threw various objects. When the final piece of expensive crystal crashed against the wall, Sally wisely suggested professional marriage counseling.

Harry refused. Dismayed, Sally urged him to get individual counseling to deal with his self-created scenarios of expected betrayal. She was not, however, about to dismiss her dear friend due to Harry's delusions.

Formerly obsessed with having Sally, Harry was now obsessed with catching her in an extramarital affair. To accomplish this goal, he came to me.

"I am positive that Sally is having an affair with Burt," said Harry, and he hired my firm to watch her when he went on business trips, and whenever she was out of town shooting a picture.

"Sally is not having an affair with Burt," I reported back to him, "nor is she having an affair with anyone else." Harry didn't believe me. He was sure that Sally was outsmarting us.

His next plan: have us install hidden video cameras throughout the house. We decided that doing so would at least give him peace of mind, so we installed the cameras. Harry seemed pleased with his new toy and couldn't wait to review the tapes that he just knew would reveal Sally's deceitful behavior.

The tapes, of course, revealed only a happy, loyal, loving wife. Harry was blatantly disappointed. So convinced was he of her infidelity, he actually confronted her with non-existent evidence, insisting that he had proof of her affair with Burt.

That did it. She exploded in a rage of hurt and fury. "I've been a loyal and faithful wife," she said angrily. "How dare you say such a thing?"

"You're obviously more than just friends," countered Harry. "He's obviously handsome—"

"In case you haven't noticed," she snapped at him, "I am obviously a married woman, and Burt is obviously gay!"

Suddenly realizing the depths of his degrading and insulting behavior, Harry chased after her in tears. Over time, and with great effort and many apologies, he wooed her back for a second chance. He no longer had her followed nor did he obsess on imaginary indiscretions.

A few months later, Sally went to South America for a motion picture. An unexpected bout of dysentery afflicted the crew, and Sally avoided the runs by trotting home to Harry. On the flight back, Sally imagined what a fun surprise it would be when Harry saw her home so quickly.

Sally not only surprised Harry, she surprised Burt as well. The two men were having sex in her marital bed.

The stunned trio remained motionless for a moment. There was no way the men could avoid Sally's wilting gaze.

"Harry, you're having sex with Burt," she blurted out as if Harry were unaware of the act or the identity of his partner.

"Yes, I know who he is, honey," came Harry's calm reply.

Sally saw the look on Burt's face, and realized her friend mistakenly assumed that the homoerotic coupling happened with her foreknowledge and tacit approval.

"I've always been bisexual, honey," admitted Harry, as if any validation were required. "I guess I should have told you."

Sally filed for a divorce. Harry and Burt moved in together. I don't know if Burt remained Sally's trainer, but I'm sure their friendship was strained by the affair.

Harry's obsession with catching Sally having her non-existent affair with Burt is something only a psychologist could explain. From my experience as a private eye, sometimes when a person says, "I *know* my spouse is doing something wrong," what they really mean is "I don't really know anything." It is the fear of being right, plus the fear of being paranoid, that motivates them to take decisive action and find out the truth.

Some affairs are sloppy, ill-concealed violations of trust. Others are elaborate schemes, planned and executed with the precision of a professional heist.

The cleverest scheme ever devised by cheating husbands was created by a group of philandering businessmen in Los Angeles. As if with most acts of conspiratorial dishonesty, it eventually came crashing down, breaking hearts and destroying families in the process.

With much trepidation, the wife of a Los Angeles executive came to my office. It was all gut feelings on her part, she admitted, but she suspected her husband was having an affair. Interestingly, he displayed none of the primary telltale signs of cheating.

He often went out of town on business trips, and every time she called him up, he was always where he said he would be. If he said he was going to be on business in Texas, for example, he would leave her his itinerary with the phone numbers and addresses of all the hotels he would be staying on his trip. When she called, he would answer, and nothing seemed out of the ordinary. Despite outward appearances, the missus' intuition told her there was something amiss with the mister.

I took the case, and when he left for his next business trip, we followed him to the airport. He parked his car in a very conspicuous spot in the parking lot. If his wife looked for his car at the airport, she would find it easily.

No sooner did he lock his car, than an attractive young woman pulled up in a late-model vehicle. He got in the passenger side, and we tailed the pair all the way to a residence in Marina del Rey. We researched the property ownership and discovered it was in the names of the husband and the other woman.

From the husband's itinerary, we got the number of the hotel in Dallas, Texas, where he was supposedly staying. I called the number, and a woman answered, "Hilton Hotel, may I help you?"

"Yes, please connect me to the room of Dr. Lyle Jenson," I requested, making up the name on the spot.

"I'm sorry," she replied, "we have no one by that name registered."

"Please look again," I begged, "we have an emergency at the hospital. This is a matter of life or death, and this is the only number we have for Dr. Jensen."

The person put me on hold for a minute, and during those sixty seconds, I prayed that she wouldn't realize that my story was an obvious lie; there was no way that anyone would have given me that fake phone number. I was counting on the "life or death" ruse to push things in our favor.

When she came back on the line, she told the truth. "This is not actually the Hilton Hotel," she said nervously. "This is an answering service in Los Angeles where the calls are forwarded to. That's why we know Dr. Jensen is not here."

We traced the call from the call forwarding number back to Los Angeles, got the address of the answering service, and investigated the answering service's ownership. It did not take long for the entire scheme to unravel. The service was created specifically to create the illusion that these specific businessmen were out of town on work-related activities when they were actually having affairs in their own hometowns.

They would set up fictitious business trips. The phone numbers in those cities, all with proper area codes, were low-cost lines with automatic call forwarding back to the answering service in Los Angeles.

When the answering service received a call, the system told them where the call was coming from, to whose itinerary it related, and the procedure for contacting the person in event of an actual emergency, either by pager or at the love nest.

A little meeting was arranged between the cheating husband and a prospective client—me. I showed him the videotape of his mistress meeting him at the airport, displayed a copy of the property deed proving his co-ownership of his lover's home, and produced copies of checks he had personally signed to the WLFY Answering Service.

He didn't put up an argument or a fuss. He met his wife's divorce settlement conditions and she went on her way, as did he.

Before he left, I asked him one question. "What was the significance of WLFY?"

"Oh," he said with a smile, "WLFY stands for We Lie For You."

SECRETS of a HOLLYWOOD PRIVATE EYE

http://wbp.bz/secrets

BETRAYAL IN BLUE

BURL BARER
FRANK C. GIRARDOT JR.
KEN EURELL

BETRAYAL IN BLUE

THE SHOCKING MEMOIR OF THE
SCANDAL THAT ROCKED THE NYPD

THE STORY BEHIND THE DOCUMENTARY "THE SEVEN FIVE"

http://wbp.bz/biba

Adapted from Ken Eurell's personal memoirs of the time plus hundreds of hours of exclusive interviews with the major players, including Adam Diaz and Dori Eurell, this book reveals the truth behind the documentary *The Seven Five.*

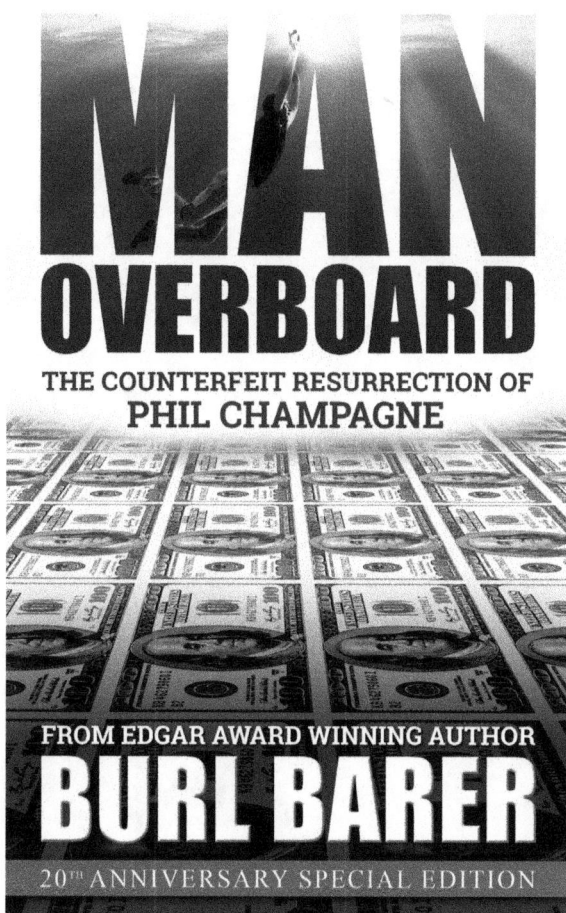

MAN
OVERBOARD
THE COUNTERFEIT RESURRECTION OF
PHIL CHAMPAGNE

FROM EDGAR AWARD WINNING AUTHOR
BURL BARER
20TH ANNIVERSARY SPECIAL EDITION

http://wbp.bz/manoverboarda

"Barer does it again! A deft and dazzling display of solid research and rapier wit—a must for all true crime aficionados."—Gary C. King, author of Love, Lies, and Murder

A TASTE FOR MURDER

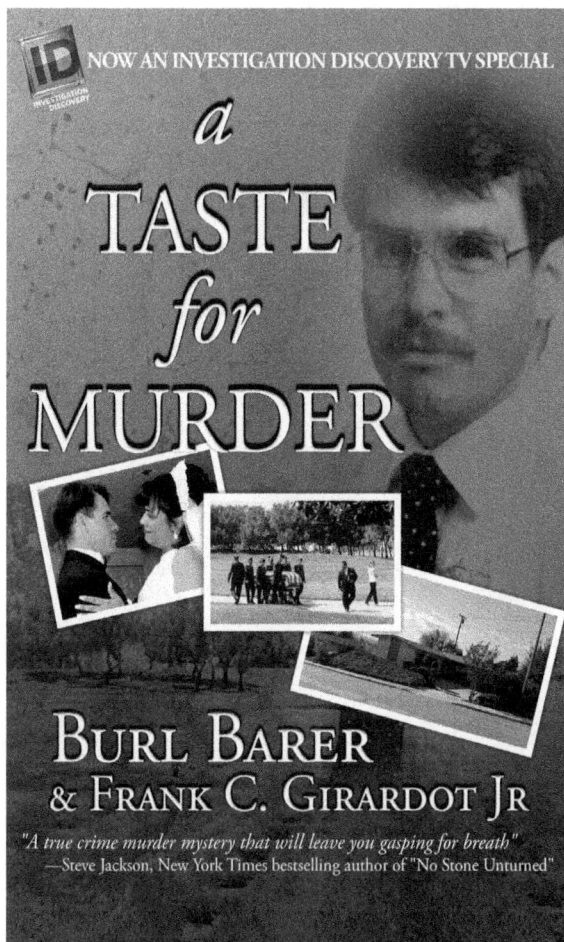

http://wbp.bz/atfma

As seen on Investigation Discovery: "A true crime murder mystery that will leave you gasping for breath." —Steve Jackson, *New York Times*–bestselling author of *No Stone Unturned*

HEADLOCK

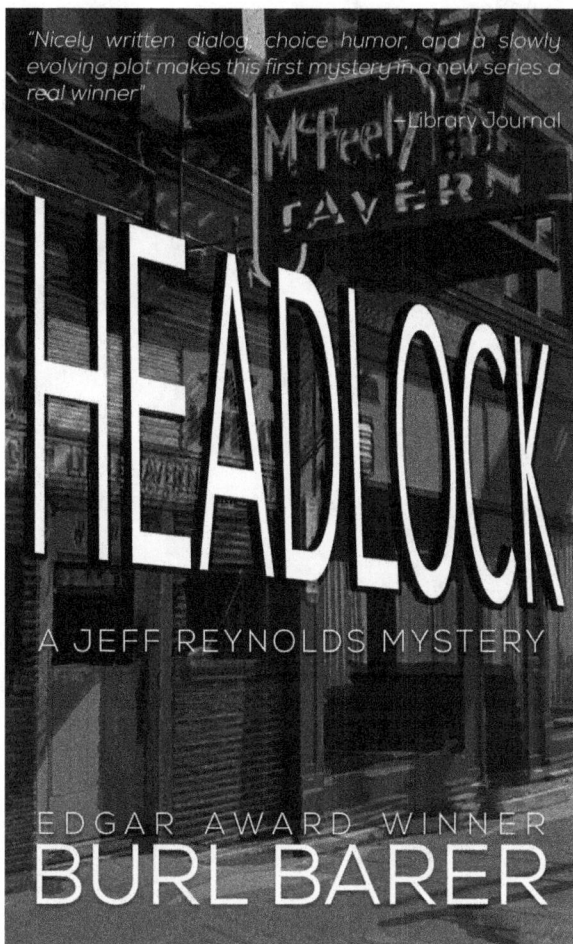

"Nicely written dialog, choice humor, and a slowly evolving plot makes this first mystery in a new series a real winner"

—Library Journal

HEADLOCK

A JEFF REYNOLDS MYSTERY

EDGAR AWARD WINNER
BURL BARER

http://wbp.bz/headlockreviews

From the New York Times–bestselling and Edgar Award–winning author Burl Barer, and featuring cameos by a few real-life mystery authors, this is a wildly entertaining PI tale in which it's hard to tell what's deception, what's delusion, and what's genuinely deadly—and all roads lead to McFeely's Tavern in Walla Walla, Washington . . .

HOT NEW RELEASES

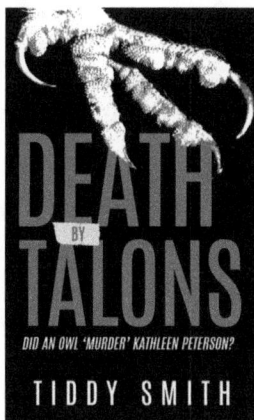

DEATH BY TALONS
http://wbp.bz/deathbytalons

LOU & JONBENET
http://wbp.bz/louandjonbenet

www.ingramcontent.com/pod-product-compliance
Lightning Source LLC
Chambersburg PA
CBHW070058030426
42335CB00016B/1931